poltics

Text: Florian Hertweck, Christian Hiller, Markus Krieger, Alex Nehmer, Anh-Linh Ngo, Milica Topalović

for the

Editorial

We are doomed to repair. This is hardly an astonishing insight in a world that ages with every passing moment. Capitalist modernity, however, with its emphasis on innovation, growth, and progress; its economic system based on consumption, overuse, and squander; and the ruthless exploitation of natural resources that this entails, has firmly engraved a throwaway mentality into our minds: Everything is replaceable. There is always a better product ready and waiting. Repair is not worthwhile. German architectural discourse has come up with a particularly striking euphemism to describe the demolish-and-replace approach: *Ersatzneubau*, or new construction replacing existing buildings. It thus comes as no surprise that today, waste from construction and demolition accounts for more than half of the total waste accumulating in Germany.

What is neglected here is that the extent of what needs to be repaired is constantly growing. After all, the total mechanization and technologization of modern life go hand in hand with a natural (or planned) obsolescence of the technologies used. However, despite the prevailing throwaway mentality, cities, infrastructures, and buildings are more often converted or kept in use than torn down. A plethora of technical devices are repaired and maintained day in, day out. Maintenance, repair, and servicing form an important sector of the economy. Key statistics reveal that today, more engineers work in the field of repair than in that of development.[1]

This is not a particularly well-known fact, as repair work is hardly glamorous and often Sisyphean. It takes place behind closed doors: an everyday, minute occurrence. It is precisely in these qualities that it unfolds its power, and precisely where the project *The Great Repair* takes its starting point, seeking to surpass the pragmatic level and point to the geopolitical, socio-economic, and ecological dependencies behind the material assemblages, infrastructures, and social interactions of our societies. When we speak of the *great* repair, those major contexts in need of repair are exactly what we mean.

And great is the need for repair given the degree of destruction of the world. The impact of the climate crisis and of dwindling resources—with the loss of biodiversity and dying forests, with flooding and storms, heat waves and droughts—is already causing death, starvation, and migration in the Global South, where large areas are becoming uninhabitable for humans and animals. In the future, military conflicts over energy, infrastructures, and food will increase as a corollary of the climate crisis, effecting inescapable battles for geopolitical control over territories and resources. Given these factors, it becomes evident that not only everyday life will be destabilized, but geopolitical architectures and borders as well. This holds true not just of the Global South, but has long applied to Europe, where in the last 30 years, average temperatures have risen 0.5°C per decade.[2]

In light of the planetary scale of these escalating crises, one might ask how such a cautious concept as that of repair might help. No doubt, many will object: Should we not, like previous modernist movements, evoke grand visions rather than proclaiming a "Great Repair"? It is in this contrast between cautious circumspection and global perspective, however, that we see the outstanding characteristic of *The Great Repair*. Considering that the major crises were triggered precisely by modernity's grand visions, we need a new paradigm.

To repair that which is broken, the first step is to assess the damage. We should, therefore, "take erosion, breakdown, and decay, rather than novelty, growth, and progress, as our starting points in thinking through the use of nature," as information scientist Steven J. Jackson suggests.[3] However, in the Global North, the powerful narrative still prevails that we will only succeed in getting a handle on the climate and resource crisis and uncouple economic growth from its environmental impacts by using technological innovation and development. In this vision of a green capitalist transformation, renewable energies are expected to cover the needs of industry and a constantly growing number of urban consumers in a climate-neutral fashion, while smart technologies regulate the flows of people, goods, and energy with ever greater efficiency, manage the recycling of materials, close energy cycles, and bind greenhouse gases. The loss of biodiversity and the leaching and depletion of the soils would, so the argument goes, be solved by the automation of industrial agriculture, by food technology, by reducing food waste across the entire supply chain, and by the mass introduction of vegan nutrition and products. The raw materials necessary would, it continues, possibly even be extracted extraterrestrially by future technologies.

This vision is coupled with the political hope that growing material prosperity on the basis of green technologies would enable the strengthening and spread of "liberal market democracies" against the "increasing threat by authoritarianism." These narratives are so appealing because, in the end, they support the political status quo: Neither politicians nor citizens need to structurally change, nor is the underlying capitalist economic system with its mechanisms of exploitation and unequal distribution cast into doubt. The danger of such a mindset stems from the fact that it pushes the necessary repair of the system down the road into the future, further intensifying the global geography of inequalities, and superficially papering over the climate crisis with an inflation of greenwashing and *innovation speak.* It is impossible to discard the contradictions of such visions: For all the technological innovations and improvements in efficiencies in recent years, the claims and the reality they purport to describe are as far apart as the ambitious goals of the Paris Climate Agreement from the real planetary greenhouse gas emissions. Despite massive efforts, the "green solution" does not yet work.

Repair society

For this reason, *The Great Repair* is putting forward a counternarrative that focuses on the human ability to redesign our relationships within the social and natural environment: from the conditions of production and social participation all the way to issues of justice; from the built environments and eco-systems all the way to the Earth's climate. As a counterstrategy to capitalist modernity's creative destruction, we advocate a focus on care, maintenance, and repair as the key action strategies. This concept of repair does not aim at reconstructing an idealized, original state, but at regenerative transformation toward a better state. Unlike in the case of (techno-)fixes, the focus here is not simply on troubleshooting functional disturbances: Repair means to bring the world "back into equilibrium," as heritage preservation theorist Wilfried Lipp wrote in his seminal essay "Rettung von Geschichte für die Reparaturgesellschaft im 21. Jahrhundert" (Rescuing History for the Repair Society of the 21st Century), quoting from an old encyclopedia.[4] As early as 1993, speaking at a conference on heritage preservation, Lipp coined the term "repair society" as a new societal guiding principle,[5] one that he understood to be, "both diagnostic and therapeutic, offering a perspective and making an appeal."[6]

In other words, we are in the midst of 'repair.'
Things are being repaired everywhere.
This refers, and I am just highlighting things

by keywords here, to general environmental measures for the air (reducing emissions), water (quality, sewer systems, consumption), the oceans (reducing the stress factors on them), soil (over-use of fertilizers), wood, forests ('dying forests,' excessive logging, rainforests). […]
Something like a 'repair of the human' has been set in motion. […] Eventually, the goal is a 'repair' of the system of labor primarily defined economically in terms of production and sales, labor that is defined in this logic as an endless chain of abundance—accumulation—waste.[7]

Shortly after Lipp, political scientist Claus Leggewie likewise proclaimed the repair society in his 1995 book *Die 89er: Portrait einer Generation* (The 1989ers: Portrait of a Generation)[8]; returning to the concept in 2016 together with Jürgen Bertling: "Die Reparaturgesellschaft: Ein Beitrag zur großen Transformation?" (The Repair Society: A Contribution to a Great Transformation?).[9] Alluding to Karl Polanyi's *The Great Transformation* (1944),[10] Leggewie and Bertling locate the discourse on repair in line with the technological history of the industrial "great transformation," which, according to Polanyi, led to the independence and hegemony of the "free" market vis-à-vis society: "Instead of economy being embedded in social relations, social relations are embedded in the economic system."[11] The consequence of this "great transformation" is the ruthless exploitation of humans and nature. According to Polanyi, this process can only be reversed if, instead of the ideal of a free, self-regulating market to which all social relationships are subordinate, a notion of a free and self-determined society defines political action. In this sense, the *Great Repair* project entails nothing less than a realignment of the fundamentals, norms, processes, and objectives of our economic system toward economies of repair and care, in order for the economy to be re-embedded in society, and society, for its part, to be re-embedded in the natural environment.

Almost in passing, Leggewie and Bertling point out the breaking point at which the project of *The Great Repair* will have to intervene:

> We can assume that manufacturing and repairing things prior to the emergence of the manufacturing system and subsequent industrialization was handled by the same set of actors. For both actions, the same skills and tools were needed, and in many cases the subsequent repair was probably already factored into the manufacturing process. Seen through the lens of the history of technology, manufacturing and repair parted ways in conjunction with the increasing mechanization of the core processes of manufacturing: material processing and design.[12]

In other words, the capitalist industrial economic system is based not only on "the process of separation of producer and the means of production," as Karl Marx described,[13] but also on the separation of production and repair, resulting in commodities that are interchangeable black boxes bereft of any social relationships. The resulting alienation is profound and extends from the conditions of production through to personal consumer behavior: The product intended for consumption possesses neither a connection to the labor processes that went into manufacturing it, nor to those that would be necessary for its maintenance and repair. On a societal level, this development goes hand in hand with a self-imposed technical immaturity, a loss in "skills and tools" with which people could design and repair the worlds in which they live. Conversely, this means that a Great Repair can only have an emancipatory impact if it provides people with repair tools. Accordingly, Silke Langenberg gave her 2018 book *Reparatur* the subtitle *Anstiftung zum Denken und Machen* (Instigation to Think and Do).[14] A Great Repair must follow the motto that architect Yoshiharu Tsukamoto from Atelier Bow-Wow formulated in the context of his research project, the *Satoyama School of Design*[15]: "Tools to the People!"[16]

This call touches on a central theme in Marxist theory, if we translate tools to signify the "means of production." Marx believed that the concentration of ownership of tools, materials, and machines as the "means of production" in the hands of a few formed the core of the capitalist system—and to overcome it (in theory), the means of production had to be reappropriated by society: They have to be socialized. In this regard, the *Great Repair* project is more modest, less revolutionary, and more grounded in everyday life. The emphasis is on increasing each individual's agency by centering not the anonymous consumption, but the caring and maintaining of the world in which they live. To paraphrase Kant, we could say: The Great Repair is humans' escape from their self-imposed techn(olog)ical immaturity.

Tools to the People

Giving the tools back to the people and re-imbuing things with the capacity to be repaired may, at first sight, seem to have a technoskeptical feel to it. However, the implying DIY and low-tech approach is often not primarily aimed against technology itself but furthers the wish to decommodify the social relationships that are embedded in production. According to Polanyi, the commodity character of the social constitutes the core problem of the current system: "Machine production in a commercial society involves, in effect, no less a transformation than that of the natural and human substance of society into commodities."[17] This development has led us into a cul-de-sac, from which we can liberate ourselves by realizing that we have fallen for a false consciousness: "But labor, land, and money are obviously not commodities; the postulate that anything that is bought and sold must have been produced for sale is emphatically untrue in regard to them."[18] It is no coincidence that many repair-based approaches focusing on forms of empowerment place at the center of their struggle the relationship to labor, to the soil, and to money.

"Tools to the people" thus actually means the empowerment of people. Leggewie and Bertling, in their contribution on "Open Source and DIY as a Post-capitalist Praxis," also home in on this notion. That is why knowledge and tools are at the center of *The Great Repair*.

However, in order to devise or reappropriate new-old tools, we must first question our existing base of knowledge, our epistemological fundamentals—and recognize that we have repressed, marginalized, and lost a whole raft of knowledge worlds and ways of relating to the world in the name of progress. This loss includes the knowledge about sustainable material extraction, building techniques, and land use; not to mention the associated experience with different forms of managing the commons. In this regard, the process of repair also leads to a new understanding of territory and of laws as specific governance instruments through which our (presently unequal and unjust) socio-ecological systems are reproduced. In light of the disastrous ecological, political, social, and economic consequences of this narrative of progress, we urgently need an alternative one. Repair as the counterstrategy to obsolescence could at least contribute to slowing down the engine of progress with its logic of perpetual destruction and reconstruction.[19]

Seen from this angle, the concept of repair must be defended time and again against the erroneous ideal of an anachronistic return to either pre-industrial economies or to some purported "natural" state. Since at least the publication of the Club of Rome report on the *Limits to Growth* exactly 50 years ago we know that we cannot rewind the clock. By confusing the observed limits to growth with the causes of the climate crisis, however, neo-Malthusian worldviews arise today, effectively leveraged against the development of the Global South. For example, historical geographer Jason W. Moore points out that a comprehensive redesigning of global nature began long before the invention of the steam engine with the early modern conquest of new territories by the nascent European empires. According to Moore, this increase in production in the *web of life* hinged on the notion of the "Great Frontiers" and the colonial practices of expansion, appropriation, and the exploitation for production of *cheap nature* inextricably bound up with it. The paradigm of the Great Repair is therefore, as stated, not aimed against technology per se, but against technology as a means of reproducing inequality and of exploiting the nonhuman world at both the planetary and local levels.

RePair and reParation

Against the backdrop of centuries of exploitation of cheap nature and cheap labor in the Global South, repair on a planetary scale cannot ignore the concept of reparations. Even if the social and ecological damage already inflicted is irreparable, we can still seek climate justice in the sense of recognizing responsibility and trying to find a way by which those who have hitherto profited from the climate-damaging economic system compensate those who are most affected by its impacts. The "Loss and Damage Fund" for poorer countries agreed to at the COP27 United Nations Climate Change Conference in Sharm el-Sheikh, despite the conference's failure as a whole, is a first step to creating a mechanism of reparations. In this context, reparations for climate damage are only one example of the much-needed processes of decolonization. *The Great Repair* seeks not only to decommodify social relations of production, as outlined above, but above all to decolonize social relations,

including social institutions, enacting a more extensive form of decolonial reparations. The concept of reparations tends to be used in the context of reparations for war damage. The party that bears responsibility for the war and then loses it must, as a rule, make reparations payments. However, Lipp points out that the categories get mixed up in the context of sustainability:

> The concept of 'repair' is related to the martial notion of reparation. [...] The losers have to pay. However, paradoxically, and new in the history of reparations, there is no winner. The reparations affect everyone. The currency they are due in is called 'repair.'[20]

politics for the repair society

We must, however, be careful not to take repair as an absolute value. It only has a social impact as a *political* category that embraces both action and negotiation at once. What needs to be repaired, how, and with what tools? What state do we aim to achieve? While fully aware of the open-ended character of the following list, we define six politics as the parameters for this open process of negotiation which, from our viewpoint, should structure the actions of a repair society.

Sufficiency

Given the rift between ambition and action, sufficiency is becoming ever more vital. By nature, however, the green-tech ideology ignores it. Sufficiency is not the opposite of efficiency. Instead, it describes the vision of a material culture in which humanity—and in particular the Global North—has to get by with less: less energy, fewer resources, less use of land, instead using what is already there more carefully. It is therefore at the opposing end of a logic of planetary material extraction and long supply chains fueling the construction industry. Sufficiency should also not be confused with austerity, which entails a reduction in a personal lifestyle borne by the marginalized members of society. Rather, it is construed as a paradigm of social planning and governance controlling the design of the built and unbuilt environment in such a way as to enable a life that is sufficient. What is decisive here is also reterritorialization, meaning the embedding of production and supply chains in regional and local contexts.

Longevity

In contrast to sustainability, which today primarily means transposing economic principles onto ecology, longevity focuses on extending the lifeline and life cycles of materials, objects, and technologies for as long as possible. In this context, recycling functions merely as the grease for an unchallenged productive system, whereas repair aims to ensure the longevity of things. The right-to-repair movement is making an important contribution to the design discourse by combatting throwaway culture and built-in obsolescence. At the same time, the reality of increasing migration, in particular the forced migration of climate refugees, demonstrates the need to rethink the impermanence and the mobility of architecture and settlement areas. Longevity is not the opposite of lightness and flexibility.

Care

Repair involves not only repairing things, but also caring for people, for nonhuman creatures, and for ecosystems. It requires that hitherto invisible labor be recognized. This includes the so far externalized costs of domestic and reproductive labor, as well as the labor of nature. On the basis of this expanded understanding, "ecosystems of repair," spanning a network of human and nonhuman relationships, can be created.

Reappropriation

Racist and colonial violence—both of a territorial and of a cultural kind—is an indispensable precondition of the capitalist production of *cheap nature* in the Global North and in the Global South. No climate discourse is therefore possible without its consideration. Practices of repair must thus factor in decolonial reappropriation of the stolen and devalued objects, places, territories, cultural practices, and epistemes.

Solidarity

The politics of solidarity are at the very center of a multiplicity of practices of repair. Here, repair is understood as a social act that promotes coexistence, communal work, social forms of ownership, commonwealth economies, and risk sharing. The focus is on the local, city, or community level, often beyond the domain of the market and the state. Researching and strengthening smaller collaborative structures and economies contributes to their increasing robustness, for example regarding the shared use of resources and adaptation to climate change.

Plurality

In the endeavor to decommodify and decolonialize social relationships, the repair society questions the one-sidedness of techno-scientific rationality and aspires for plurality instead. This in particular means the endeavor to pluralize knowledge production outside the state- and market-validated knowledge cycles, opening them up to different systems of knowing and making. This includes practices that are based on Indigenous, crafts, or bricoleur-like knowledge and solve problems with the resources available. This way, expert knowledge is cast into question and the constellation of actors changed. Instead of emphasizing novelty and individual origination, plurality focuses on collaborative forms of knowledge production and self-empowerment.

Self-repair

These current debates on repair, care, and maintenance resonate strongly in architectural and urban research, which in response has the potential to stimulate other discourses and practices thanks to the discipline's specific repair knowledge. After all, strategies of repair have always formed an important element of architecture. Starting with Leon Battista Alberti's book *On some defects which cannot be provided against, but which may be repaired after they have happened,*[21] via the Arts and Crafts movement, all the way to Carlo Scarpa's approach to the historical built environment or the *as found* concept ventured by Alison und Peter Smithson. Of special importance is the social practice of maintaining urban fabric by the squatter's movement as was the case in Berlin and other cities during the 1970s and 1980s—approaches combining repair with appropriation strategies from below, as well as urban repair and other large-scale planning projects responding to the destruction caused by the Second World War, the impacts of deindustrialization, and shrinking cities.

With *The Great Repair*, the focus is not least the self-repair of architecture as a discipline: the repair of its notion of work, its work processes, its understanding of authorship, its education system, and its forms of communication. However, this is no longer a bygone search for inter- or transdisciplinarity, where the discipline still provides a safe haven to which, metaphorically speaking, one can return after having ventured into unknown territory. On the other hand, architecture's self-repair as a discipline does not mean giving up on situating oneself. After all, feminist critique has revealed that in the cultural, political, economic, and social domains, we always have to deal with situatedness and framings binding us personally in more than one way. The politics of the repair society challenge us to think and act intersectionally if we are to achieve social emancipation. If the Great Repair is humans' escape from their self-imposed techn(olog)ical immaturity, then self-repair is the discipline's escape from its self-imposed social immaturity.

The Project

The Great Repair is a project of ARCH+ gGmbH in cooperation with Akademie der Künste, Berlin, the Department of Architecture at ETH Zürich, and the University of Luxembourg's Department of Geography and Spatial Planning. The project covers two issues of *ARCH+* as well as an exhibition and events program that will take place from October 14, 2023 to January 14, 2024 at Akademie der Künste, Berlin. This present issue serves as a theoretical introduction, the second issue will present repair practices and be published as a catalog to coincide with the opening of the exhibition on October 13, 2023.

Acknowledgments

The project would not have had such depth without the support and trust of Akademie der Künste, Berlin, in particular of Johannes Odenthal, its former Program Director, and his successor, Johanna M. Keller. Our sincere thanks go to all our funding partners, in particular the German Federal Cultural Foundation and Wüstenrot Stiftung, all the authors, artists, and not least our colleagues Marija Marić and Nazlı Tümerdem, as well as the *ARCH+* team, in particular Nora Dünser and Felix Hofmann.

We would like to express our profound gratitude to Hortensia Völckers. Without her courage and her vision of culture as a social challenge, we would not have been able to realize such ambitious research, discourse, and exhibition projects as *projekt bauhaus*, *Cohabitation*, or *The Great Repair* during her time in office as Artistic Director of the German Federal Cultural Foundation.

1   See Stefan Krebs et al., eds., *Kulturen des Reparierens: Dinge. Wissen. Praktiken* (Bielefeld: transcript, 2018), 20: "If we consider the employment structure of engineers as the central technical actors then most engineers today are not active in the field of development and construction, but in maintenance and repair."

2   See The World Meteorological Organization, "Temperatures in Europe Increase More than Twice Global Average," press release of November 2, 2022, accessed November 29, 2022, public.wmo.int/en/media/press-release/temperatures-europe-increase-more-twice-global-average.

3   Steven J. Jackson, "Rethinking Repair," in *Media Technologies: Essays on Communication, Materiality and Society*, eds. Tarleton Gillespie et al. (Cambridge: MIT Press, 2014), 221.

4   Wilfried Lipp, "Rettung von Geschichte für die Reparaturgesellschaft im 21. Jahrhundert. Sub specie conservatoris," *ICOMOS Hefte des Deutschen Nationalkomitees 21, Das Denkmal als Altlast? Auf dem Weg in die Reparaturgesellschaft* (1996), 146.

5   See Wilfried Lipp, "Vom modernen zum postmodernen Denkmalkultus? Aspekte zur Reparaturgesellschaft," in *Vom modernen zum postmodernen Denkmalkultus? Denkmalpflege am Ende des 20. Jahrhunderts*, eds. Wilfried Lipp and Michael Petzet (Munich: Bayerisches Landesamt für Denkmalpflege, 1994), 6–12; translated as "From the Modern to the Postmodern Cult of Monuments?: Aspects of a Repairing Society," accessed February 23, 2023, www.icomos.de/icomos/pdf/06_lipp_1993_en_jb.pdf.

6   Lipp, "Rettung von Geschichte" (see note 4), 144.

7   Ibid., 146 f.

8   See Claus Leggewie, *Die 89er: Portrait einer Generation* (Hamburg: Hoffmann & Campe, 1995).

9   See Jürgen Bertling and Claus Leggewie, "Die Reparaturgesellschaft: Ein Beitrag zur Großen Transformation?," in *Die Welt reparieren: Open Source und Selbermachen als postkapitalistische Praxis*, eds. Andrea Baier et al. (Bielefeld: transcript, 2016), 275–86.

10   Karl Polanyi, *The Great Transformation* (New York: Farrar & Rinehart, 1944).

11   Ibid., 73.

12   Bertling and Leggewie, "Die Reparaturgesellschaft" (see note 9), 276.

13   Karl Marx, *Capital*, vol. I, accessed February 2, 2023, www.marxists.org/archive/marx/works/download/pdf/Capital-Volume-I.pdf, 526.

14   Silke Langenberg, ed., *Reparatur: Anstiftung zum Denken und Machen* (Berlin: Hatje Cantz, 2018).

15   See Yoshiharu Tsukamoto and Siena Hirao, "Lernen im Feld: Die Satoyama School of Design," *ARCH+ 249, Learning Spaces* (September 2022), 196–203.

16   This is a claim Tsukamoto made in conversation with the curators and which he will elaborate on together with Momoyo Kaijima for their planned contribution to the exhibition *The Great Repair*.

17   Polanyi, *Great Transformation* (see note 10), 58.

18   Ibid., 88.

19   See Daniel M. Abramson, *Obsolescence: An Architectural History* (Chicago: University of Chicago Press, 2016).

20   Lipp, "Rettung von Geschichte" (see note 3), 148.

21   Leon Battista Alberti, "Book Ten. Chap. 18," in *Ten Books on Architecture* (1755), trans. James Leoni, complete reprint (London: Alex Tiranti, 1955).

p. 124

p. 95

ARCH+ team for this issue:
   Nora Dünser (managing editor), Franziska Gödicke, Christian Hiller, Felix Hofmann, Marlene Huster, Sarah Knechtel, Markus Krieger (project leader), Daniel Kuhnert, Victor Lortie, Alex Nehmer (project leader), Anh-Linh Ngo (editor-in-chief)

Guest editorial team:
   Florian Hertweck, Milica Topalović with Marija Marić, Nazlı Tümerdem, and Santiago del Hierro, Leo Paulmichl

Cover: Bas Princen, *Djenné Mosque*, 2010
Each spring on the day of *crépissage*, the Great Mosque of Djenné in Mali, which is made of adobe tiles, is protected against the rainy season in a collective act of maintenance by a new plaster coat made of clay slurry, sand, and rice husks. This collective practice of repair dates back to the very first Great Mosque that was built on this spot back in the 13th century. The edifice became dilapidated in the 19th century owing to local conflicts; in 1907 it was rebuilt on the old foundations. The planning of the building was later attributed to the French colonial power, and symmetries and hierarchies of order were projected back onto the polytechnic training the French engineers had enjoyed. This narrative is, however, not uncontroversial: Architectural historian Jean-Louis Bourgeois argues that the architecture is the work of local masons headed by guild leader Ismaila Traoré, as it bears no traces of the use of colonial surveying techniques. This photograph by Bas Princen taken in 2010 as a part of a series with the same name, shows the monument during a major act of reconstruction during which the in part centuries-old adobe tiles protected by the annual plaster were repaired.

Repa
and
Repa

ir

raton

Separating the

Jason W. Moore and Raj Patel in conversation
with Milica Topalović, Alex Nehmer, and Nitin Bathla

Repair from the Fix—

Our modern world is based on the cheapening of nature *and* human life, argue environmental historian Jason W. Moore and economist Raj Patel. In conversation with guest editor Milica Topalović, Alex Nehmer of ARCH+, and architect Nitin Bathla, they discuss how to repair the damage caused by the colonial capitalist world system without resorting to fixes that merely displace these crises.

Toward a

Photo essay: Bas Princen

Reconstruction Ecology

Milica Topalović *The Great Repair* aims to develop a panorama of thinking and practices of repair which respond in different ways to "the broken world" in which we live. The work that you have done individually, but also together for your book *A History of the World in Seven Cheap Things*, provides an encompassing diagnosis of how we have got into this state, but you also reflect on possible counterstrategies. Could you start by briefly restating the thesis of your book?

Jason W. Moore At the center of our book was the attempt to identify turning points in the long span of capitalist world history which have led to a devaluation of webs of life, including humans. Our view of these developments follows a perspective we call "world-ecology." This term does not describe the "ecology of the world," but rather emphasizes that capitalism is not just part of ecology, it is an ecology—a bundle of relations that entwines power, capital, and life. These relations are not purely "social," they are at the same time producers and products of environmental conditions. And conversely, the web of life is also not only a product but also a producer of historical change. The concept of world-ecology is offered as an antidote to the Cartesian "Man versus Nature" paradigm that lies at the heart of the modern world and that to this day is inscribed in conventional modes of thinking about history and webs of life. Capitalism as world-ecology is very much the history of the civilizing project and its real abstractions. Nature and Society, Man and Woman, Black and White, etc.—these became instruments of domination, *real abstractions* with enormous material power. That means they don't just describe and categorize the world but they have served practically to dominate and cheapen the lives of almost all humans and the rest of nature, above all by means of four "cheap things": labor, food, energy, and raw materials. Since the age of the Conquistadors, these organizing principles fundamentally make and shape our world in the interests of the One Percent. The world-ecology conversation thus also took shape as a protest against, and an alternative to, the conventional modes of thinking about environment and society that emerged and developed over the past 50 years among both mainstream critics, and also many eco-socialists and ecological Marxists. To ignore these violent and real abstractions of "society" and "environment" and to adopt uncritically the terms of the bourgeois fetishes of growth, the economy, etc., is not only to invite failure but to guarantee it.

MT How would you reflect on the notion of repair from the perspective of world-ecology?

Raj Patel Talking about these real abstractions in our discussion of "Seven Cheap Things," the idea of the "thing" and its cheapness are key concepts. When we say that capitalism makes and takes nature's free gifts, we don't imagine those gifts dangling there waiting for capitalism to take them. In order for capitalism to appropriate, to force them into processes of exchange and profit, it has to identify and differentiate. What happens is thus a process of reification, the formation of a real abstraction that transforms the web of life away from a series of relationships into individuated things—commodities, units of account, and the temporal purchase of labor—which then is ready to be captured by accountants, often free but never without cost.

Thinking about repair, we should be analytically rigorous, and distinguish a repair from a *fix*. Borrowing from David Harvey's notion of the "spatial fix"—which describes capitalism's strategy of regulating crises temporarily through geographical and technological expansion—we can understand *fixes* as processes that do not solve capitalism's inner contradictions but merely displace them. These *fixes* manifest as frontiers, which, driven by forces of endless accumulation, continually expand the principles of the capitalist order across the planet. As David Harvey observes, colonialism and accumulation by dispossession is the fix for crisis. Marx already pointed this out: After writing at length about the circulation of money into commodities and back into money—an endless cycle of accumulation—he suddenly changed the subject in the last chapter of *Capital: Volume 1* to talk about colonialism. For this is what enables the constant cycle of furthering, deepening and exhaustion, and reinvention of frontiers.

MT A lot has happened since the book appeared, from the Black Lives Matter movement to the election and defeat of Donald Trump, to the COVID-19 pandemic, and the war in Ukraine. Do these events cast new light on the arguments in your book?

RP One of the points where I believe we pushed the thinking forward in *Seven Cheap Things* was by reflecting on the cycle of war-money-war, analogous to the central Marxist transformation of money into commodities and back into money. If the *Great Repair* is the opposite of the condition we are in right now, then for a transformative repair to happen, we need to understand capital's destructive and steadfast dependency on cycles of conflict. Arms spending is reaching unprecedented heights, everywhere. The war in Ukraine is today the most publicized but far from most expensive example of money being transformed into weapons with a view to make money out of crisis. These crises manifest themselves in places like India or Brazil where security-minded states have manufactured many alibis for soaring arms spending. It's not an accident that we are seeing, again, the cycle of war-money-war, in border conflicts but also armaments used against indigenous communities, used in the process of deepening the frontiers of the state and of capitalist extraction, while we are simultaneously approaching the end of the cheapness of these things.

JWM The frontiers are exhausted. I'm surprised at how often the Left—much more than the business press even!—argue that the era of Cheap Nature still has a long way to go. The exhaustion of frontiers is not simply depletion; it implies financialization, social movement struggles, and geopolitics. Just look at the IMF's all-commodity price index which has doubled over the past two years. And while rising energy prices are driving the new commodities boom, it's not limited to energy; food inflation is also huge, inflicting catastrophic damage to the working class. The problem is that frontiers are exhausted, but the frontier *strategy* of Cheap Nature continues and with an increasingly pathological force. This is the problem of American unipolar hegemony as it emerged after the overthrow of the Soviet Union. If we were writing this book in 2022, we would make the argument that American regime-change politics is at the center of any conception of climate justice. This became clear to me as we were writing the chapter on Cheap Money, which is not about money in a narrow economic sense, but about how modern conquest was financialized from the beginning, and how those conquests transformed the wealth, plenitude, and work of planetary life into *capital.* The horrific body count of "disposable" indigenous and African workers in the early silver mining and sugar growing frontiers produced wealth but not capital; that transformation required armies and bankers. Every stage of capitalism has required new forms and expanded volumes of Cheap Nature. These Cheap Natures were secured by force, organized by great superpowers and their military-industrial complexes.

As we confront the planetary inferno today, this tendency has not receded, but advanced. As the opportunities for appropriating Cheap Natures receded in the late 20th century, the American Empire has intensified its Cold War logic of militarized accumulation. This is a stubborn fact generally ignored by mainstream environmentalism. Don't take my word for it. The Military Intervention Project at Tufts University has identified over 500 military interventions in US history. More than a third of those have occurred since 1999. At the same time, the Pentagon is the world's largest institutional emitter of carbon dioxide. Meanwhile, the US and Russia have begun training and courting African militaries—many of them involved in a recent string of coups. The specter of Cheap Nature wars—already underway in the war in the Ukraine—haunts Africa, and fuels great power rivalry everywhere. While Europeans cry out for "degrowth," many of the same elements are calling for rearmament and war—the German Greens are a good example. The crisis of Cheap Nature and therefore of capital accumulation is, for the great powers, a death spiral towards world war. Most environmentalists have been silent on this reality.

From this standpoint, an internationalist front of what Marx and Engels called the associated producers and reproducers of life is today more necessary than ever. Unfortunately, the forces on the Left who advocate for an internationalist and anti-imperialist front to climate justice are weaker than ever, while the counterforces appear to be stronger than ever. Here the academic discourse that favors ideas of settler colonialism and decoloniality emptied of their class relations is especially troubling.

Alex Nehmer For us, architecture and urban design are of particular interest. What role do they play in these processes of cheapening? How would you link these frontier strategies to the built environment?

RP The idea of the city only makes sense in dialectical relation to the non-city, which come to be narrated as "the countryside." To illustrate this, let's look for instance at *The Allegory of Good and Bad Government*, a series of three frescoes painted by Ambrogio Lorenzetti for the Palazzo Pubblico in Siena in 1338/39. The frescoes depict the effects of good and bad governance on the city and on the countryside, and they show their dialectic relation. We can see the city itself as demarcated by frontiers; in the case of early medieval cities quite literally with walls beyond which lies the territory from which extraction is necessary in order to constitute the city. This is a depiction of the city as both parasitic on, and oblivious to, frontiers beyond the urban. But not just beyond the urban: It is not as simple as saying that wherever you see a wall, inside is the urban and outside is the countryside and the zone of extraction. There are frontiers within urban areas as well that are mined, for finance, for the debt of working-class people. In some of the financier reports the language of mining is used explicitly to think about certain urban populations as populations from whom wealth ought to be extracted. It is important to see the urban as constituted through frontiers.

JWM Here I would bring in our comrade Neil Brenner. Together with Christian Schmid he has put forward a planetary urbanization thesis that resists methodological city-ism, which means taking the urban as a "basic unit," much as Raj and I resist, in a different register, taking society as a basic unit. The problem with "basic unit" approaches is that they embody the principles of bourgeois reductionism—basically the philosophical expression of early modern primitive accumulation. The planetary urbanization thesis, by contrast, allows us to link built environments in the so-called cities and in the so-called countryside. The built environment is not just about cities. Nothing in these operational landscapes, to borrow Brenner and Schmid's term, can be adequately conceptualized without the profound capitalization and militarization of agrarian geographies, which is at the heart of frontier-making.

Coming back to the question of repair and fix, the discussion of ecological reparations could be the beginning of conceptualizing a political strategy of what I would call a *reconstruction* ecology. *Reconstruction* in multiple registers: In the climate crisis, every major city on earth located next to a coastline will have to be moved, the electrical grids will have to be reconfigured, housing, water and food systems will have to be reimagined. This requires a profound act of imagination. Looking at the socialist experiences of the Soviet Union and China in particular, and Cuba in a different register, could be extremely valuable for that.

AN A large part of environmental discourse focuses on fossil fuels. In architecture as well, the decarbonization of the built environment is urgent, as construction is one of the largest direct and indirect users of fossil energy. In your analysis, however, you don't prioritize the question of Cheap Energy above other processes of cheapening.

War

Tyranny

Avarice

Justice

How do you see the necessity of decarbonization and its relationship to counterstrategies in other fields?

RP I live in Texas, where our most famous resident now is Elon Musk. Let's set aside the vast amount of carbon he puts into the air through his rockets in his desire to colonize and create a new frontier on Mars. Merely his idea that if we all drive a Tesla everything is going to be fine is just a re-inscription of a certain kind of imperial politics of consumption. In response to the extraction of lithium from Bolivia, for instance, and the associated coups that overthrew the legitimate government of the Plurinational State of Bolivia, he literally said: "We will coup who we want." While the engines of capitalism require propulsion, it is important to understand that the structures that support it can be bent to pretty much anything. We could decarbonize and go into full Musk tomorrow, and we'd still be in the Imperium, and still be in a world of *Seven Cheap Things.*

JWM It is unsettling to me to see the return of, not just a profoundly Eurocentric, but a profoundly Anglocentric vision of capitalism as the dominant interpretation of the origins of planetary crisis. This fetishization of the industrial revolution—the view that the crisis is fossil-fuel-driven—is misleading. It's empirically partial at best. And it's a way of obscuring the capitalist and imperialist relations at the heart of the crisis. In *Seven Cheap Things*, Raj and I point out that it is the *plantation* revolution, not the industrial revolution, that is the beating heart of the relations that produce the climate crisis today. A deeper study of history of the so-called industrial revolution makes clear that it doesn't begin with the coal mining revolution—which, by the way, began two and a half centuries earlier. It also doesn't begin with the steam engine. It begins with the cotton gin, and the appropriation of *Gossypium hirsutum* cotton, a particular strain of cotton developed by indigenous peoples, then the expulsion and extermination of those indigenous peoples, the creation of plantations and the revival and expansion of slavery. To draw on the great historian Barbara Fields, the plantation's priority was not to produce racism but profits. Racism was necessary to that process, ideologically necessary in order to sustain Cheap Labor and racialized super-exploitation. Once we begin to look at the plantation revolution in the web of life, it fundamentally changes how we see the climate crisis. It is not "anthropogenic," but rather capitalogenic. The plantation revolution incubated the climate class divide, climate patriarchy, and climate apartheid. Those are the drivers of today's climate crisis, not the results of it.

MT The distinction you made between repair and fix is very helpful here. There is a lot of "fixing" going on in mainstream European and American politics right now, in the plans for the Green New Deal for instance. What would an actual repair look like instead?

RP We can understand the fix as a way to keep a broken system going, rather than repairing it. A fix is entirely different from a transformative reconstruction as a way of rebuilding with different forces in the driving seat. To reconstruct the economy is to involve reparative work. Reparations for patriarchy for example. Given that currently the household is one of the agents of the perpetuation of empire, the reconstruction of the household is another litmus test of the redistribution of power. This will require very difficult conversations, personal reconstruction, and collective transformation. Will comrades who identify as men have to engage in some therapy? Of course we will. We are constructed through these real abstractions and letting them go is not easy but that's the work of reconstruction. The psychoanalytical work that the climate crisis demands belongs not in oak-paneled rooms but on shop floors and in fields, offices, and classrooms. This reimagination is a collective act of libera-

The cotton gin, invented by American Eli Whitney in 1793, mechanically separated the cotton from the seeds. This not only massively boosted productivity but also increased the need for enslaved workers on the American plantations.

Cotton mill owned by the Lancashire Cotton Corporation in Failsworth, Manchester, about 1935
Cotton from slave plantations, the exploitation of workers and children, and coal and steam are all central elements of the historical industrial mills.

tion which we could understand as a form of self-repair. Never under capitalism have the majority been asked about the world we would like to live in. To dream, and dream seditiously, is something that many humans need to practice, for we have been prevented from doing it for centuries. And the shop floors and community centers and classrooms and kitchen tables where these dreams will be shared are themselves subject to reimagination.

JWM Here again we can look to history. This emphasis on "the new socialist man and woman" which appears in every great socialist revolution insists that these are collective, class, and cultural processes of struggle. An important moment of reconstruction involves an overhaul of bourgeois habits and structures of feeling and mind in order to reckon with the challenges of building an egalitarian world, both in terms of consciousness and, then, in terms of built environments of every kind.

I would also point to another moment of reconstruction: Reconstruction ecology hearkens back to Black Reconstruction in the American South after the Civil War. The Radical Republicans saw that the plantation aristocracy had reassumed the reins of power and were proceeding to establish an ecology of power, profit, and life in the South that was as ruthless and violent as the antebellum slaveholding regime. In response, the Republicans sent soldiers to reimpose the conditions for democracy. It was a brief historical moment of new possibilities and tremendous productive unrest. This reminds me of Machiavelli's age-old quote about the distinction between armed prophets and unarmed prophets. I think much of the Left in the Global North

Albrecht Dürer, *The Expulsion from Paradise*, 1510
In her 2004 book *Caliban and the Witch*, feminist theorist Silvia Federici linked Dürer's depiction of the expulsion of Adam and Eve from Paradise with the expulsion of farmers from their commons, a process that was starting throughout western Europe at the time when Dürer produced the woodcut. Women were especially hard hit by the transformation to a money economy, which, Federici suggests, forced them into devalued reproductive labor.

has the entirely misleading assumption that the reconstruction of the world in a just and egalitarian way can proceed as if, once we secure a majority in parliament, we can legislate the One Percent out of existence. There is nothing in the history of capital and empire that suggests that the One Percent will go down without a fight. As we are seeing with the invocation and intensification of regime change politics, the lessons of Machiavelli's insight remain indispensable. We need a revolutionary climate politics that fights for planetary justice and centers reconstruction.

Nitin Bathla Raj, you have worked in particular on the field of agroecology as a counterparadigm to the capitalization of agrarian geography. What course of action do you envision in this field of reconstruction?

RP Land reform is the first objective. But how do you get land reform when the person who owns the most private farmland in the United States is Bill Gates? In order for agroecology to work, you need to understand that agroecology is not just a technique to do right by the soil, not just about planting some soy, corn, beans, and squash, and stopping the use of Monsanto's wicked chemicals. In fact, it is about a reconstruction of everything from the household to the modes of operation of the economy.

I find myself in full-throated alignment with the landless peasants. In India, however, we also have Zero Budget Natural Farming initiatives which in some places are wedded to a cer-

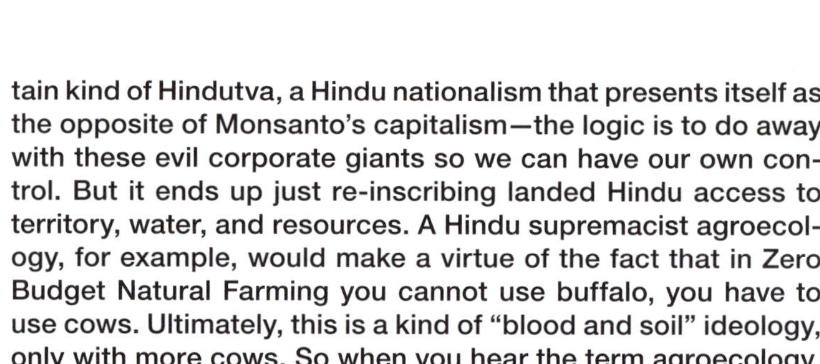

tain kind of Hindutva, a Hindu nationalism that presents itself as the opposite of Monsanto's capitalism—the logic is to do away with these evil corporate giants so we can have our own control. But it ends up just re-inscribing landed Hindu access to territory, water, and resources. A Hindu supremacist agroecology, for example, would make a virtue of the fact that in Zero Budget Natural Farming you cannot use buffalo, you have to use cows. Ultimately, this is a kind of "blood and soil" ideology, only with more cows. So when you hear the term agroecology, be very suspicious and ready to interrogate the ways that agroecologists think.

MT Agroecological reconstruction looks very different in the context of Switzerland compared to a country in Africa for example. About 70 percent of Swiss agriculture subsidies incentivize forms of agriculture damaging to the environment; at the European level the numbers are similar. But these subsidies could be redirected. In your view, what are the institutions that are potentially allies in such an undertaking? To what extent can we rely on the state?

RP How can one deploy the state when the state clearly remains the elite committee for the bourgeoisie? This is a difficult question of practical politics. If there are democratic moments where the state can be tilted towards doing the right thing—and Switzerland is unusual in its possibilities of direct citizen mobilization—that seems to me to be a force for good. But what are the movements organizing to achieve these ends? Is it the bourgeois environmentalists who just want to treat their bodies as a temple and therefore don't want glyphosate in it? Or is it a movement driven by the interests of landless people? Concerning farming subsidies, I think the interesting question is not only to which forms of agriculture they go, but also to whom they go. In the United States Black farmers owned 16 million acres of land at the beginning of the 20th century, by the end of the century it was only 4.7 million acres, which amounts to a loss of $326 billion. What happened there? Well, there was a series of farm subsidies and a market that was geared towards making sure that white farms grew bigger. The Biden administration recently floated an idea to address the history of racial discrimination in US farm assistance by forgiving loans to black farmers. Here in Texas, it was met with a series of lawsuits by white land owners. So here again, a "blood-and-soil" ideology comes into play at the expense of those whose lives have been cheapened.

But we are not seeing calls on the state to engage in widespread land reform. Instead, in India for example even long sacrosanct land ceilings are being breached as the power of capital is encroaching on the state. So I think what is interesting is precisely the political organizing around repair that might point us toward more generative politics.

MT What do you see as effective forms of political struggle in this context?

RP I was very excited to be reminded that the Dalit Panthers, who formed in India inspired by the US Black Panther Party, are celebrating their 50th anniversary this year. The working class around the world is in an emergency that needs to be met, and the state is useful only in managing that emergency, through the expediencies of food banks and emergency food aid for example, while never being ready to address the root causes of why the poor remain hungry. The Black Panthers understood that both revolution and survival to that point were important, and that this would require a shared and multiple international class struggle. The movement may be crushed, but its ideas still circulate. They survive in forms of internationalist politics around the world from the Landless Workers' Movement in Brazil, to the Abahlali baseMjondolo, a socialist shack dwellers'

OIA·
Concord

Peace

Peace

Temperance

movement in South Africa that organizes land occupations, establishes communes, and campaigns against forced evictions and for social housing.

JWM Well, I wish there were more politics. Movements like Black Lives Matter and before them Occupy Wall Street ultimately failed to formulate a political vision. The destruction of working-class power in the US especially has contributed to an anti-statism that has crippled the political imagination. But social power without a political vision—a vision of building working-class power and a political vehicle to impose those interests on the state-corporate-party apparatus—will go nowhere. Without a political vision, we are doomed to "resistance" and defeat.

NB Teaching at the ETH Zürich and other universities I can see that among students and young practitioners in architecture and urban planning there is a wide interest in world-ecology and critical thought in general, and there is an intention to direct this interest into activism. What would be your advice to them?

RP I would advise that they engage in class suicide. Universities are temples for bourgeois reproduction—social reproduction and the reproduction of capital. We need to put the resources of these institutions of theft in the hands of the workers and learn from them how we should redeploy these resources. Maybe these decolonized and working-class-dominated spaces of learning will get called universities, but only after a process of reconstruction. The hardest part is, how do we, as academics, hold ourselves accountable? If we are not exposing ourselves to disagreement including from our working class comrades, then our politics isn't really politics.

MT Where would you start to repair the education system and curriculum?

JWM Yet inside the university we are not even allowed to say the word "class." Class politics is a taboo subject. We need to remind ourselves, as the New Left did in the 1960s, that the universities are part of the problem. The universities are in fact knowledge factories, to quote Mario Savio. Within the knowledge factory—and let's remember that factories as such are not bad, only their bourgeois form—there are pockets of liberated spaces. But even here, we see serious divisions: between permanent faculty and adjuncts; research faculty and teaching faculty; professors and graduate students; academic and non-academic workers, from departmental administrative staff to janitors; and of course, between all these groups and the students. The professoriate's track record of solidarity with graduate student workers and non-academic workers is, to put it politely, extremely uneven. Let's not pretend these questions of solidarity within the knowledge factory are incidental to the kinds of research and thinking that dominate the world university system. The knowledge factory reveals its strong class character in reproducing a professional managerial class that is historically anti–working class, imperial, and willing to make all sorts of compromises with capital. One of the chief functions of The University is to produce forms of managerialism—in terms of technical skills but also outlook. Not just management in the narrow sense of the workplace but also for example social work and social policy as the management of the poor layers of the working class. Nowhere is this tendency more pronounced over the past 50 years than in the case of environmentalism. Environmentalism in its dominant form today is essentially planetary management. In an era of planetary inferno, managing the problems of capitalism—and reproducing academic business-as-usual—will not produce the kinds of radical socio-ecological change we so urgently need. Without a critique of the University and its complicity in the climate-academic industrial complex—to adapt a phrase from the 1960s—all of these intersectional, critical ideas will be just that: ideas. They will remain entirely compatible with the continued rule of the One Percent and probably put to work in favor of some Davos style techno-authoritarian sustainability project. The time for polite academic conversation is over. If we really believe that we are in the midst of an extraordinary tipping point in world history, we need to break with academic conventions. We need to pose the dangerous questions.

Bas Princen, *Room of Peace*, 2014
Inkjet print on rice paper

The photo series consists of detailed images of the Virtues and Vices in Ambrogio Lorenzetti's fresco *The Allegory of Good and Bad Government* (1338/39) in the Palazzo Pubblico in Siena.

"We Have to Adopt a Materialistic Approach!"

Olúfẹ́mi O. Táíwò in conversation
with Alex Nehmer and Markus Krieger

Photo essay: Richard Misrach

The philosopher and political scientist Olúfẹ́mi O. Táíwò calls for thinking climate justice together with reparations for historical injustice. With ARCH+ editors Alex Nehmer and Markus Krieger, he discusses how his materialist understanding of repair can be made fertile for the urgently needed transformations in architecture.

Alex Nehmer One aim of our project *The Great Repair* is to not think of "repair" as a restoration of the past, but as transformation towards a better future—which is why your understanding of reparations was of particular interest to us. In your book *Reconsidering Reparations* you describe reparations as a practice of worldmaking oriented towards a more just future. What do you mean by that?

Olúfẹ́mi O. Táíwò In *Reconsidering Reparations*, I explored the connection between climate justice and reparations for transatlantic slavery and colonialism. In this context, reparations respond not just to any history of injustice but to the particular injustices which have built the world. I mean *built* in the literal sense. The fact that we have a planetary-scale economic and political system is a direct causal result of these specific historical events and injustices. If we understand the history of global racial empire as the construction of the world, then it is a short step to tasking reparations with what I call the "constructive view," which takes the position that we should rebuild the world, this time with justice as its organizing principle.

The idea of an organizing principle or a design principle is deeply built into how I think of reparations and justice in general. Racial stratifications can be seen as a design principle of the unjust planetary-scale system which we inherited from global racial empire. When we respond to concrete institutions or even concrete physical structures within that world, we can ask questions which give us different ways of thinking about repair. Let's say we come across a power line that provides energy exclusively to a rich neighborhood but which is now broken. We could think of repair in a purely mechanical sense here: The power line is down, we put it back up, get it back into working order. However, this sense of repair is tied to an old design principle: What this piece of machinery was supposed to achieve functionally represents a state in the past. But we are not tied to that mechanical understanding. We can ask, what role *could* this object play? What if we expanded energy access beyond this rich community to the neighboring communities? We could think of that as a kind of repair, not from the point of view of yesterday's organizing principle but of a new organizing principle. Who do we think should have energy access and what opportunities do we have, given the present state of the world, to make energy available to them? This would involve new kinds of design decisions that we don't leave to the past but we ourselves would have to take up in our process of relating to the world.

Once we think of repair in this expansive way, we're not even chained to the past at all. We can just skip to the question of who should have energy access. Maybe we expand energy access by repairing or expanding the existing grid. Maybe we build entirely new grids. But in either case we are guided by forward-looking decisions based on our political commitments. What do we want the world to look like and how do we make things accordingly? Physical things like grids, institutional things like organizations, moral things like norms. How do we make those in a way that meets our new design principles in a world that has been built on bad organizing principles?

Markus Krieger In your book you differentiate the constructive view from other concepts of reparations.

OT There are two families of other views I discuss in *Reconsidering Reparations.* One is the "harm repair view." This notion focuses on the people who have been marginalized and disadvantaged

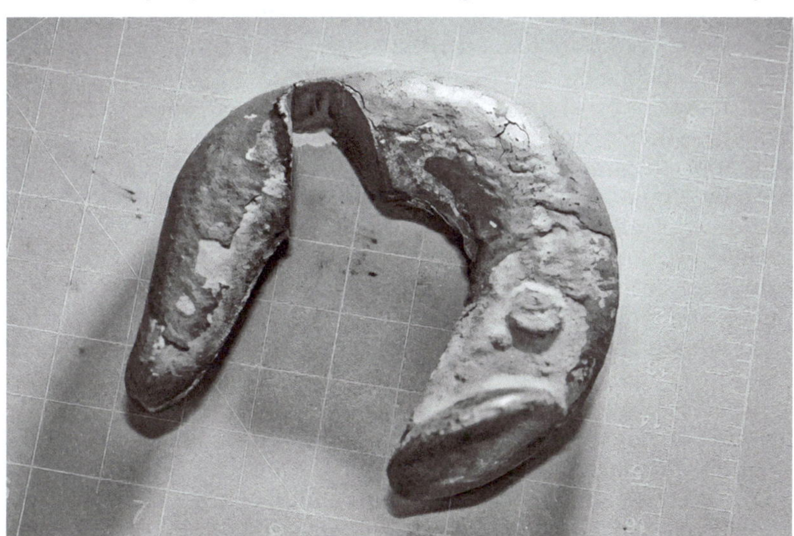

Failure of a steel hook on a high-voltage pylon that had fallen into disrepair in the absence of maintenance was found to have caused the "Camp Fire" of 2018. Not least owing to a drought exacerbated by climate change, this resulted in the deadliest and most devastating wildfire in Californian history.

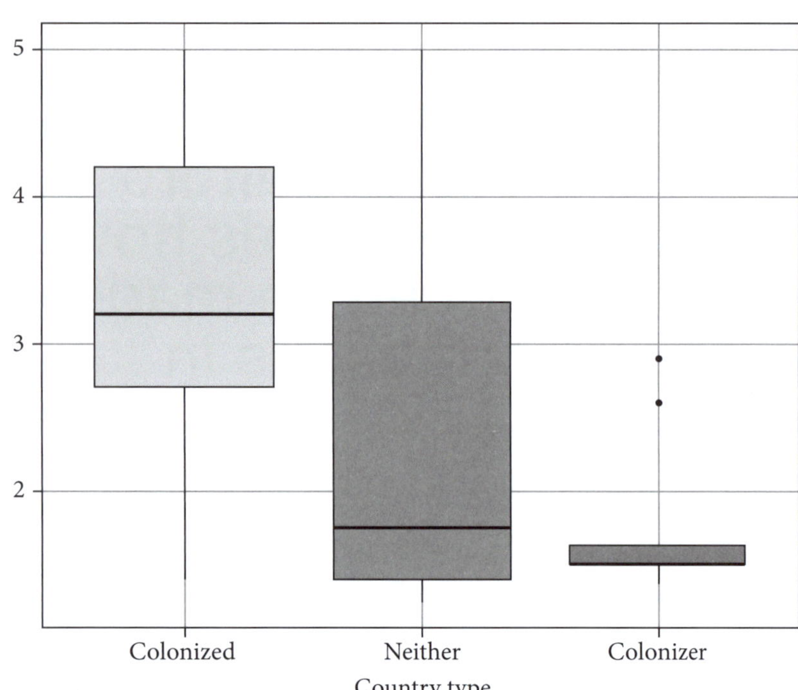

Climate vulnerability index (5 = highest vulnerability)
Graphic in Olúfẹ́mi O. Táíwò, *Reconsidering Reparations* (New York: Oxford University Press, 2022), 171.

by the history of global racial empire and therefore have fewer welfare and life opportunities than they should have. What reparations are tasked with in this view is to increase people's welfare by giving them cash, land, or assets in order to make up the difference between the level of welfare they're at and the level of welfare they should be at. In this way, reparations would also address some of the injustices of the past. The "relationship repair view" states that social relations have been harmed by the history of global racial empire. People who are racially marginalized might rightfully distrust their neighbors or the government. The idea is that we can fix these relationships through reparations, that they can serve as a tool of reconciliation.

While I think both notions get important things right, they don't necessarily involve changing the global political system and the economic distribution systems which explain why some people have more life chances than others and why some people don't trust other people or institutions. While we should strive for some people to have more money than they currently have, and we should want to mend relationships, we should also want to change the structures themselves.

MK The burning of fossil fuels is the single largest cause of anthropogenic greenhouse gases; it is responsible for over two-thirds of all global emissions. In this perspective, one must also understand the architectural and urban history of the Global North since industrialization as fossil-fuel-based space production. Focusing solely on emissions, however, does little to show how the climate crisis destructively intersects with the historical injustices and ordering principles you emphasize. For example, the Crystal Palace in London, constructed of steel and glass, was not only at the origin of the fossil fuel turn in architecture, it was also a space for the display of colonial power. Your book can be read as a response to such entanglements. You call for reparations to be thought together with the climate crisis. Why do you make this connection?

OT The basic perspective I have on reparations is a broadly materialist one. It is about creating actual structures, both physical and institutional, in response to the climate crisis and the legacy of global racial empire, and in doing so, creating the material and political conditions for life. Especially the life of human animals, but with important consequences for nonhuman creatures as well. Justice, from my materialist perspective, is a description of what particular designs and structures do or do not achieve. When we fail to be holistic in our thinking about the kinds of political challenges we're taking on, like when we redesign structures in response to specific problems such as the climate crisis, we might redesign those institutions in ways that solve one problem while creating others. As is unfortunately common in the history of racial capitalism, we solve a problem for some people by shifting it onto other people.

It is not that every aspect of today's global racial empire is rooted in the impacts of climate change. But every aspect of tomorrow's global racial empire will be. In the history of the world system that we have inherited, fossil fuels and changes to the energy system alongside the industrial revolution had a large role in enabling those who exerted colonial power during past generations to so do. The control over future energy systems—over the continued use of fossil fuels in the most apocalyptic case, but even over changes made to address the climate crisis—might be exerted in ways that re-entrench or even worsen existing patterns of historical domination. For example: We could build electric vehicles with minerals extracted by Indigenous and Black people in Chile and the Democratic Republic of Congo in ways that worsen political conditions and people's self-determination in those places. Nevertheless, we would make some progress with respect to emissions and think of this as a political victory. But both the climate crisis and reparations are going to call on us to fundamentally remake our political and economic structures. And the ways in which we remake our structures in response to both must inform each other.

MK In urban discourse, climate change is often framed as an adaption problem. In the discussion about measures to establish climate safety, a key notion is the "resilient city." But architecture, urbanism, and agriculture adaptations are based on both financial and material access to resources. Your work crucially points out that disparities in adaptive capacities result in large differences in climate vulnerability not just between the Global South and the Global North but also within countries.

OT If we want to know how the climate crisis will interact with global racial empire's distribution of advantages and disadvantages, one place to start is looking at how global racial empire already distributes environmental risk and vulnerability *right now.* Take pollution as an example: Most countries that were not colonized during the last 500 years have a comparatively low mortality rate due to pollution: fewer than 50 deaths per 100,000; whereas in countries that were colonized the mortality rate is more than double that. The two groups of countries live in different environmental realities.

Wealth and power imbalances cause major differences in adaptive capacity. This translates, for example, into differential access to physical infrastructure and warning systems that can be used to respond to the climate crisis. Or differential access to vaccines and medication that can be used to respond to public health crises, which are themselves also bound up with the climate crisis and broader ecological collapse.

AN Under the theme of repair, we also address practices of reconstruction after environmental disasters. For example, the response to the massive destruction caused by the flooding of the German Ahr valley in 2021 or rebuilding efforts after the 2011 earthquake and tsunami in Japan. With the climate crisis getting even worse in the coming years, architecture will have to be increasingly employed in such a setting. In your work you argue against a depoliticized view of environmental disasters, highlighting that such catastrophes and

Richard Misrach, from the series *Untitled [New Orleans and the Gulf Coast]*, 2005

Hurricane Katrina was one of the worst natural disasters in the history of the US and destroyed large parts of the East Coast in 2005. US photographer Richard Misrach documented the state of the communities that had been emptied by it—and the messages that the inhabitants and helpers left behind.

ORIENTAL RUGS
ANTIQUE AND NEW
DONT TRY.
I AM SLEEPING
INSIDE WITH
A BIG DOG,
AN UGLY WOMAN,
TWO SHOTGUNS
AND A CLAW HAMMER
9/11/05 YOU
MISS YALL COME
CARNIVAL
MY PARA RA
COME BACK
ZULU, BACCH
PROTEUS
MUSES.
HEY TAR
SOMETHING

I AM HERE
I HAVE A GUN

Sorry

the resulting damages are far from solely "natural," but distributed along the lines of historically and politically shaped inequalities. What could rebuilding practices look like that take this into account?

OT The preexisting structures of inequality are one of the main causal determinants of the actual distribution of suffering that results from natural disasters. They may be caused by wind and rain, but it is the natural world interacting with our social system that explains the social results. The example I use in my book is Hurricane Katrina. People who were able to respond to the advance warnings were disproportionately more affluent, able-bodied, younger, and often racially advantaged. The way that environmental disasters affect people strongly relates to who our social systems have been designed to protect, and who they have been designed to render vulnerable. We could counter that by for example redesigning the distribution of resources like disaster insurance or rapid response networks. Bangladesh, for example, has a very robust cyclone response system. It is a multi-layered early warning system that combines weather monitoring and communication technologies with a social warning system made up of a large network of volunteers. Importantly, half of these volunteers are women, in order to better support women who had previously been disproportionately affected by disasters. We should build systems like this in more places. But of course, there are also actual physical structures that are climate-resilient and energy efficient, and we have to build and distribute them in ways that don't just track preexisting privilege. Market principles are distributive mechanisms which ensure that the people who have the most consumer power get first access. This means there needs to be some other way to ensure the public provision of various forms of climate-resistant physical architecture as well as the political and economic architecture to respond to the history of injustices that accounts for our current moment.

AN In her article "The Migrant Workers Who Follow Climate Disasters" published in *The New Yorker* in November 2021, journalist Sarah Stillman outlines a disaster-recovery industry that is currently mushrooming in the US in response to growing numbers of fires, floods, and hurricanes. She exposes how large disaster-restoration firms make a profit from these catastrophes while exploiting mainly immigrant workers and putting them at risk of injury and death. That must surely be one of the most striking examples of old inequalities built into current ways of responding to crises.

OT Yes, exactly. It is surprising that we haven't seen more of it already. Perhaps owing to the "short term-ism" of the market. I think we are going to see much more of that in the years going forward and we have to put a stop to it.

MK You also highlight the danger of new forms of colonialism through "green" technologies, especially those linked to large-scale land acquisitions. There are now industrial processes to manufacture carbon-neutral steel with hydrogen for example. In order to meet the calculated increase in demand for "green hydrogen" in Germany and the expansion of renewable energy needed to meet it, land areas in northern Africa have been targeted as production sites, among others. There are also efforts in the construction sector to promote a shift away from building mostly with concrete and steel to timber construction. The hope is that buildings could function as carbon sinks, but this would need large-scale afforestation which is very land-use intensive. Where do you see the dangers in efforts such as these? Would it still be possible for them to bring more justice instead of new inequalities?

OT It really matters *how.* Many of the conversations we have about climate politics revolve around these categories: Green hydrogen, solar or wind power, and so on, are they good or bad technologies? To answer those questions, we have to look at the

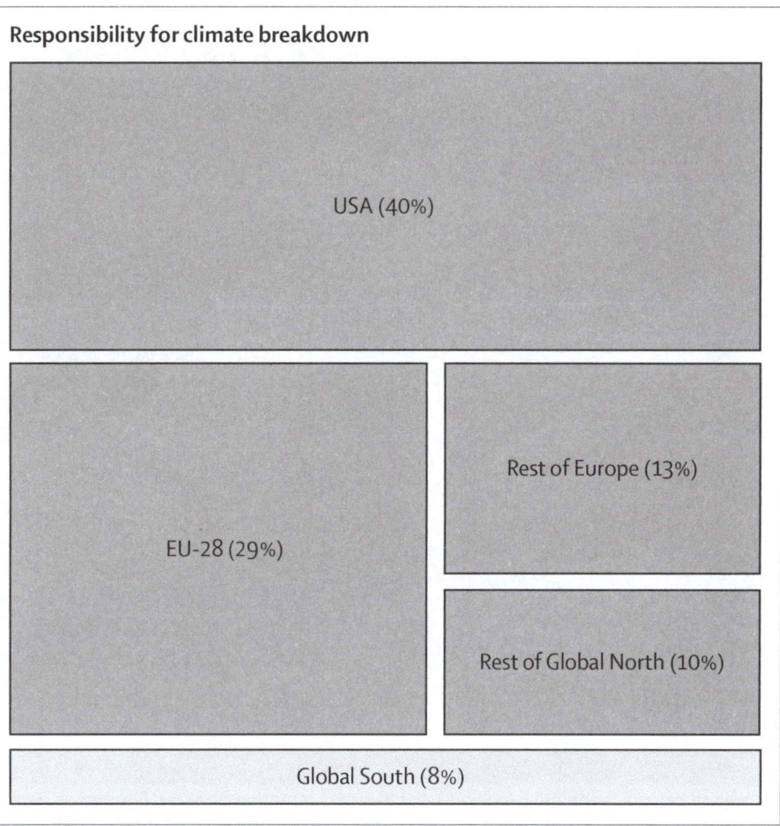

Responsibility for climate breakdown according to data from 2015:
Global North includes the US, Canada, Europe, Israel, Australia, New Zealand, and Japan; *Global South* South America, Africa, the Middle East, and Asia

Jason Hickel, "Quantifying National Responsibility for Climate Breakdown: An Equality Based Attribution Approach for Carbon Dioxide Emissions in Excess of the Planetary Boundary," *The Lancet Planetary Health* 4, no. 9 (2020): 403.

details: Where are we putting the wind farm, exactly? Who gets to decide? Who benefits?

I'm worried about climate colonialism in particular. This notion describes a situation where you take something that is at least in principle good, like wind or solar farms, and implement them with policies which exploit or worsen relations of domination between places. This is at play, for example, in the ways individual countries account for their emissions. Many countries simply relocate their emission-causing industries to other parts of the world. If you develop afforestation projects as compensation but do that on land in the Global South, you are often just exploiting the unequal political costs of land use. People with interests around land use in Germany will be harder to evict for a state than people in Namibia might be. The eviction or violation of the land use rights of Indigenous peoples has been a major issue globally, especially in the nature conservation industry. As I said, we have to figure out the responses to these things down to the details. But generally, community control over climate projects and forms of governance that cement that control would be a first line of defense against climate colonialism.

AN What role could technology play within a transition towards more justice? You argue for example for a more nuanced view of geoengineering against the tendency, particularly on the Left, of simply writing it off. One common criticism is that technological solutions depoliticize our response to the climate crisis, turn it into a matter decided over by experts instead of by democratic negotiation. How could we think geoengineering in a non-technocratic way?

OT I should first say that I am extremely skeptical of geoengineering. I see the possibility of geoengineering contributing something positive to the world as being very remote. The only reason

By means of non-technical processes such as reforestation or algae farming as well as technical plants for direct air capture, CO_2 that has already been emitted can be re-captured and stored. This representation by the DESIGN EARTH collective from their series *The Planet After Geoengineering* (2021) shows a process developed by oil companies for drilling oil that injects the CO_2 into porous stone and thus permanently removes it from the planetary carbon cycle. The CO_2-reduction must not, however, be used for "Net Zero" arguments to justify continued use of fossil fuels—in 2020, they still accounted for 84 percent of global primary energy consumption. The precondition for any serious climate justice project remains the end of the fossil-fuel economy, as epitomized by the slogan *Leave it in the ground.*

why it is even worth thinking about is that the possibility of the climate crisis contributing something very negative to the world is not at all remote. I think a lot of the criticisms of geoengineering are spot on, but we have to weigh criticisms against the alternatives rather than just dismiss them. The fact that something is imperfect is a better reason against doing it if there is a perfect or at least less imperfect thing to do. Here, I think what the less imperfect thing to do would be remains an open question. We are not in a situation where there is some set of options lying around that would be obviously efficacious, politically palatable, and likely to work in a just way. Banning research into geoengineering solely on the assumption that it will be impossible to control it politically makes no sense. If we are technically capable of developing such technologies, then surely we can imagine, and actually build, political structures to control them, just as we should create democratic structures in other areas. There aren't models out there at this scale that I know of, but you could for instance imagine citizens' assemblies making decisions about many areas in climate politics, including research production and, perhaps even more importantly, land use management and the provision of energy—what some have called energy democracy. Communities themselves should get to decide how energy is produced, under what circumstances, how it is distributed, and have direct decision-making power over all those matters. That would be, like all political systems, a highly imperfect way of making decisions, but warrants at least thinking about in principle and is worth trying out.

MK You have also written about carbon removal and carbon capture and storage technologies. If we take the possibility of car-

bon-neutral cement, for example, carbon capture technologies seem to be part of the solution to reduce so-called process emissions. But beyond reducing *new* emissions in production through technology, there is the bigger question of how to "repair" the already damaged atmosphere. What is your opinion on these fields of action?

OT In response to arguments about carbon removal, people often point to the unscrupulous ways these arguments are being used, especially by fossil fuel companies to legitimize the continued use of and investment in fossil fuels. This is indeed a tactic to depoliticize our response to the climate crisis and one that makes carbon removal a lifeline for fossil fuels. But it is also true that silence on the discussion of carbon removal in the rich countries, particularly high-emitting rich countries, is being used to help hide their historical responsibility for the climate crisis and ecological destruction. It is not just one set of unscrupulous actors using the idea of carbon removal to their advantage, it is also another set of unscrupulous actors downplaying the idea of carbon removal. There is no path forward compatible with justice that doesn't include significantly reducing new carbon emissions. However, that is not enough: The bottom line is that we have already emitted too much carbon and we have to remove some of it. From a justice perspective we can't just wash our hands of past emissions.

The question from there is not whether to do it or not, but what are the best ways of doing that and how do we distribute the costs and benefits? Many things that would remove carbon aren't especially technological, growing trees or seaweed and adapting alternative forms of agriculture for instance. Ideally, those kinds of approaches could harmonize with other goals like increasing the incomes of farmers and providing more nutritious, more resilient food systems. If we can't achieve sufficient carbon removal this way, then we will have to critically examine technological solutions and at the same time challenge the vested interests and the lies of the Exxons of this world. We have to remove them from the driver's seat, and figure out what happens with those technologies in community-controlled, publicly administered settings.

AN One of your main arguments is that reparations must also entail redistribution. Taking decarbonization as an example, what could that look like practically?

OT A great way to fund some of the carbon removal would be by taking it from the fossil fuel companies—markedly the ones who helped destroy climate politics by promoting climate denial—whether it is by punitive fines or by nationalizing them. On a global level, we could implement a wide variety of carbon removal approaches that take into account the historical responsibility of the rich countries, which have emitted a great deal, without exporting the associated political problems to other parts of the world. If you are one of the former colonizer countries, you figure out where to put a direct air capture facility, where to grow kelp, or find other suitable methods, and you finance it. In this way, carbon removal could become a tool for rectifying historical climate injustices.

MK Which existing institutions and instruments could play a role in this redistribution?

OT One example that has already been adopted by many cities is participatory budgeting, a way of making public direct democratic decisions over public funds. It started in Porto Alegre as an innovation of the Brazilian Workers Party and has been exported to Mozambique, India, and the US. In a lot of these places, to date only a small fraction of the respective city budget comes under participatory budgeting practices. But this percentage could just be increased. That could be a clear, measurable way to not have to invent anything new but nevertheless

WHAT
NOW
?

BROKEN DREAMS

Destroy
this
memory

Keep the
Faith
WE
Will
Rebuild

MK   redistribute power and money in ways that contribute to more just worldmaking.

What role could architects take on in this context? Take cave_bureau as an example: a young practice based in Nairobi that infuses their work with decolonial and ecological thought. Their project *Maasai Cow Corridor* addresses a colonlal-era law that banned the grazing of cows in the city and proposes to reappropriate an infrastructural corridor in Nairobi for the Maasai to move through the city with their herds of cows. In this way, the practice reinterprets a part of Nairobi's current fossil-fuel-based infrastructure initially planned by colonial ambitions towards a more just spatial condition. What role can this kind of project-based approach play in the bigger framework of reparations? And how do we move to a global scale of worldmaking from there?

OT   I think this plays a central role. I have tried to stress in my book that the constructive view of reparations is literal, we actually need to build things. Some of those things will be intangible things like institutions or norms, but a lot of those things are literal, physical objects like buildings, solar panels, and yes, cow corridors! Changing the ways that our cities are designed and who gets to decide over them is deeply part of the worldmaking project, on a global scale as well. But to achieve it at a global scale we have to start at a local scale. This process is not likely to start at the IMF. We have to start locally and from the ground up, that is, doing whatever we can do at that level of politics and building the support, approval, and evidence that is needed to challenge larger structures from there.

AN   In my political work I am involved in activism against the European border regime. There it sometimes seems impossible to bring about positive change because all the things we're up against—from refugee detention centers to draconian laws that criminalize migrants—are not the root problem, but just symptoms of and held in place by racism. How can we start on a small scale as you describe when what it seems we actually have to challenge is the racism behind these injustices?

OT   This is a very important question that makes me emphasize again and again: We have to adopt a materialistic approach! Of course, there is a larger abstract structure of racism. Nonetheless, at the bottom, in any given historical era, it manifests in a set of institutions and norms. Racism is a set of determinate people in determinate political positions exercising their will and their bigotry, or their apathy, as the case might be. You can tear that down brick by brick, not because we need to challenge every single detention center and shut them all individually, but because it does communicate a challenge to detention centers *in general* if you challenge one. People understand that the detention center over here is related in political rationale and purpose to the detention center over there. That is part of why the state is so enamored of the brutal repression of attempts to fight any of these symptoms. It is not because they need this particular node of the network, but it is because they understand that what is being challenged is the entire network of oppression. We should understand the scale of what we are up against, but we shouldn't let it trick us into thinking that we can't do anything about it. Some nodes of the network might be better targets than others and we don't have to take out everything all at once. We can start with something particular and material in front of us. This is how divestment movements have put huge amounts of capital into jeopardy, not because they worked at *every* institution, but because they worked at *some* institutions, and everyone at the other institutions had to wonder whether theirs was next. I think this is how we are going to make progress.

Rescuing History for the Repair Society of the 21st Century sub specie conservatoris

Text: Wilfried Lipp

The concept of the "repair society" was coined in 1993 at the conference *From the Modern to the Postmodern Cult of Monuments?* in Passau, Bavaria.[1] Admittedly, there is an inflation in such hyphenated labels to characterize society. [...] [Terms such as] "media society," "communications society" and "information society," [...] "risk society" and "event society," [...] "service society," "performance society" and "acquisitions society," and all the labels connected to affluence and growth such as [...] "consumer society," the "affluent society," or the "throwaway society" [...] signify a comparative characterization of society.[2] Just as little as can the aforementioned comparable designations, the "repair society" cannot lay claim to exclusive validity [...]. There is a key difference to the other concepts in that they are solely meant diagnostically, while "repair society" is conceived to be both diagnostic and therapeutic, offering a perspective and making an appeal.

The labels of "consumption," "overabundance,"[3] and "throwaway" branch out like the ribs structuring a folding paper fan representing the "affluent society," which points directly to the "repair society." Flip the fan over and you will see its reverse side: the experience of scarcity.[4] It stands as it were behind the phenomena that lead to "repair" and make it inevitable. [...]

Fundamentally, we can distinguish between three (in part interlinked) positions [in the current debate around scarcity]:

– the biological eco-system position with the assumption of factually limited resources. Meaning: Food, air, water, soil, etc. are not unlimitedly available and therefore are becoming ever more significant in terms of scarcity.

– the economic approach which foregrounds the problem of allocation.

– scarcity understood as a variable in the process of society. In the framework outlined here, it is above all this third position that is of interest. [...] En route to the "affluent society" what initially counts is: What gets wasted is that which has no scarcity value. Scarcity once identified is then overcome by production and/or "exploitation." Here, the paradox (according to Luhmann) is: Scarcity generates (produced) squander (keywords: "consumer" or "affluent society"), whereby owing to the consequences of a fast-spreading democratization of consumerism the paradox repeatedly means that new scarcities arise. Under the heading of economic growth, wastage causes waste in order to make space for accelerative new production (keyword: "throwaway society"). [...]

The new and novelty value (which, incidentally, Alois Riegl termed the "beatus possidens" of society)[5] are the engine driving the economy, but at this speed, product novelties can no longer be achieved "objectively." The result is a race of "fake innovations," the permanent career of "fashion" and the "fashionable,"[6] the endless repetition of the "dernier cri" ("innovation society"). This race is, on the other hand, measured according to the "speed of obsolescence": Fast and ever faster aging is the price of the new at all costs. [...]

Repair

In other words, the question is: How to escape this? The—hypothetical—answer: Rescue by "repair." First up: "Repair" is not our destination harbor like Virilio's teleport, but an anchorage on the routes traveled by cultural movement and the process of civilization. In short: "Repair" has a transitory character. When it has been performed, new horizons open up.

"Repair" is an everyday term which is why it is also suitable (just as are "event" or "risk"), for making more far-reaching connections. It is easy to imagine what it means. The term, derived from the Latin "re-parare" and then from the French entered English in the mid-14th century and was construed to mean "to mend, put back in order, restore, to return to sameness."

In everyday parlance, to repair initially refers to both the visual, aesthetic side to objects and to the function side. "Improving"

1   Wilfried Lipp, "Vom modernen zum postmodernen Denkmalkultus? Aspekte zur Reparaturgesellschaft," in *Vom modernen zum postmodernen Denkmalkultus? Denkmalpflege am Ende des 20. Jahrhunderts*, eds. Wilfried Lipp and Michael Petzet (Munich: Bayerisches Landesamt für Denkmalpflege, 1994), 6–12; translated as "From the Modern to the Postmodern Cult of Monuments?: Aspects of a Repairing Society," accessed February 23, 2023, www.icomos.de/icomos/pdf/06_lipp_1993_en_jb.pdf.

2   John Kenneth Galbraith, *The Affluent Society* (Boston: Houghton Mifflin, 1958).
3   See Gerhard Schulze, *Die Erlebnisgesellschaft: Kultursoziologie der Gegenwart* (Frankfurt/Main: Campus Verlag, 1992).
4   Gerhard Scherhorn, "Die Unersättlichkeit der Bedürfnisse und der kalte Stern der Knappheit," in *Das Naturverständnis der Ökonomik: Beiträge zur Ethikdebatte in den Wirtschaftswissenschaften*, eds. Bernd Biervert and Martin Held (Frankfurt/Main:

Campus Verlag, 1994), 224–40.
5   Alois Riegl, *Der moderne Denkmalkultus: Sein Wesen und seine Entstehung* (Vienna: Braumüller, 1903); trans. Kurt W. Forster and Diane Ghirardo, "The Modern Cult of Monuments: Its Character and Origin," in *Oppositions* 25 (1982): 20–51.
6   René König, *Menschheit auf dem Laufsteg: Die Mode im Zivilisationsprozeß* (Munich: Carl Hanser Verlag, 1985).

and/or "restoring their functionality" are the fields primarily associated with "repair"; its opposite images are "damaged" or "broken."

The premodern term for repair in German is "flicken" or patch.[7] Like many other premodern phenomena, the term "flicken" gains a new lease of life in the postmodern world as "patchwork," specifically in fashion but metaphorically also to characterize a social identity (patchwork identity).[8]

Until the 19th century, there was an unbroken tradition of repurposing and reusing, converting things and overlaying them, and "repair" thus an integral factor in development. In the course of the 19th century, as historicism emerges dominant, so this tradition falls apart into the fields of "old" and "new" and also of "new" as "old" and "old" as "new." The history of monument conservation and restoration during this period documents this division very clearly.[9] In more recent modernity, "repair" undergoes the process of specialization and then, for example owing to the complexity of objects (e.g., high-tech products), tips over into a rising proneness to repair and/or actually inability to repair and/or succumbs to the economically dictated verdict of repair, meaning an imperative of renewal.[10]

Parallel to specialization, differentiation, or also obsolescence of the object-related "repair," the concept was transposed onto other areas of life, as a glance at the relevant literature shows. Under the all-encompassing meaning of "returning to sameness," "repair" is now to be encountered in the widest variety of areas. Ecologically in connection with: depletion, exploitation, overuse, squander, waste; as "repair" of the environment (key word: *Grün kaputt*, "Green is broken").[11] Urban in connection with: dilapidation, neglect, a focus on new builds, a loss of architectural quality, architecture as a "throwaway good or article for consumption"—as "urban repair." Biologically-medically the concept of "repair cells" exists; interactively-socially the talk is of "repairing" relationships, conditions, and standards; economically, there is the "repair" of finances, the proverbial "plugging of budget gaps" (negative) and the metaphor of "patching things up."[12]

In other words, we are in the midst of "repair." Things are being repaired everywhere. This refers, and I am just highlighting things by keywords here, to general environmental measures for the air (reducing emissions), water (quality, sewer systems, consumption), the oceans (reducing the stress factors on them), soil (overuse of fertilizers), wood, forests ("dying forests," excessive logging, rainforests). In cultural technology, the paring back of regulations and land consolidation are the order of the day; in terms of spatial planning, an attempt is being made to counteract urban sprawl; in the world of finance, "repair" comes under restoring budget health and ecological tax systems, with "eco-balance sheets" being envisaged as a new basis for calculating the value of products and materials.[13]

Socially speaking, the reform and conversion of the social welfare system are invoked, the wastage, excess, and abuse of social welfare benefits bemoaned. Something like a "repair of the human" has been set in motion,[14] and in the daily political debates some speak openly of victims of financial restoration with a view to the possible consequences of a "repair" "downwards," to the standards as regards burdens to be borne and restrictions set.

One special focus of the repair perspective is on the field of labor and unemployment. The end of the current valuation of labor is forecast, and a form of labor liberated from the yoke of the growth compulsion called for.[15] Eventually, the goal is a "repair" of the system of labor primarily defined economically in terms of production and sales, labor that is defined in this logic as an endless chain of abundance—accumulation—waste.

People are also busy developing ethical repair projects: enterprises to find meaning in the crisis of meaning—to counteract the latter, proposals for a new morality, programs for a change in mindset, and alternative ways of life.[16]

7   Gottfried Korff et al., eds., *Flick-Werk: Reparieren und Umnutzen in der Alltagskultur*, brochure accompanying the exhibition at Württembergisches Landesmuseum Stuttgart October 15 – December 15, 1983 (Stuttgart: Württembergisches Landesmuseum, 1983).
8   Heiner Keupp, "Auf der Suche nach der verlorenen Identität," in *Verunsicherungen: Das Subjekt im gesellschaftlichen Wandel*, eds. Heiner Keupp and Helga Bilden (Göttingen: Hogrefe Verlag, 1989), 47–69.
9   See, among others, Ernst Bacher, ed., *Kunstwerk oder Denkmal? Alois Riegls Schriften zur Denkmalpflege* (Vienna: Bühlau Verlag, 1995) […].
10   Friedrich Schmidt-Bleek, *Wieviel Umwelt braucht der Mensch? MIPS: Das Maß für ökologisches Wirtschaften* (Basel: Birkhäuser, 1994) […].
11   See on this, among others, Bernhard Glaeser, *Umweltpolitik zwischen Reparatur und Vorbeugung: Eine Einführung am Beispiel der Bundesrepublik im internationalen Kontext* (Opladen: VS Verlag für Sozialwissenschaften, 1989); Ralph Graf, *Umweltpolitik: Zwischen symbolischem Handeln, Reparatur und Zukunftssicherung* (Mainz: Podium Progressiv, 1992); Rolf Hamann, *Die Umweltpolitik der Bundesrepublik Deutschland zwischen Reparatur und Vorbeugung: Eine ökonomische und ökologische Bewertung, dargestellt am Problemfeld "Wasser"* (Oldenburg: Universität Oldenburg, 1991); Industriegewerkschaft Metall, ed., *Umweltschutz zwischen Reparatur und realer Utopie: Wege aus der Bedrohung* (Cologne: Bund-Verlag, 1988); Dieter Wieland et al.: *Grün kaputt: Landschaft und Gärten der Deutschen* (Munich: Raben, 1988).
12   See on the aspect of repair: Ronnie Schöb, *Ökologische Steuersysteme: Umweltökonomie und optimale*

In the field of aesthetics,[17] the efforts of monument conservation, of urban image concepts and the like can all clearly also be seen under the sign of the extended aspect of repair. It is harder to discern such a linkage in the sphere of the arts. The above-cited underlying meaning of to repair, "returning to sameness," could, if misunderstood, point a possible answer in the wrong direction. It could then lead (combing the tangle of chaos, deconstruction, and randomness to form a single skein) into the danger zone of the normativity of a harmonizing "canon," a unifying "new order," a monopolistic "style." This underlines the risks and responsibility innate in the "repair" undertaking.[18] "Repair" must not be redirected into a one-way street, not be focused on the one thing that is salvage for all. "Repair" is not a tool of one-dimensionality but a key in the concept of plurality.

The repair society

Back to the more immediate criteria for the meaning of "repair" and the attempt to draw up a systematic *sub specie conservatoris.* From the outset: "Repair" and avoidance are intimately interconnected. A "repair society" is always also an "avoidance society."[19] Sparing and nurturing are integral terms, boosting efficiency and trends towards sufficiency (frugality)[20] are fundamental obligations underpinning the following relationships.

Repair—abundance—logjam

The "space" of repair is to be located between production and waste. "Repair" creates an extension of product time, i.e., of "time value." This means a slowing down and reduction of production, thus a careful consideration of resources, of what exists and is available. The precondition for this is guaranteeing the fundamental capacity for something to be repaired, and key in this context are adherence to repair intervals and maintenance. What is called for is a qualitative improvement in products which guarantees long-term repair cycles and/or service life, coupled with the compatibility of the product with others.[21] For products coming under the scope of monument conservation, a catchy slogan was recently coined: "500 Year Guarantee." Thanks to its long-term thrust, "repair" rescues us from the "logjam," undoes the paradox of scarcity through abundance.

Repair—innovation—Production—creativity

In this context, the prescriptions are: an end to fake innovations, a minimization of quantities, and an improvement in the quality of new products. This should in the short term also have a positive economic component without (as is usual) making things cheaper meaning a loss in quality.

On principle: "Repair" is not inimical to technology and/or progress. However, it does call for reflection on what progress and technology mean,[22] and points in a different direction. What is required here is a substantive creativity—as opposed to mere design.[23] "Repair" is at any rate not some static, restorative concept, but is one energized by creativity in the sense of the dialogic of creative break and new creation. If, to paraphrase an Aristotelian insight, culture while always being a human project also always as such implies a changing, rethinking, a dreaming beyond and discovery over and above what exists already as culture,[24] then the imperative must be to treat this existing evolution of culture with care and if necessary repair it in order to tap into new, comparable potentials.

"Repair" is thus a concept denoting continuity, located on the side of memory and tradition. Through "repair," a historically aware and responsible form of creativity persists and arises. "Repair" in this sense sets our objectives for creativity, and that includes aesthetically speaking. In continuation of Max Weber's concept of an "ethics of responsibility,"[25] we could speak here of an "aesthetics of responsibility," in particular with a view to economic and ecological sustainability and much more besides.

Besteuerung (Frankfurt/Main: Campus Verlag, 1995) [...].
13 Schmidt-Bleek, *Wieviel Umwelt* (see note 10), 271.
14 See Ferenc Fehér and Agnes Heller, *Biopolitics* (Aldershot: Avebury, 1994).
15 Jeremy Rifkin, *The End of Work: The Decline of the Global Labor Force and the Dawn of the Post-Market Era* (New York: Tarcher, 1995); Hellmut Butterweck, *Arbeit ohne Wachstumszwang: Essay über Ressourcen, Umwelt, Arbeit, Kapital* (Frankfurt/Main: Campus Verlag, 1995).
16 Representative of this is Karl-Heinz Hillmann, *Wertwandel: Zur Frage soziokultureller Voraussetzungen alternativer Lebensformen* (Darmstadt: Wissenschaftliche Buchgesellschaft, 1986) [...].
17 Schmidt-Bleek, *Wieviel Umwelt* (see note 10) [...].
18 See Günther Moewes, *Weder Hütten noch Paläste: Architektur und Ökologie in der Arbeitsgesellschaft. Eine Streitschrift* (Basel: Birkhäuser, 1995), 71 ff.
19 Ibid., 83.
20 Ernst Ulrich von Weizsäcker et al., *Factor Four: Doubling Wealth, Halving Resource Use. A Report to the Club of Rome* (London: Routledge, 1997).
21 Schmidt-Bleek, *Wieviel Umwelt* (see note 10) [...].
22 Of interest in this context: Ivan Illich, *Tools for Conviviality* (New York: Harper & Row, 1973) [...].
23 Friedrich Schmidt-Bleek and Ursula Tischner, *Produktentwicklung: Nutzen gestalten: Natur schonen* (Vienna: Wirtschaftskammer Österreich, 1995).
24 See the entry by Robert Spaemann: "Natur," in *Handbuch philosophischer Grundbegriffe*, vol. 2, eds. Hermann Krings et al. (Munich: Kösel, 1973), 956–69; see also the entry by Reinhart Maurer, "Kultur," in ibid., 823–32.

RePair—history

As an ethic-aesthetic concept of continuity, "repair" is per se geared to continued existence. People have as good as repressed the fact that "duration" has had a dominant weight in human history ever since the genesis of advanced civilizations. It was modernity that first replaced the category of "duration" through that of accelerated change, revolution, progress, the temporary, the provisional, the ephemeral. [...]

The historical concepts of fortifying, regaining, or perpetuating "duration" were primarily politically motivated—with aesthetic consequences: Renaissance, Renovatio, Restauratio, Restitutio, Regeneratio, Recorso. "Repair" is more comprehensive than these historical terms and expands them to include the dimension of the ecological and the economic with specific ethical and social focuses. In a world of overuse and exploitation, with an enormous consumption of world and of culture and history, both material and immaterial, the file of possible therapies must include: "Repair," which rescues history by its stubbornly defying consumption. "Repair" is the integrative formula for rescuing history.[26] As such it could—by rejecting a ruined world—also function as a relay for a new kind of social contract in which "assuring ourselves of the past," "recognizing the limits of resources," and "agreeing on a concept of justice" would function as leading principles.[27]

RePair—monument conservation

[...] It bears restating that "repair" already played a role *expressis verbis* in 19th-century monument conservation. Thus, in the stipulations laid out in *Grundzüge einer Instruction* issued in 1850 by the Austrian "Central-Commission für die Erforschung und Erhaltung der Baudenkmale," sections 12 and 17 address the "necessary" and "possible repairs."[28] On the back of a consistently social common sense notion of "repair," monument conservation could be better received by the outside world and be increasingly differentiated within the discipline. In a continuum of repair, continued and new use, monuments would thus no longer be disavowed as a burden left over from the past. Monument conservation is challenged to differentiate not the concept of the monument per se but rather the practice of monument conservation, especially in view of the potential mass of monuments of industrial architecture built in the 19th and 20th centuries.[29] The question as to the social relevance of monument conservation in a repair society is also answered if we compare the terms conventionally used to date: Conservation is in the final instance not concerned with society, is ahistorical with its reliance on abstract ideal types, paradigmatically as "history at a standstill." Restoration, which takes is cue from some (fictitious) original and/or the trope of an "organic state" that has come to an end, has an aesthetic historical thrust; renovation, by contrast, focuses on the aesthetic present. Revitalization is essentially an adaptation to current needs, functionally referring to the present; reconstruction is defined as referring to the present by means of a reference backwards in time; reproduction (simulation, copy) is a random repetition for random ends, in a positive spin the democratization vehicle of participation.[30] Outside the (post-)modernist simulation paradigms geared to appearance, show, staging, and design,[31] "repair" does not seek to replace all these terms (they all have a status and history in monument conservation), but gives them a different foundation and thrust. Thus, conservation and restoration can definitely be read as modes of a repair project geared to greater contexts; however, by way of a significant example, one needs think only of the debate conducted so vehemently in recent years over reconstruction.[32] In the sense highlighted here, reconstruction undertaken from the viewpoint of monument conservation (for all the well-founded skepticism) can be considered as an attempt to repair "history." One should at any rate not completely ignore the moral aspect of the intention to "rectify," "make amends," and distinguish it from revisionist or merely aestheticist trends.

25   Max Weber, "Politics as Vocation" (1919), in *Weber's Rationalism and Modern Society*, eds. Tony Waters and Dagmar Waters (New York: Palgrave Macmillan, 2015).

26   It bears remembering in this context that the German Unification Treaty enshrines "preserving the existing substance," which thus includes monument conservation, and indirectly also repair, in law. See Manfred Ackermann, *Der kulturelle Einigungsprozeß. Schwerpunkt: Substanzerhaltung*, in Forum Deutsche Einheit, *Perspektiven und Argumente*, no. 7 (Bonn: Friedrich-Ebert-Stiftung, 1991).

27   The concluding sentences are phrased accordingly in: Daniel Bell, *The Cultural Contradictions of Capitalism* (New York: Basic Books, 1976).

28   Walter Frodl, *Idee und Verwirklichung: Das Werden der Staatlichen Denkmalpflege in Österreich* (Vienna: Böhlau Verlag, 1988), 192 ff.

29   Georg Mörsch, "Zur Differenzierbarkeit des Denkmalbegriffs," in *Denkmal. Werte. Gesellschaft: Zur Pluralität des Denkmalbegriffs*, ed. Wilfried Lipp (Frankfurt/Main: Campus Verlag, 1993), 241–43 [...].

30   This is the sense in which we should read the intention to erect in 1999 in Weimar (the year the city was European Capital of Culture) alongside Goethe's garden house a pendant as a recreated replica in order to spare the original, which was being subjected to intolerable strain. See "Weimar ist kein Museum," conversation with Bernd Kauffmann, *FAZ*, November 25, 1995, 31.

31   See Stefan Müller-Doohm and Klaus Neumann-Braun, eds., *Kulturinszenierungen* (Frankfurt/Main: Suhrkamp, 1995).

Needless to say, a specific definition of "repair" with regard to monument conservation still has to be developed, but the practice of monument conservation, above all in areas close to the crafts trades, is well ahead of theory formation in this regard anyway.[33]

However, as is always the case when transposing something onto a general level, it bears to be on the look-out for erroneous trends and abuse. There is a danger of "repair" being reduced to a mere buzzword or catchphrase.

Last but not least: "Repair" does not identify or double up the past and has nothing to do with what Günther Anders termed a "craving for the old." In a society in which according to Mario Bretone it is becoming ever more uncertain whether it even needs history to construct an image of itself and where "only a thin layer of ice seems [...] to link our present to the past,"[34] "repair" gives the past and the future a chance.[35] In a situation which was critically explored recently under the heading of "Is the future already over?"[36]—in which at any rate the past is becoming ever longer, the future gobbled up in the compression of time and speed and thus becomes ever shorter—"repair" means to postpone, to gain time,[37] to consolidate, in order to—after it is achieved, at a later point in time—open up new horizons.

Taking Nature into Account is the title of the latest report to the Club of Rome edited by Wouter van Dieren,[38] in line with the postulate of sustainability. "Take the stock of things into account," Gottfried Benn admonished us many years ago. Linking up these two approaches, the conference in Dortmund could by way of the repair society's specific task as regards heritage protection, declare a "cultural species protection," a kind of "Greenpeace for Cultural Heritage" in order to make people more aware than hitherto that the cultural heritage is also dramatically threatened and is a swiftly dwindling resource, alongside nature the second pillar on which life rests.[39]

Postscript: The concept of "repair" is related to the martial notion of reparation. Everyone knows what a "reparations debt" is. In the "Culture Drama,"[40] in its provisionally last scene, last act, this means that one of the many decidedly successfully offensives launched by modernity has been lost. The time after "the mental orgy."[41] The losers have to pay. However, paradoxically, and new in the history of reparations, there is no winner. The reparations affect everyone. The currency they are due in is called "repair."

This essay was first published in 1996 in ICOMOS – Hefte des Deutschen Nationalkomitees, vol. 21. Reprinted here in an abbreviated version with the kind permission of the author.

32   See Michael Petzet, "Rekonstruieren als denkmalpflegerische Aufgabe?," in *Denkmalpflege Informationen* A/81, ed. Bayerisches Landesamt für Denkmalpflege (1995).
33   Paradigmatically, for example, in Wolf Schmidt, "Reparatur historischer Holzfenster," *Denkmalpflege Informationen* D/17, ed. Bayerisches Landesamt für Denkmalpflege (1993) [...].
34   Mario Bretone, *Zehn Arten, mit der Vergangenheit zu leben* (Frankfurt/Main: Campus Verlag, 1995), 83.
35   See on this, among others, Hans-Peter Dürr,

Die Zukunft ist ein unbetretener Pfad: Bedeutung und Gestaltung eines ökologischen Lebensstils (Freiburg: Herder, 1995).
36   *Salzburger Nachrichten*, August 28, 1995.
37   See Peter Koslowski, "Die Baustellen der Postmoderne: Wider den Vollendungszwang der Moderne," in *Moderne oder Postmoderne?*, eds. Peter Koslowski et al. (Weinheim: Acta Humaniora, VCH, 1986), 1–16.
38   Wouter van Dieren, ed., *Taking Nature into Account: A Report to the Club of Rome Toward a Sustainable National Income* (New York: Springer-Verlag, 1995).

39   See in general the research project at Universität Hagen, *Umwelt als knappes Gut* (led by Michael Toyka-Seid).
40   This is the title of the compendium by Wolfgang Lipp, *Drama Kultur*, Sozialwissenschaftliche Abhandlungen der Görres-Gesellschaft, vol. 22 (Berlin: Duncker & Humblot, 1994).
41   Jean Baudrillard, *The System of Objects* (1968), trans. James Benedict (London: Verso, 2005), 179.

Repairing as Preparing

Wilfried Lipp in conversation with Florian Hertweck, Silke Langenberg, Alex Nehmer, and Markus Krieger

Florian Hertweck The concept of the repair society that you first introduced at a conference in 1993 sketches out the lines of vision of our issue on *The Great Repair*: repair as sufficiency, longevity, solidarity, reappropriation, plurality, care, and self-repair. "Repair," you wrote back then, was an "integration formula to save history. As such, it could, as a rejection of a ruined world, also function as a relay for a new kind of social contract" in which the key principles would be "assuring ourselves of our past," "recognizing the limits of resources," and "agreeing on a concept of justice." Has some part of your promise come true in the intervening 30 years?

Wilfried Lipp Some partial successes have without doubt been achieved in the field of heritage preservation, as the innermost ring of repair, as it were. A different awareness of the problem has arisen. And fortunately in past decades much lost ground has been rediscovered, researched, and put into practice, namely in the realm of an exact knowledge and ability to use historical handicraft techniques—which is, after all, the prerequisite for repair in the classic, literal sense of "returning to sameness," mending in continuation of the original fitness of work and material. However, practice all too often fails because of a lack of framework conditions. Politically and socially, the stance toward the exploitation and consumption of resources, wastage, and the throw-it-away mindset has started to shift. But repair, internalized as a practice that is a matter of course, has not yet been fully and genuinely accepted as an attitude. Although in the course of the three decades things have become even more urgent. In principle, I am pleased, but it does all trigger very ambivalent feelings in me that the concept of the repair society that I introduced in 1993 now has a truly explosive edge to it, given the dramatic constellation of current developments. I hope this gives it a far faster impact.

Silke Langenberg Where does the "repair" project take us today?

WL In the flow of transmission processes conjured up by the daily media, we have arrived at a field where repair still stands for the traditional measures of mending and making things functional again. Windows, doors, roof trusses, furniture still form the classic repertoire of repair, followed by technical appliances—refrigerators, washing machines—tasks for repair specialists. Overall, however, repair today stands for something much more comprehensive: Repair has become a positively impregnated

In Silke Langenberg's repair course at the HM Hochschule München University of Applied Sciences, Paulina Kampmann focused on repairing a copy of a Fabergé egg.

In the 1990s, the then Regional Conservator of Upper Austria and later president of ICOMOS Austria, Wilfried Lipp, coined the term "repair society" in a pioneering essay, parts of which are reprinted in this issue. In conversation with guest editor Florian Hertweck, heritage theorist and architect Silke Langenberg as well as ARCH+'s Alex Nehmer and Markus Krieger he reflects on the term's topicality and how it can be made productive for *The Great Repair* project.

general term and is part of ecology's conception of itself. Within the broad radius of this concept of repair are issues of sustainability, adaptability, and reuse as opposed to neglect, waste, and the squandering of resources. Repair encompasses nature, climate, environment, people. We are witnesses, indeed coparticipants and contributors to a new, quite differently weighted and in a sense elementary philosophy of conservation. The terms "original," "authenticity," and "aura" have moved into the background. The goals have changed. The slogan of the proclaimed turn of the times is: *Reparatur der Zukunft* (Repairing the Future). This is also the name of an ongoing series of broadcasts by the Österreichischer Rundfunk (Austrian Broadcasting Corporation).[1]

The appellative announcement expresses concern for the future and means repair must happen now—comprehensively—in order to put a future worth living back on track. Tools must be tested, paths found, innovations made, strategies devised. In a word: The course must be set. In this context, repair is rethought and further developed—entirely in the sense of a course of repair: from the strengthening of what exists to the creative, inventive thrust for what is to come.

Alex Nehmer In our *Great Repair* project, repair likewise is not aimed at restoring some original state or preserving the status quo, but rather at redesigning the world—in the direction of a better state. In your 1996 essay on the repair society, you already emphasized the transitory nature of repair. In your opinion, what does the concept of repair mean in this regard, and how can it be understood as transformative rather than as restoration?

WL My piece on the repair society, or so the subtitle read, was written *sub specie conservatoris.* The expansion of the concept of repair to include "society" took place in full awareness of the fact that the methods of preserving, conserving, and reusing such as are existentially necessary and had remained intact in everyday practice across all cultural histories through to modernism were swiftly no longer a matter of course. It was and still is my conviction that repair in the sense of continuity and preservation can only gain sway (again) if it is embedded in our everyday understanding of the world and the environment. To realize that a comprehensive systemic change of course is indeed necessary. That is a *conditio vitalis.*

The fact that the *Great Repair* project is declared to be an undertaking aimed at the "world's redesign" in the direction of a better state is a logical advance on that original key idea. The domain of cultural heritage should actually have an avant-garde function, act as a paradigmatic role model in this context. However, your question begins paradoxically with a contradictory definition of repair: Repair is not aimed, it states categorically, at restoring an original state or at preserving the status quo … so could it be that repair in the traditional sense has no place under the overarching heading of the *Great Repair*?!

On the back of that conflict, questions as to the transitory and transformative character of repair have to my mind an almost suggestive feel to them. Could it be that the terms "transformative" and "transitory" are meant to serve in the context of the *Great Repair* project as legitimation for defining repair per se as a category of change against the broad horizon of the possible? Repair would then become a dubious conceptual envelope for all manner of conceivable measures to "redesign the world." How is that?

Transformative means "to make something into something different." And transitory means temporary. When in 1996 I identified the transitory character of restoration work and raised this in the debate on monument conservation it was, on the one hand, an echo of the historicist illusion of a specific, static, ideal image as the objective of restoration; on the other, it was the simple recognition of the fundamentally processual character of reality. Even the academically most scrupulous restoration work creates a (new) state that has never existed before and thus makes something into something (subtly) different. Since restoration work and repairs are never definitive, they are also transitory. However, that does not mean that something is made into something *completely different.*

In fact, the affordances innate in the very DNA of things should block that. By which I mean that nature and the world of things require *eo ipso* a certain appropriate approach to them. In my opinion, this also holds true for cultural heritage and the assets created by civilization. The imperative of affordance determines the limits of physical and aesthetic damage, of excess and wasteful usage, the limits of the transformative per se: integrity as the intactness of things—as the ideal norm of affordance.

That said, countless examples show that contrary to all affordances something can be turned into something completely different, and they show how a label with positive connotations can contain contents that are anything but. For example, what is not to be found in things labelled organic? What gets concealed behind terms such as "sustainability" or "eco"? On closer inspection, frequently the objectives involved are anything but those that are stipulated. And given the open contours of the *Great Repair* project what could not be segmented behind the legitimating proof of "repair"? To give it an ironic spin: Repairwashing makes it possible—together with greenwashing it provides the perfect pulverization of any world rescue.

In the field of architecture and monument conservation, incidentally, the 1964 Venice Charter was abused by the strategic misinterpretation of Article 9 to justify rigid, deliberately contrasting modernization interventions by simply ignoring the limiting framework of the conditions set in the article. In fact, the article only refers to the case that it is necessary for aesthetic or technical reasons to restore something of which we do not know what it looked like. However, the subsequent clause was taken out of this context and made into an alibi for any intervention, reading that "any extra work which is indispensable must be distinct from the architectural composition and must bear a contemporary stamp."

In order to exclude this risk to the Great Repair from the outset the repair society would need to focus on something like new principles of design. The days of immoderation really do belong in the past. There is no lack of aesthetic concepts and markings that can provide the backbone here, such as integrity, appropriateness, or compatibility, which can provide sufficient orientation. However, the actual definitions still need to be set in the framework of the targets to be pursued by the repair project.

Markus Krieger Sociologist Oliver Nachtwey speaks, in line with broader social trends of the 20th century, of the last 30 years in Germany as having come under the sign of social decline. Against the background of the increasingly precarious nature of labor and growing social inequality, Nachtwey resorts to the image of the escalator that for some individuals still travels upwards, but for the majority constantly runs downwards. Your text appeared prior to these developments but already after the neoliberal turn initiated by Thatcher and Reagan (what Nachtwey calls "regressive modernity"). And it addresses social inequalities only from an abstracting distance. Would you like to bring your notion of a resource-sparing repair society up to date by including social justice? Where do you see the linkage between the material and social levels?

WL A resource-sparing repair society would be an extraordinary contribution, not to say precondition, for social justice, without doubt a key relay to a better balance being struck between abundance and scarcity. To this end, however, a different concept of economics would be necessary: Let us bring to mind that old oxymoron of "less is more" that also became important in architecture theory (among others thanks to Heinrich Tessenow, Adolf Loos, and Mies van der Rohe). In the field of economics in 1973 Ernst Friedrich Schumacher made the idea into a now forgotten slogan at the time of the oil crisis and rephrased it poignantly as *Small Is Beautiful.* So it is not as though the Great Repair would not have a foundation in the history of ideas and economics.

MK In your text you argue that a constant repair prolongs the "temporal value" of an object, as a result of which production as a whole decelerates, and resources are spared. In our understanding, this emphasizes the processual character of repair, whereby labor and productivity play a central role with reference to the object maintained. If, moreover, you also point out that in the final analysis the

"system of a labor primarily geared economically toward production and unit sales" needs to be repaired, then one can discern the affinity to the contemporary degrowth discourse that calls for a revaluation of labor and a reduction in working hours. Precisely in architecture focused on new builds, our own labor productivity is tied to the speed of resource consumption. Was such a reconceptualization of labor inscribed into your text? How would you rate questions of labor and productivity today?

WL A revaluation of labor with a view to productivity and resource wastage would be the logical consequence. Fundamentally, all "making" entails changing what is already there, on the one hand of nature and on the other of things that were already made by humans. If repair is based on the principle of sparing resources, then labor needs to be assessed in terms of the degree to which it sparingly and caringly handles what exists. Not resource wastage but resource thriftiness must be the maxim for ethically responsible economic activity. And that crucially includes being honest in the energy balances. Each step in production is a step consuming energy. What then reaches the consumers as a commodity is always the product of energy being wasted. In terms of the complexity of the promises it cannot fulfill, the euphemistic energy-saving industry (photovoltaics, wind turbines, e-cars, facilities technology, heating/cooling technology, etc.) is an example we should take as a warning as to how the repair project must not allow itself to be co-opted and sent in the wrong direction.

AN In your lecture on the repair society to the 1993 conference you argued that the city requires an expanded, "fluid" concept of the monument.[2] You asked, "Is there a preservation of change?"—a question that remained open at the time. In architecture, at present there are increased efforts to convert buildings, give them new uses, and experiments with circular construction methods, urban mining, etc. To what extent are such approaches that consider existing buildings as a (raw materials) resource fit to follow your notion of permanence and longevity? Do we need new concepts of care and preservation that include constant change?

WL Is there a preservation of change? Yes, to put it very simply and deliberately redundantly: with a caring and considerate approach to what exists. "Urban mining" may be urgently required in certain areas such as the waste and circular economies. And expanding it to architecture makes sense if one thinks of the volumes of vacant buildings in commercial wastelands. Removal, reclamation, and recycling are definitively challenging goals of a Great Repair campaign. However, a generalizing expansion to *everything* built would at best also drag historically and culturally infused existing buildings into the danger zone of a "resource-gaining" demolition ball that possibly even swings under the fake label of "repair."

In the question on concepts of care that cover constant change one can sense the assumption that repair is per se an expansive category of change. I have already remarked on the terms "transformative" and "transitory." Changes made under the heading of repair have a scope of possibility. There are evidently dangers and temptations for transgression.

Let us take a simple everyday example: repairing a roof made by carpenters in the 19th century. Repair in the conventional sense would replace damaged, no longer reparable parts and insert new wood into the existing structure in keeping with the rules of appropriate craftsmanship. For a "modern" repair, (in part) new sections made of different materials would be used and thus a different technical concept introduced. If repair is associated with a conversion as regards the aspect of use for example for residential purposes when it comes to insulation, lighting, energy, etc., then that primarily results in the construction "disappearing," at least visually. Under the primacy of use, the roof structure "disappears" entirely in terms of its materiality and is replaced by upzoning. So where in this chain of examples are the limits of the philosophy of the Great Repair? Clarification and elucidation will require clear orientation guidelines on the scope of repair interventions. The heritage protection laws provide a legal basis for this.

Framework conditions that take a careful approach to the existing buildings and resources must as an imperative include the creation of a system of incentives. Repair must be tangibly worthwhile. Incentive systems are already on the political agenda in adjacent fields such as energy and the climate. Repair objectives as well should be defined with precision and as such made politically appealing. A discourse between equals on the compatibility of climate and repair goals is long since overdue. The most recent example from Bavaria does not inspire confidence in this regard: The draft amendment to the Bavarian heritage protection law gives grounds to fear the rigid subordination of heritage protection to the primacy of climate needs under the banner of "reconciling heritage protection and climate protection."[3]

How resilient the peripheries of the notion of repair are, especially when reaching out to human civilization as a whole, is a challenge that will require courage and expedient creativity to master it—a nuanced "repair creativity."

SL   What is the role of architects in this context?

WL   I think they should be the main avant-garde spearhead of a preservation- and repair-oriented approach to architecture. In pursuit of these goals, this course would probably also have to be included in their training. In current pedagogical practice, after all, a major focus of the—let's call it creative—approach to historical architecture lies in exploring possibilities for change and intervention within ever-expanding tolerances. In an inventory-based architectural avant-garde, technical design innovations would be required for many details that need to be resolved under the influence of repair. An endless catalogue of tasks—but with less attention yield for the ego. This presupposes that perceptions would have to change, the frameworks of compatibility of old and new would have to be tailored more tightly, more precisely, and with higher quality.

SL   What is your prognosis for the future of repair?

WL   This also creates a new basis for the concept of repair in monument conservation. New opportunities arise because, in a holistically expansive repair policy, repair practices conventionally geared toward preservation should be taken for granted. But: no development without ambivalences. A not inconsiderable danger lies in the fact that in the ranking of measures counted as repair, hierarchies and dominances arise which have a detrimental effect on cultural heritage. The concept of "repair" should not be over-strained holistically and we should resist its appropriation by completely different interests. Instead, we should understand repairing as an integral imperative of preparing the future. It is therefore important to take advantage of opportunities, form alliances, and take a position as well as do the work of educating and creating meaning. Because preserving, caring, and protecting are simply among the fundamental ethical obligations of a repair society grounded in ecology.

A great challenge was the composition of a broken chicken's egg, to which end dental tools were used.

The interview and the reprint of Wilfried Lipp's essay on the repair society were developed in cooperation with Silke Langenberg. The questions she asked and Wilfried Lipp's answers to them come from her book Upgrade: Making Things Better *(Berlin, 2022), published by Hatje Cantz. The complete interview between the two is to be found there under the title "Obligations of the Repair Society," 70–83.*

1   Accessed August 31, 2022, oe1.orf.at/collection/667884.
2   Wilfried Lipp, "Vom modernen zum postmodernen Denkmalkultus? Aspekte zur Reparaturgesellschaft," in *Vom modernen zum postmodernen Denkmalkultus? Denkmalpflege am Ende des 20 Jahrhunderts*, eds. Wilfried Lipp and Michael Petzet (Munich: Bayerisches Landesamt für Denkmalpflege, 1994), 6–12.
3   Bavarian State Government press release, "Wir bringen Klimaschutz und Denkmalschutz zusammen," August 2, 2022, accessed August 31, 2022, www.bayern.de/wir-bringen-klimaschutz-und-denkmalschutz-zusammen.

Part
the
R
soa

cs for
epar
ety

sufficiency

Text: Florian Hertweck

The world-wide consumption of resources continues to rise steadily. Earth Overshoot Day (i. e., the symbolic point in time at which we humans have used up all natural resources the Earth can produce in one year) comes earlier each year. In 2022, it occurred as early as July 28, meaning that in the five following months of the year we lived at the expense of the future. The concept of sufficiency (from Latin *sufficere*, English to suffice, to be enough) recognizes the ecological boundaries and focuses on reducing the consumption of raw materials, energy, and land. This means fundamentally calling into question economic growth in the customary sense.[1] As a new planning paradigm, sufficiency is not geared at a change in human behavior, but at a transformation of infrastructures, soils, services, and work processes that enable humans to consume as few resources as possible. Accordingly, "repairing is sufficient," as Jürgen Bertling and Claus Leggewie state, "because it unquestioningly reduces the demand for new products"[2]—and, we could add, for land.

Hannes Meyer, *Co-op Interieur* (detail), Basel, 1926

Tejo Remy, *Rag Chair*, 1991

However, restrictions at the personal level will also be required. What is important here is that sufficiency does not treat all humans equally, but makes certain to factor in social and spatial justice.[3] This combination of "a critique of growth, ecological boundaries, and questions of distribution make sufficiency a complex and highly contested issue."[4] The concept not only challenges politics to revise subsidies and tax incentives such as the commuter allowance and homeowner subsidies. It also calls upon architects and urban and spatial planners to create positive narratives of sufficiency and drive and moderate processes with which conflicts of transformation can be negotiated. Indeed, sufficiency requires architects to reorient themselves in a much more fundamental manner: Demands for a moratorium on the sealing of soil, on demolition, and even on new construction compel us to work with existing buildings. While for generations the design of new builds was architecture's top priority, the focus is now on the transformative and regenerative repair of what already exists.

1   See Bund für Umwelt und Naturschutz Deutschland e. V. (BUND), Friends of the Earth Germany, *Perspektive 2030: Suffizienz in der Praxis. Wie Kommunal- und Bundespolitik eine nachhaltige Entwicklung in den Bereichen Mobilität, Material-verbrauch, Energie, Landwirtschaft und Ernährung gestalten können* (Berlin: BUND, 2017); Institut für Energie- und Umweltforschung (ifeu), ed., *Energiesuffizienz: Strategien und Instrumente für eine technische, systemische und kulturelle Transformation zur nachhaltigen Begrenzung des Energiebedarfs im Konsumfeld Bauen/Wohnen* (Heidelberg: ifeu, 2016); Manfred Linz, *Suffizienz als politische Praxis: Ein Katalog*, ed. Wuppertal Institut für Klima, Umwelt, Energie (2015); Thomas Princen, *The Logic of*

Sufficiency (Cambridge: MIT Press, 2005); Wolfgang Sachs, "Die vier E's: Merkposten für einen maßvollen Wirtschaftsstil," *Politische Ökologie* 33 (1993): 69–72.
2   Jürgen Bertling and Claus Leggewie, "Die Reparaturgesellschaft: Ein Beitrag zur Großen Transformation?," in *Die Welt reparieren: Open Source und Selbermachen als postkapitalistische Praxis*, eds. Andrea Baier et al. (Bielefeld: transcript, 2016), 278.
3   See Anton Brokow-Loga and Frank Eckardt, eds., *Postwachstumsstadt: Konturen einer solidarischen Stadtpolitik* (Munich: oekom, 2020).
4   Maike Böcker et al., *Wie wird weniger genug? Suffizienz als Strategie für eine nachhaltige Stadtentwicklung* (Munich: oekom, 2020), 13.

Less is More —
On strategies of Sufficiency

Dismantling and restoring parking lots is one way to repair land sealing in the *Zwischenstadt*. The image shows a collaborative deconstruction of a parking lot carried out as part of the *Holes in the House* project by Mio Tsuneyama and Fuminori Nousaku in Tokyo.

for the Socio-Ecological Production of Space

Text: Florian Hertweck, Markus Miessen

It is as astonishing as it is understandable that narratives of progress based on technological innovation are of far greater appeal in the climate debate than perspectives critical of growth. Astonishing, because these narratives are based on something which does not yet exist in the first place. And understandable, because they intimate that green technologies could create economic growth uncoupled from environmental impacts, which would mean that neither the electorate nor politicians need to initiate structural changes. In this context, it is no coincidence that the coalition treaty underpinning the present German government took as its headline "Dare More Progress."

The success of the technofix narrative also stems from the conceptual weakness of the alternative narrative: sufficiency as the decisive thrust of a Great Repair. The attempt below to outline a sufficiency theory for architecture and spatial planning is intended, first, to overcome this weakness. And, second, to counter the "end of confidence"—to adopt Wolfgang Pehnt's term for the architecture of the late 20th century—by sketching a "new confidence" for our discipline. The objective is not just to sketch a narrative for socio-ecological transition in a broken world, but also to describe a *theoria cum praxi*, with all its related risks.

What is sufficiency?

Sufficiency—as a concept in the sustainability debate—was originally developed as the third pillar of the transition toward a post-fossil society. While efficiency is geared to the most productive use of materials and energy, and consistency seeks to change our form of production by expanding the use of renewable energy sources and establishing a circular economy, sufficiency focuses directly on an absolute reduction in the energy and resources required. The best energy, so the compelling argument, is that energy which is not consumed and accordingly does not need to be generated, transported, and stored. While this triad of efficiency, consistency, and sufficiency was initially designed as a dialogue between green growth and degrowth, these fronts are currently hardening in the face of the immense challenge of decarbonization and the shortage of resources. The combustion of fossil resources is responsible for almost two thirds of all anthropogenic CO_2 emissions worldwide.[1] In the next two decades, we need to reduce their use in Germany essentially to zero, as our contribution towards enabling human survival on Planet Earth.[2] Given the ever fiercer climate catastrophe, this makes sufficiency the single key element of transformation in the direction of sustainability and grants it a status over and above efficiency and consistency.[3] Following on from Wilfried Lipp,[4] we locate the repair society within the spectrum of sufficiency, because a reduction in materials, energy, and space implies a critical inquiry into what already exists, and thus caring for it, maintaining, and repairing it.

That said, the concept of sufficiency also has its weaknesses. One difficulty is that sufficiency has hitherto primarily concentrated on changes in personal lifestyles. Under the heading of *voluntary simplicity* or *downshifting* it had referred to a motto diametrically opposed to the technofix narrative: "You must change your life."[5] Not only do structural changes take a backseat in this line of argument, it can also be easily exploited politically. For example, the Greens' justified questioning of the sensibleness of continuing to construct detached houses in Hamburg or their proposal to introduce a Veggie Day proved politically disastrous. Philipp Lepenies has recently shown how "proposed prohibitions" can be instrumentalized on the part of neoliberal politics and populist media in favor of the technofix culture by whipping up emotions and hysteria.[6] Objective discussions are nipped in the bud by constructing a purported opposition of Prohibition versus Freedom. However, sufficiency should not be equated with self-limitation and comprehensive personal renunciation. A theory of sufficiency for architecture and spatial planning must address planning and design in the broader sense and not exclusively focus on changes to personal routines.

Another problem with the concept of sufficiency stems from the fact that it suggests everyone should consume less. The more unequal societies are, the more cynical any call for self-restriction must seem to less privileged people, not to mention the colonialized, exploited societies of the Global South. Sufficiency cannot spell a path to the subsistence minimum for the less privileged while the upper classes live in the comfort of an optimum existence. Participation and social justice must be key characteristics of sufficiency. The proposal for a theory of sufficiency put forward here as the planning basis for European urban landscapes seeks to ensure social justice in Europe, whereby overcoming or at the very least containing the externalization society must be the objective of a repair strategy.

In the final analysis, sufficiency—similarly to degrowth or *décroissance*—is not a particularly attractive slogan. In French, the term used is *sobriété*—but who wishes to always be sober? More appealing

As a protest against a planned new building to replace the former AMAG workshop in the Schwamendingen district of Zurich, in 2021 the Zürcher Arbeitsgruppe für Städtebau ZAS* (Zurich Urban Design Working Group) staged the building as a doomed "cruise ship" with "sun deck, cabins, casino, engine room, and shore walks." ZAS* pleads for more openness in dealing with existing buildings.

adjectives were thus appended, such as in the case of *sobriété heureuse* (happy sobriety) or *hedonistic sufficiency*. What is probably the best-known oxymoron in the history of architecture, Mies's pithy formula of *Less is more* provides the required poignancy, among other things, because it can also easily be applied to areas over and above the domain of the aesthetic: less traffic, more quality of life; less fodder, more food; less top-down, more bottom-up … While more materials, energy or surface area can no longer constitute a social-ecological gain in the age of social-ecological crises, less need not be boring (to recall Robert Venturi's dictum that *Less is a bore*). As much as any other, architects need to provide the proof for this.

Sufficiency against the backdrop of the degrowth city

"Anyone who believes exponential growth can go on forever in a finite world is either a madman or an economist." Environmental economist Tim Jackson uses this 1973 quotation from economist Kenneth E. Boulding to introduce his book *Prosperity without Growth*.[7] In fact, we have known of the planetary limits to growth since the 1970s.[8] As early as 1966, Boulding distinguished between the "cowboy economy" that knows no boundaries, only the great wide open to be conquered, and a "spaceman economy," whose actors view the Earth as a spaceship on which both resource deposits and waste dumps are

limited.[9] His call for a *great transition* to an economic system that corresponds to the ecological system with its limited resources is sadly just as topical as ever: Despite the general recognition that, today, we face a climate crisis and resources are scarce, we are still stuck in the middle of the cowboy economy. Against this backdrop the degrowth perspective calls for a socio-ecological transformation of the economy (and not the economization of ecology). As Ulrich Brand puts it, the focus is not on forcing a recession or "reveling in crises," but on a "controlled process of change to a different, socio-ecologically sustainable, just, and solidarity-based form of production and living."[10] This is not *change by disaster*, but *change by design*—a challenge that must inspire especially architects and other actors in spatial production.

There are plenty of points where the degrowth discourse can be meaningfully extended to urban development:[11] starting with Martin Wagner's notion of a more or less self-sufficient urban region developed back in the 1920s[12] via Cedric Price's 1964 *Potteries Thinkbelt* project and Oswald Mathias Ungers and Rem Koolhaas' 1977 manifesto on *The City in the City: Berlin as a Green Archipelago*, which was explicitly developed as a model for a "zero-growth Europe," and on to the urban repair initiated in Bologna in 1969 and the *Instandbesetzungen* ("rehab squatting") in Berlin of the 1970s. "Cities," or so Anton Brokow-Loga and Frank Eckardt suggest, should today bid farewell to the idea "of continuing to develop through constant planning, construction, and growth."[13] In their critique of growth, Brokow-Loga and Eckardt in particular address the horizontal expansion of cities and the related intensive sealing of surfaces. In response, they propose a transformation of the city that, on the one hand, emphasizes selective growth, on prospering and "blossoming" socio-ecological infrastructures and commonweal economies in the field of agriculture, energy generation, or housing construction. On the other, "globalized, profit-oriented, fossil-based/industrial sectors of the economy that do not serve the common good and cannot be transformed sustainably (e.g., motorized personal and air transport, industrialized agriculture, the armaments industry, advertising, parts of globalized trade) should be scaled back and de-privileged."[14] Obviously, such a transformation cannot happen without conflict, precisely if "the capitalist control of the means of production, of urban spaces and of land and the soil is challenged and changed."[15]

But what is meant by "city" in the first place in the context of the degrowth city? Thomas Sieverts already relativized the classic concept of the city 25 years ago in his work on the *Zwischenstadt*: "[I]t must be recorded that throughout the whole world the 'city' of the modern age extends into its environment and thus creates the peculiar forms of an urbanized landscape or a landscaped city. Following a venerable tradition we still call distinct regions of settlement 'cities'. Or we describe them with such abstract concepts as 'city agglomerations', 'areas of concentration', 'urbanized landscapes', etc., because we note how inappropriate the concept of 'city' is when applied to these fields of settlement as they evoke completely different associations."[16] Taking this up, we should speak less of degrowth cities and far more of degrowth *Zwischenstädte*. However, while the contours of the transformation of the centers is becoming slightly clearer in the guise of concepts such as the 15-Minute City or the Solidarity City, there is still a question hanging over the conversion of the *Zwischenstadt*. What shape does *change by design* take in patchworks of detached housing estates and commercial parks, in villages that are located in the vicinity of swarm cities and are dominated by daytime commuters, in large settlements and in "technical lands," meaning in airports, data centers, mining districts, military encampments, and power stations? Is it so easy to simply proclaim the end of suburbia? Can the regionalization of the city give way to an urbanization of the region, or in the future will we speak of degrowth cities on the one hand and growth suburbs on the other?

In response to the Club of Rome reports, the Center for Alternative Technology (CAT) was formed in 1973 in a disused slate quarry in Wales. The organization, which still exists today, has experimented with renewable energy, energy efficiency, and sufficiency since its beginnings and set itself the goal of democratizing "alternative" technologies and creating an emissions-free Great Britain.

Sufficient architecture

Yamina Saheb, one of the co-authors of the WGIII section of the IPCC Sixth Assessment Report on mitigating climate change, points out that architecture is lagging behind compared to all other sectors, and that architects and urban planners have to date neglected to design for sufficiency.[17] So, how to design for sufficiency?

In order to be able to address this question on a large scale, we first need to grasp *change by design* on the scale of the individual building. If sufficiency is considered to mean less material and less energy inputs, then the *economy of means*, a concept innate to architecture, is a logical answer. It is already to be encountered in the thought of Marc-Antoine Laugier, who in the 18th century followed Vitruvius in defining the principle of the primitive hut. The latter offers an original image of sufficient architecture per se as it is destined solely to protect people against the rain and the sun. Laugier considered the city to be a forest and called for its "great repair."[18] In fact, he already offered an early formulation of the social thrust of sufficiency. As a witness of the intense property speculation of his day, he criticized the waste "in structures and other useless things" and linked this to the exploitation of less privileged people.[19]

The image of the primitive hut with the desire for an *economy of means* leads from Classicism via New Objectivity and Brutalism on to self-built structures, lightweight structures, and from here to so-called New Realism. It is precisely through a creative reduction of materials that the protagonists of New Realism arrive at a poetics of the expressive shape and create *more* space, not least in the area of affordable housing. At the same time, this approach—as largely driven by Anne Lacaton and Jean-Philippe Vassal—emphasizes longevity at two different levels: first, in the conceptualization of the architecture itself, something which entails also thinking of its flexibility and mutability in terms of the uses to which it is put. In this regard, architect Gilles

The cover image by Samuel Wale for the English translation of Marc Antoine Laugier's *Essai sur l'architecture*, published in 1755, shows the construction of a primitive hut.

Delalex speaks of adolescent rather than obsolete ruins, of neutral structures that allow for the introduction of quite different functions and are never themselves finished in the sense of complete but instead develop over time with new uses.[20] Second, New Realism seeks to ensure longevity by focusing on existing buildings: "In this sense, architecture and urban planning no longer serve to write over what went before and instead to accept what already exists, with the intention being to strengthen it in terms of its intrinsic urban logic,"[21] wrote Anh-Linh Ngo, André Kempe, and Melissa Koch in their editorial for *ARCH+ 240, New Realism in French Architecture*. While Lacaton & Vassal, if the occasion suggests it, also decide not to build, other proponents of New Realism do indeed build on a grand scale and not infrequently using high-emission reinforced concrete. Thus, the ecological rhetoric is often given greater say than the ecological metrics, meaning all that is created is the mere appearance of sufficiency.

Another path leads from the *economy of means* to self-built structures. "Building things yourself," so sociologist Lucius Burckhardt wrote in the introduction to the 1981 Werkbund volumes *Für eine andere Architektur*, "is not everybody's cup of tea; but the fact that some people have built their own houses gives the population confidence in dealing with buildings. So we see once again that laypersons are able to design their own homes, to renovate an old house, or convert it."[22] In this light, with self-built structures and the associated new focus on existing buildings, architecture becomes more "reparable." Self-built structures, Burckhardt continues, can succeed in "making us independent of supplies and wear-and-tear, encourage us to act sparingly and intelligently, and to make the right use of our resources."[23] In the same vein, in their publication on the repair society Jürgen Bertling and Claus Leggewie consider "the relationship of the culture of repair to the sociality of societies which are characterized by a wide-scale division of labor, alienation, and wastage, and are therefore challenged by social initiatives that under the overarching banner of 'conviviality' call for new practices of collaboration and civic self-empowerment at all levels of everyday life right through to the sphere of institutional politics."[24]

If less is more, then, as Rem Koolhaas once remarked, is not nothing perhaps everything? At least, voices calling for us to stop erecting new buildings and to stop demolishing buildings are growing ever louder.[25] Perceived by many as a provocation, a moratorium on new buildings and demolition first and foremost challenges architectural obsolescence as the result of the logic of exploitation driven by the market economy.[26] For, "the present calculation of investors to amortize invested capital in about one generation and then destroy a building" is, as Thomas Sieverts writes, "irresponsible."[27] In a manner similar to Lipp, Sieverts accordingly insists on the idea of heritage preservation being extended to the entire built and unbuilt environment. A comprehensive concern with the potentials for future (new) uses of existing buildings implies not only the consistent focus of monument protection on the value in use, but also creativity in how private ownership rights are handled when it comes to making already extant built/converted space available in line with the principles of just distribution of space. Architecture that is sufficient combines the principles of the primitive hut with those of

The architect and urban planner Thomas Sieverts was scientific director of the IBA Emscher Park (1989–99), which became for him an outstanding example of the positive cultural occupation of former industrial sites. It later formed the starting point for his examination of the urbanized landscapes between the centers of the Ruhr region and influenced the concept of the *Zwischenstadt*, a term he later coined.

bricolage, by placing the transformation of existing surfaces and spaces in full focus, preferentially conceiving of these as low-tech light structures that rely on an economy of means, and enabling simple realization and repair that can potentially be undertaken by the users.

Sufficiency in Spatial Planning

As early as 2003 landscape theorist Sébastien Marot wrote, "The century of expanding cities has passed. Ours is now the time of deepening territories."[28] However, the status today is a far cry from a circumspect and deeper urban–country relationship. In the last 30 years the area covered by settlements in Germany has grown by almost one million hectares, and every day 66 hectares of land are sealed owing to the construction of infrastructures, housing, and commercial spaces. Yet it is clear to all that in order to preserve biodiversity, to buffer heat islands, and not least to achieve the desired decarbonization every square meter of organic and planted soil is needed with its potential to bind CO_2.

Alongside this, the architecture and urban planning discourse in recent decades has devoted much effort and hope to developing concepts that contain urban sprawl: by concentrating urban planning programs in large structures; by creating clear edges to settlements in order to protect the countryside; by rededicating monofunctional zones in urban districts; by emphasizing densification concepts and internal development measures. However, the urgency of the climate crisis and the scarcity of resources should encourage us to go a decisive step further and terminate sealing of soil surfaces not only in order to counter urban sprawl into the countryside but also to ensure the protection of all organic and planted soil in the *Zwischenstadt*. A moratorium on soil sealing could bring to an end the ever-fiercer competition for the use of expected land for development and at the same time stimulate the deeper territorial use advocated by Sébastien Marot: The result would be an agro-ecological transformation of unbuilt areas and a more intense use of built areas. This implies the equal status of spheres of infrastructures and settlement areas with their green zones, on the one hand, and the usually human-made natural spaces, on the other.

A Great Repair of the urban landscapes undertaken in this light would revise the 150-year-plus hegemony of urbanism and the associated plans. Moreover, in this way the paradigm of metropolitanization that has dominated recent decades would be overcome. Even if we must necessarily still plan using a trans-scalar view, the focus can no longer be on forming high-performance metropolises that are destined to win the day against transregional, national, and international competition. At the scale of municipalities, a stop to soil sealing would terminate the disastrous linking of their financing to the use of land because no new commercial zones could be designated outside the city limits. Inside the cities, it would bring an end to the speculative strategy of letting certain sites lie vacant because, once sealed, the pressure to build on them would rise and, if unsealed, they would no longer be worth anything. Essentially, a moratorium on soil sealing would function like a bypass for the issue of land that is so essential to the socio-ecological transition, even if instruments to reform land use such as leaseholds would continue to apply.

The settler movement in Vienna, which organized itself after World War I in response to housing shortages and unemployment, began building unauthorized "wild settlements" and from 1921 to 1933, with the support of the city, erected over 8,000 settlement houses made of pressed concrete bricks — like the Rosenhügel settlement here.

Deeper territorial use implies, as it were, a radical mixture of functions, of agroforestry and agrophotovoltaics through to the consistent conversion of monofunctional areas into neighborhoods with mixed uses. However, such a conversion is only possible with a sufficiency approach in terms of mobility. Only in the rarest of instances is mobility an expression of personal freedom; instead it must fulfill fundamental needs: getting to work, grocery shopping, or getting the children to school. It is no coincidence that mobility is the fourth necessary function in the Athens Charter because there it links the now separate human functions of living, working, and leisure time. With the finalization of the property and land markets, swarm cities have evolved and these functions have grown ever larger. In this process the less privileged people have to live ever further outside the cities. Owing to the insufficient expansion of public transportation systems and urban development geared to centrality they are the most dependent on automobiles and have to bear high mobility costs. Sufficiency in the field of mobility has to counteract this process of squeezing the less fortunate to the margins and go hand in hand with comprehensive alternative local supply and transportation services in structurally weak and thinly populated communities far from the city centers. That can be achieved by means of communal working spaces, flexible working hours, mobile supply concepts, and a better coordinated range of social infrastructures among the communities.

Sufficiency in mobility spells more quality of life and opens up an extensive reservoir of areas and spaces for sustainable urban development. From parking space, garages, and multistory carparks, or inner-city highways and arterial roads through to commercial estates and shopping centers—our urban landscapes offer a wealth of opportunities for repair. What is decisive is that the socio-ecological conversion of these spaces (contrary to green-tech projects devised without heeding context) incorporate the context in which they are located. Adding stories to a building incorporates the social and energy transformation of the entire building, constructing on top of garages changes the use of the garage, constructing on top of parking spaces changes the function of the building for which these parking spaces were originally built. These acts of repair are potentially transformative and regenerative. Different methods emerge here: first, a constant reset of existing buildings, acts of conversion, additions on top of or adjacent to buildings in cities that at the same time protect areas that are not built over; second, developing the areas and spaces that the fossil era has spawned, such as parking spaces, shopping malls, etc., above all in the *Zwischenstadt*. What counts there is, alongside the renaturation required, to increase densities in line with sufficiency criteria and to diversify monofunctional districts. Above all, what is needed is an accessible alternative range of services in less densely populated districts in order to guarantee basic functions locally.

Co-creation as the new collectivity

A project such as the Great Repair can be developed neither exclusively from the top down nor from the classic perspective of planners. Rather, it requires a social basis that (on the scale of quarters and in the *Zwischenstadt* with programmatic higher densities in certain

The Sea Saw houses in Brighton were built in the 1990s by the residents themselves using the timber frame construction method developed by Walter Segal and updated by the office Architype. With 24 units, they were the largest such housing estates in England at the time. As a result of Margaret Thatcher's policies, the buildings could not be financed by the state through mortgages, as had been the case with earlier housing estates of this kind, such as Walters Way or Segal Close in London, so Sea Saw was made possible through a housing association that organized the projects as a cooperative and gave tenants a discount on their rent in return for their work, their "sweat equity."

In contrast to Western European consumer societies, which were organized on the basis of a division of labor, automobility in the GDR was essentially characterized by the repair, maintenance, and care work of the users, which trained individual knowledge and skills in dealing with vehicles. This photo of the collective repair of a Trabant and bicycle dates from 1958.

locations) provides points of engagement with a direct social and spatial reference. No romanticized participation projects are required and, instead, the focus must be on taking people seriously as active players in the transformation process. Involving them does not mean soliciting their preferences, but initiating processes and creating spaces of possibility.

In order to set the conversion of monofunctional spaces in motion, we must from a planning perspective start exploring multidimensional and programmatically diversified communal spaces that in the context of the transition can become local places where people can assemble. These spaces, and Manfredo Tafuri once termed them counter-spaces, enable democratic-collective processes of negotiation in the direct vicinity of where people live. Urban planning close at hand fosters enthusiasm. The role of governance would then be to enable and support such a process of co-creation along with other forms of self-organization, for example building and energy cooperatives or solidarity-based agriculture. These processes need to be designed and backed up by planners who act as the moderating experts. The task of architects is now to grow a new political-ecological aesthetic of collectivity.

The strategy for sustainable urban/rural development thus interlocks the values of the degrowth city (non-profitability, selective growth, social justice, cooperation) with the conversion of the various spatial typologies of the environment as built or not built (such as urban highways and arterial roads, commercial estates, office complexes, parking lots on the one hand and recreation areas, woods, fields, rivers, and wasteland, on the other) using a conceptual toolbox (activation, intensification, hybridization, vertical additions to existing buildings, etc.) and enabling participation, indeed stimulating co-creation. The Great Repair is a planning project that expects immense creativity and commitment on the part of architects. And it is a democratic project because without transparent processes of negotiation and a consensus on new guiding principles and objectives, it will always be hard to gain acceptance for sufficiency. It is by no means the end of architecture but rather the beginning of a new culture of planning that directs architects' urge to build down new paths.

Instandbesetzung as a practice of independent renovation of illegally occupied apartments—as demonstrated here at a recycling demonstration on Oranienplatz—was a reaction to widespread demolition and "clear-cut renovation" in West Berlin in the late 1970s and significantly influenced the IBA Altbau 1984/87 on cautious urban renewal.

1   Figure SPM.1 ex: *IPCC WG3 Report*, accessed September 15, 2022, www.ipcc.ch/report/ar6/wg3/figures/summary-for-policymakers/figure-spm-1.

2   Actually more than a footnote: In Germany, greenhouse gas emissions need to be reduced by 55 percent by 2030 if the country is to adhere to the targets set in the Paris Climate Agreement. By contrast, there are no such goals as regards reducing the consumption of raw materials; here consumption levels in Germany run at a huge 16 tons per capita. This is not factoring in the resources such as water and earth needed to process these raw materials, and which get used or polluted.

3   See Thomas Princen, *The Logic of Sufficiency* (Cambridge: MIT Press, 2005).

4   See his essay in the present issue.

5   This is the concluding sentence of Rilke's sonnet "Archaischer Torso Apolls" (*Neue Gedichte*, vol. 2 [Leipzig: Inselverlag, 1908]) and was chosen by philosopher Peter Sloterdijk as the title of his 2009 book, trans. Wieland Hoban (Cambridge: Polity Press, 2013).

6   Philipp Lepenies: *Verbot und Verzicht: Politik aus dem Geiste des Unterlassens* (Berlin: Suhrkamp, 2022).

7   Tim Jackson: *Prosperity without Growth: Foundations for the Economy of Tomorrow*, 2nd ed. (London: Routledge, 2017), 1. According to Jackson, Boulding uttered the sentence during a hearing before the US Congress in 1973.

8   In 1971, Nicholas Georgescu-Roegen demonstrated in *The Entropy Law and the Economic Process* that natural materials are absorbed into economic processes but only valueless waste is then excreted by the processes. In 1972, the Report to the Club of Rome proved that fossil-fuel resources were finite. That same year André Gorz spoke of a *décroissance* of production.

9   Kenneth E. Boulding, "The Economics of the Coming Spaceship Earth," in *Environmental Quality in a Growing Economy*, ed. Henry Jarrett (Baltimore: Resources for the Future/Johns Hopkins University Press, 1966), 3–14.

10   Ulrich Brand, "Sozial-ökologische Transformation konkret: Die solidarische Postwachstumsstadt als Projekt gegen die imperiale Lebensweise," in *Postwachstumsstadt: Konturen einer solidarischen Stadtpolitik*, eds. Anton Brokow-Loga and Frank Eckardt (Munich: oekom, 2020), 34.

11   See Bastian Lange et al., eds., *Postwachstumsgeographien: Raumbezüge diverser und alternativer Ökonomien* (Bielefeld: transcript, 2020); see also Brokow-Loga and Eckardt, *Postwachstumsstadt* (see note 10); Institut für ökologische Wirtschaftsforschung, *Blog Postwachstum: Stadtplanung*, accessed August 20, 2022, www.postwachstum.de/tag/stadtplanung.

12   Joachim Trezib, "Das 'Neue Berlin II' von Martin Wagner: Modell einer Post-Wachstums-Ökonomie," *ARCH+* 228, *Stadtland: Der neue Rurbanismus* (Spring 2017): 82–89.

13   Anton Brokow-Loga and Frank Eckardt, "Einleitung: Der sozial-ökologische Wandel der Stadtgesellschaft," in their *Postwachstumsstadt* (see note 10), 16. See also the interview in the present issue.

14   Matthias Schmelzer and Andrea Vetter, "Stadt für alle jenseits des Wachstums: Was kann die Stadtforschung aus der Degrowthdebatte lernen?," in Brokow-Loga and Eckardt, eds., *Postwachstumsstadt* (see note 10), 53.

15   Brand, "Sozial-ökologische Transformation konkret" (see note 10), 38.

Over the next ten years, the Hawkwood nursery in London, run cooperatively by the OrganicLea initiative, will be expanded using self-build techniques. The spatial program of the expansion made of natural compostable materials, which is being developed in collaboration with the architectural firm Practice Architecture, includes a community hall, a kitchen, several educational buildings, and spaces for volunteers.

16   Thomas Sieverts, *Cities Without Cities: An Inter-pretation of the* Zwischenstadt (London: Spon Press, 2003), 2. In his foreword to the English edition, Sieverts notes the difficulty of translating the term *Zwischen-stadt*. It describes "an 'in between' state," "in which the old contrast between city and country has dissolved into a city–country continuum." Ibid., x.
17   See Jennifer Hahn, "Architecture 'lagging behind all other sectors' in climate change fight says IPCC report author," *dezeen*, April 6, 2022, accessed August 20, 2022, www.dezeen.com/2022/04/06/ipcc-cli-mate-change-mitigation-report.
18   See Marc-Antoine Laugier, *Essai sur l'architecture & Observation sur l'architecture*, Edition intégrale des deux volumes (Brussels: Pierre Mardaga, 1979), 222, 314.
19   See Geert Bekaert, "A l'école du bon goût," in Laugier, *Essai* (see note 18), vi, xi. See Joseph Rykwert, *On Adam's House in Paradise: The Idea of the Primitive Hut in Architectural Theory* (New York: The Museum of Modern Art, 1972), 43 f., which some-what relativizes Laugier's social thrust compared to Rousseau.

20   Gilles Delalex, "The Ruins of Adolescence," in *Positions on Emancipation: Architecture between Aesthetics and Politics*, eds. Florian Hertweck and Nikos Katsikis (Zurich: Lars Müller, 2018), 72 f.
21   Anh-Linh Ngo et al., editorial to *ARCH+* 240, *Neuer Realismus in der französischen Architektur* (Fall 2020), 2 f.
22   Lucius Burckhardt, "Selberbauen, ökologisch bauen, regional bauen," in *Für eine andere Architektur: Selbstbestimmt bauen und wohnen*, eds. Michael Andritzky et al. (Frankfurt/Main: Fischer, 1981), 10.
23   Ibid.
24   Jürgen Bertling and Claus Leggewie, "Die Repa-raturgesellschaft: Ein Beitrag zur großen Transforma-tion?," in *Die Welt reparieren: Open Source und Selber-machen als postkapitalistische Praxis*, eds. Andrea Baier et al. (Bielefeld: transcript, 2016), 280.
25   See also Daniel Fuhrhop, *Verbietet das Bauen! Streitschrift gegen Spekulation, Abriss und Flächenfraß* (Munich: oekom, 2020); Charlotte Malterre-Barthes, *A Global Moratorium on New Construction*, accessed August 20, 2022, www.charlottemalterrebarthes.com/practice/research-practice/a-global-moratorium-on-

new-construction/; Ministry of Energy and Spatial Planning, *Luxembourg in Transition: Spatial visions for the zero-carbon and resilient future of the Luxem-bourg functional region*, accessed August 20, 2022, www.luxembourgintransition.lu; *Abriss-Moratorium*, open letter to Federal Minister of Construction Klara Geywitz, accessed September 30, 2022, abrissmoratorium.de; see Emeline Cazi, "Rénovation, densification, chasse aux logements vides … l'habitat, un modèle à déconstruire," *Le Monde*, June 3, 2022.
26   See Daniel M. Abramson, "From Obsolescence to Sustainability: Back Again, and Beyond," *Design and Culture* 4, no. 3 (2012): 279–98.
27   See Thomas Sieverts, "The Principle of Heritage: Preservation and Its Generalisation in the Anthropocene," *disP: The Planning Review* 53, no. 1 (2017): 103.
28   Sébastien Marot, *Sub-urbanism and the Art of Memory* (London: Architectural Association, 2003), 86.

"Sufficiency is a concept for politics and planning, Not for the individual person"

Anton Brokow-Loga and Katrin Großmann in conversation with Alex Nehmer, Florian Hertweck, and Markus Krieger

Material Cultures was founded in London in 2019 by Paloma Gormley, Summer Islam, and George Massoud. The nonprofit organization combines design, research, and teaching for a post-fossil built environment. Developed in a design studio in 2020, *Low Carbon City* draws on principles from Ebenezer Howard's garden city model. It re-localizes the production of architecture from renewable materials. Residential and community buildings and factories are placed in close proximity to one another.

How can we think together ecology and social justice in the urging transformations in architecture and urban planning, instead of the one being played off against the other? This is discussed here by urban researcher Anton Brokow-Loga and urban and spatial sociologist Katrin Großmann with guest editor Florian Hertweck as well as ARCH+'s Alex Nehmer and Markus Krieger.

Alex Nehmer Anton, you're researching the degrowth city. Why is it important to sever the link between cities and growth in the first place? And what kind of growth are we talking about here exactly?

Anton Brokow-Loga When, in a degrowth discourse, we talk about uncoupling cities from growth we are primarily talking about economic growth. The idea is not to make cities less appealing so that fewer people want to move there. However, there are complex linkages between economic and demographic growth, which is why it is worth making a brief detour into history at this juncture. The notion of infinite economic growth arose in the course of industrialization, profit maximization, and capitalist accumulation—in other words, in the Global North the age of urbanization went hand in hand with a quite unprecedented expansion in urban economies. The idea of continual economic growth thus became deeply inscribed in social institutions and also in what we refer to as the city. By this I mean not only the constant expansion of material infrastructure such as streets and houses but also legal and fiscal structures. The financing of municipalities in Germany, for example, depends on competition for trade tax revenues and for inhabitants. Municipal administrations and local public corporations are therefore subject to the competition between locations. Through economic policy measures, commercial parks are being extended forever deeper into the surrounding areas. Areas required for housing likewise expand, whereby they are at the same time distributed more and more unevenly between inhabitants. Another example is the mobility transition, where people tend to forget that the focus should actually be on reducing transportation, not on simply changing the type of engine used.

All these things lead to a continuation of the thrust to expand and the orientation toward growth. At present, it is hard to separate the very idea of what actually is successful urban life from economic growth. At the macro-social level, gross domestic product is still regarded as a main indicator of prosperity, although it in fact says little about what people's real quality of life is like. What is becoming ever clearer at present is that the growth compulsion entails both ecological destruction and social injustice. For this reason, a key issue is how we can create alternative value orientations, other role models that place a concern for the common good and for ecological and social justice firmly in the foreground. In this context, severing any linkage of urban policy to a compulsion to grow can function as an important stone in the overall mosaic of transformation.

Katrin Großmann What is missing in your list is the level of the state. Centralization is also induced by the state and the administration. For a century now, the "system of central locations" developed by geographer Walter Christaller has determined thinking in regional planning. It is inscribed into our patterns of interpretation on how regions should be designed and planned. This leads to the assumption that infrastructure "naturally" belongs in the nodes. That is no natural law, but in the sum of the decisions it results in growth in the cores and in a centralization of administrative resources. At the same time, demographic growth in cities has a lot to do with deprivation in rural areas.

Florian Hertweck Katrin, among other things you have done research on shrinking cities. The degrowth concept is often accused of essentially hinging on shrinkage, on an artificial recession. Where do you see the difference between the degrowth city and the shrinking city? Is there in fact no overlap between them?

KG No, actually there is not. Degrowth is a self-chosen normative orientation: People want to orient themselves to other models for social development. Shrinking cities have only rarely set out to do that; on the contrary, often they are infused with a yearning for renewed growth and prosperity. And because the resources simply do not exist, the relevant actors find it hard to shape shrinking cities. Most of the municipalities in question have slid so deeply into debt that their room for maneuver is very restricted and much has to be shouldered by volunteers.

FH So no shrinking city has yet succeeded in transforming itself into a degrowth city?

KG No, and that doesn't make sense anyway. We should expect the resource-strong

Against a backdrop of climate collapse and biodiversity loss, A Global Moratorium on New Construction calls for a correspondingly drastic change: Don't demolish, don't build new, work with what is already there.

locations to be the first to engage in such experiments and innovations. With what right could one instruct a municipality that is struggling to "enjoy it, shrinking is great." Degrowth is a discourse driven by a young urban academic milieu and the majority of the members of that group do not reside in shrinking cities. To this extent I consider such a call to be wrong, even if some do indeed make it.

ABL I agree, we need to make a clear distinction here. The immensely precarious municipal authorities and spaces in which we observe shrinkage cannot act as the prototypes for a degrowth society. Nevertheless, there are relevant links to be forged here. For example, questions as to what kind of deceleration and reduction our society requires. However, we must remain critical of power relations and inequalities when it comes to reduction processes. The question as to who acts first—the big city with a large amount of political, cultural, and economic capital or a shrinking town without access to these resources—is comparable with the debates that have taken place for decades at the world climate conferences: Should it be emerging market and developing countries in the Global South or the industrialized nations that must be deprivileged? In the case of degrowth, not everyone must shrink to the same extent. That said, it is crucial to understand that shrinking municipalities are considered deficient first and foremost because of our growth-focused hierarchical system.

For the Balearic Islands' public housing association Institut Balear de l'Habitatge (IBAVI), a team of civil servant architects designs social housing buildings. The buildings are constructed with renewable raw materials and natural stone from re-localized and low-carbon production.

Markus Krieger It also seems advisable to distinguish between the degrowth city and other urban visions, such as the sustainable city or the smart city.

ABL These ways of thinking are completely unlike that for degrowth: Other visions of future urban development, such as that of the smart city, seek to boost the city's technological potential. The focus is thus on technology-oriented processes that are expected to make life more pleasant. Often such approaches view urban life from the angle of efficiency: Where can payroll be reduced? How can rule violations be predicted by AI? The models and algorithms that the cities are then expected to adapt and with which humans are meant to conform are, however, created by transnational corporations with specific interests of their own, such as data, profit, and influence. Any reduction in discrimination and the creation of "equal living conditions for all" is not on their agenda in the first place. It is important to bear in mind that the smart city is primarily an entrepreneurial vision, a vision for the city as enterprise. This could hardly be more different from the holistic perspective of the degrowth city with its strong adherence to the common good, redistribution, and negotiation.

Moreover, degrowth also incorporates other relationships, such as that between the city and what research has long since labeled the "hinterland," and also a global and above all a globalization-critical perspective, such as is often missing from visions of the smart city and also of sustainable urban development. Copenhagen, for example, which is exceptionally successful in marketing itself as a sustainable and in particular a bicycle-friendly city, in the process conceals its indirect emissions. In almost all the accounts drawn up by the municipal authorities it hardly plays any role where and at whose cost the objects of everyday life (from clothing to food) are produced. To factor all that in we precisely need a degrowth perspective. Local solutions are important, but we should not be satisfied to simply render the surface more beautiful and greener. We must also re-localize global supply chains.

FH What do you take re-localization to mean?

ABL A process of disentangling economic linkages. The concept has figured in globalization-critical debates for decades now. The plan was for it to also be realized in the implementation of Agenda 21 as resolved in 1992 at the UN Earth Summit in Rio de Janeiro and which focused on sustainable development at the economic, ecological, and social levels. Instead, things went the other way: Transnational corporations and lobby groups have been hell-bent on pursuing their interest in expanding value chains by eliminating importation restrictions and customs tariffs and expanding the global networking of economic regions. The result was the downgrading, indeed degrading, of centuries-old relationships between cities and the regions surrounding them.

Today, this affects many fields, such as nutrition, where soybean is shipped halfway round the world to be used as cattle fodder in order to satisfy Europe's hunger for meat. In the recent times of crisis, road construction projects wait sometimes for months for specific materials which for reasons of price can only be procured from remote regions of the Earth. Those are examples that show how dysfunctional this system is. In the construction sector, one key issue must be to unravel these linkages. Here, re-localization means specifically only using new materials that are available close at hand, to build within the existing urban fabric, and to reclaim construction materials from buildings that have been dismantled. If a material cannot be obtained locally then we should radically reduce its use.

That is a tall political order. It would be fatal if economic re-localization led to political closure, to closure at the level of migration policy and identity policy. The free flow of people and social interaction must be at the forefront of things.

FH It is important, and this also applies to a transition in construction, what we understand the term city to mean in the first place. It is now 25 years since Thomas Sieverts brought out his work on the *Zwischenstadt*, which he describes as "an 'in between' state," "in which the old contrast between city and country has dissolved into a city-country continuum."[1] Since then, we have seen a continually growing expansion in such *Zwischenstädte*. The contours of the degrowth city are gradually becoming discernible. But how to apply the degrowth paradigm to the condition of the *Zwischenstadt*?

ABL A degrowth city based on solidarity is not some metropolitan concept. The emphasis is most certainly not exclusively on downtown areas that are to remain or become attractive. No, it is about places to live, and small and medium-sized towns are a key element here as more than half of all Germans live in places with between 5,000 and 100,000 inhabitants. The degrowth city must find answers to people's lived realities.

That said, the expansive settlement structure that the term *Zwischenstadt* denotes, and which is still being pushed forward, needs most definitely to be revisited. Commercial parks are still being designed as single-story settings, with parking lots adjacent to them with no photovoltaics. The development is forever only horizontal, because people evidently still believe, or our political-economic system would have us believe, that land is an infinite resource, which is of course not the case. To my mind, as yet there is no clear path forwards to be seen. However, a municipal cap on land consumption, such as the 30-hectare goal, needs to be set in stone, in our federal system presumably at the federal state level. Inter-communal cooperation could then result together with the neighboring communities in a circular land economy.

One thing is implied in all this: deliberate dismantling. This already seems to be legitimate in the case of fossil fuel infrastructures. We in fact need much more research and strategies on consciously increasing densities, for examples in the *Zwischenstadt*, and the dismantling of other areas. What is equally important here is to recognize the realities of life. If for legitimate, scientifically justified reasons you take a stance against detached houses, then you must not forget that this type of building is related to a specific welfare regime and practice of personal provisions for old age that cannot be jettisoned that quickly. The key term here is a just transition.

MK The challenges of a just transition apply to the construction transition in its entirety, especially if the focus is on existing buildings as an instrument to reduce emissions: Architects4Future demand in a draft legislation they have developed together with GermanZero that the annual rate of energy efficiency renovation be increased from 1 to 4 percent. Katrin, in your research you have explored the consequences of policies that focus only on energy efficiency and do not factor social issues into the equation.

KG Things would perhaps be better if the focus were actually on energy efficiency. However, on the market the focus in fact is actually often not on that at all and instead on upgrading existing buildings and boosting the return on investment. Where energy efficiency is indeed the objective, and the example of strongly committed housing cooperatives demonstrates this, large investments are required as well, and rents rise, but at least an attempt is being made there to cause as few social costs as possible. On the free market, the problem is usually the modernization levy that can be charged on tenants, which encourages speculation. Any act of modernization, be it energy-related or otherwise, is an upgrade. The administrative authorities think that all households should be jumping for joy if their buildings are retrofitted because it lowers energy costs. However, it would be naïve to believe that households who live at the bottom rung of the housing market in homes that have not been modernized will in the long run not once again end up in bad and cheap segments of the housing market. Either they have to move out immediately after the modernization because they can no longer afford the new, as a rule clearly more expensive, rent, or they are gradually forced out over the course of the years. Many subsidies simply attempt to increase the pace of energy efficiency renovation. The EU is increasingly pushing the pedal with programs such as the Green New Deal, Renovation Wave, Fit for 55 and so on. All these packages are economic growth packages, promising green growth. Yet specifically in the case of Fit for 55 there is much criticism owing to the lack of social instruments or resources.

In this context the problem can also no longer be grasped in terms of (green) gentrification. I for one believe that reality is currently overtaking the concept of gentrification. Because we are not talking here about quarters, but entire cities that are exposed to a price increase. To date, energy efficiency renovation has functioned to drive segregation and we very urgently need ways to put a brake on this.

FH What would the alternative be?

KG The modernization levy needs to be abolished. Grants for energy efficiency renovation should in particular be given to owners who focus on the common good and in housing markets that don't automatically blossom. In shrinking regions, it is almost impossible to shoulder the investments, specifically in so-called rural areas, for the many private households in old houses that are economically very run down. There, it must be

the job of the state to subsidize this modernization in the first place. In housing markets in big cities, we need political instruments that prevent speculative investments. That actually starts with the fact that rarely is a real assessment made whether an energy efficiency renovation has actually been carried out. In Berlin—so colleagues tell me—at times insulation is simply glued on top of insulation. It suffices to claim that something has been modernized in order to increase the rent.

For very many years, the state has shied away from committedly subsidizing energy efficiency renovation and has pushed the costs back to tenants and then on to landlords and back again under the heading of the "tenant-landlord dilemma." Public subsidies can also be tied to the type of economic use of the housing. To my mind, a precondition for subsidizing energy efficiency renovation should be that it is pegged to non-profit-oriented, charitable, cooperative, and municipal use of the housing.

AN Our project *The Great Repair* juxtaposes a series of alternative politics to that of the growth paradigm. This conversation is presented in the chapter on the politics of "sufficiency." From your vantage point, to what extent can this provide orientation for the transformations ahead?

KG Many approaches are geared to the behavior of low-income groups of the population and are intended to help them save energy. Nonsense! These groups can show others how to save energy, as they *have to* do it. Irrespective of whether it is heating, electricity, or mobility—the lower income decile in Germany consumes a minimum and the upper decile almost four times as much. A Slovenian colleague of mine, Lidija Živčič, therefore talks of "energy decadence" as the real problem. If we were to start charging taxes that made such energy decadence clearly more expensive and therefore as good as no longer affordable, we would already be heading in a better direction. Then we could make a basic level of energy consumption free of charge and in one fell swoop we would be rid of the debate we just had about complicated forms of relief that are then actually not enough. If we talk about sufficiency and saving, we should start with those who consume the most—and not always at the bottom.

ABL This is why we so urgently need to focus on the inequalities in our society as the basis for the debate on sufficiency. Nevertheless, what Katrin just described tends to be the customary state of affairs. I have also encountered situations where a municipal authority issues a sufficiency guide for poor households, published with a public grant. For example, including tips on energy saving in large housing estates in a city in eastern Germany. This simply serves to fuel precisely the narrative that the ecological always comes at the cost of those who are at a material disadvantage anyway. That certainly needs to be changed.

FH If we're talking about sufficient housing, then we also need to talk about mobility. In growing cities, there's an extremely large volume of traffic, and it causes a large part of the CO_2 emissions. Most people are compelled to live outside cities and to commute into them to work. What would sufficiency mean in this context?

KG Everything converges in the issue of housing: The cost of living is largely determined by the choice of where you live. As a rule, housing costs are fixed, whereas you have a little scope when it comes to mobility and energy costs. This leads to a phenomenon that is well known in research on poverty: People in precarious circumstances take decisions that fly in the face of their own interests. Capacities are so limited and the pressure to act so great that some households, for example, attempt to ease the burden of housing poverty but the trade-off is energy poverty and mobility poverty and, moreover, time poverty, as the commute eats up so much of their time that little remains of the day, and there is scarce time for personal interests and social activities. I find myself repeatedly asking what purpose there is in calling for sufficiency in such situations.

ABL There are no simple solutions to this. One possible approach has been on the table for decades now, namely the compact city where everything is close at hand. I believe that this offers a key to designing settlements in line with human needs. Working, living, and provisions for a social life need to be considered as an integrated complex. For example, what should the infrastructures look like for a *Zwischenstadt* modeled on the 15-minute-city in order to lower traffic levels? This could be achieved via the detour of sufficiency. Sufficiency has the advantage over degrowth that it has definitely been more strongly accepted by practitioners. There are major players in urban development who have gained experience with it and conducted studies on it. However, sufficiency cannot be a task set for an individual person and that can also not be the objective. From my point of view, sufficiency is a concept for politics and for planning, and not for individual persons. The people in Copenhagen, for example, do not use bicycles because they have a more pronounced green conscience than do we, but simply because the material infrastructures for cycling are safe and easy to use, meaning cycle paths, covered cycle racks, and so on.

FH Affordable housing must be created where people demand the right to the city. The German Federal government wants to create 400,000 new apartments a year as part of its housing construction campaign. The units will inevitably cause more emissions and will presumably not be built by using existing housing but on newly sealed land. How do you see that from a degrowth perspective: Are we witnessing a conflict between social needs and ecological needs, Anton?

ABL We will be hard pushed to avoid a moratorium on new builds. And we at any rate need a social debate on this. In the final analysis, 400,000 new apartments a year cannot be realized, something made abundantly clear by the end of the construction boom caused by the emerging recession in the sector. The more central argument is, however, that we simply cannot afford a new-build program if we adopt a planetary perspective informed by climate science.

From the social point of view, it's not necessary in the first place. Since the 1960s, per capita living space has almost doubled in what used to be West Germany. That's surely what should be our key starting point. On a spatially restricted planet it is impossible to constantly increase the amount of personal living space. What Katrin mentioned in the context of energy consumption also applies to the distribution of living space by income group: A healthy mean would be tolerable for the planet, but the increase in living space, particularly due to the above-average spatial requirements of the upper ten percent, is at the expense of the general public as a whole. So if we talk about living space sufficiency we must ask how it is currently distributed. Who lives in overcrowded apartments below the poverty line and can definitely not reduce their living space? Who lives on his or her own in a space of 150 square me-

ters and can afford horrendous heating costs? To my mind, there's simply no way around a state redistribution policy based on taxation.

However, if housing is to be built after all, then that could be negotiated in the moratorium. It would have to exclusively be affordable housing that is secured by the organizational model used: either by cooperatives, syndicates, or projects that do not generate profits through privatized housing. At present, high-end housing is being built, and this completely ignores where the demand lies. Under the protection of the narrative that more new builds would make housing more affordable overall, here social issues are played off against ecology. However, that contradiction can, to my mind, be solved by politicians and planners taking a long-term view.

Moreover, the construction industry must morph into a conversion industry. Housing construction is immensely slow moving. About 80 percent of the residential buildings in Germany are over 30 years old. We can't make sure there is a sufficient stock of affordable housing at the pace at which we are busy building housing, even if we were to resolve from now on only to construct social housing. For that reason, I believe the solution has to be to focus on existing buildings, on conversions and extensions of existing infrastructures. The changes in working patterns caused by the COVID-19 pandemic, for example, already indicate that going forward large swathes of office premises will be vacant in downtown locations. We need viable concepts on converting them into housing. And we also need, even if this sounds more trivial than the realization will then be, we need more shared infrastructures and meeting places as common spaces within the urban fabric. "More public rather than private luxury"—from the sufficiency perspective that could be a meaningful slogan to proclaim.

KG The inequalities in the distribution of living spaces is in part also caused by the tight housing market, for example by the remanence effect: Pensioners remain living in four-room apartments although they can no longer handle the housekeeping—but moving into a smaller apartment now entails a higher rent. Price increases have thus resulted in a "lock-in." That is not something that can be mastered using the models for social housing construction deployed to date, which Andrej Holm rightly terms business subsidies for private developers with an interim welfare use. Housing is such a basic good that it does not belong in the hands of the market. Like energy, it must simply be part of the social contract. In this context, the government would be recognized as the regulating agency and would, in return, assume responsibility for our basic needs. This is already being implemented in education, and the state must also shoulder the basic provision of housing and energy such as to allow everyone to participate with dignity in our society. This means either at an affordable price or, in the basic version, free of charge, just as is the case with education. Anything and everything over and above that can gladly cost a lot—which brings us back to the keyword "decadence."

By contrast, a new-build program would only amount to repair within a system that is neither social nor ecological in thrust. However, the huge distortions that the market produces have to date rarely been questioned. Above all not in the framework of the idea of the sustainable city which was introduced decades ago, but which has changed absolutely nothing.

MK In your opinion, why did it achieve so little?

KG Because the primacy of the economy was not tackled. The postulate of sustainability has only led to alliances between ecological and economic efforts, to illusions such as "green growth" that then supposedly brings everyone prosperity.

When a food distribution center in Basel was converted into the ELYS Culture and Trade Center in 2021, a new large facade surface was created. For this, baubüro in situ asked window producers within a radius of around 100 kilometers for "stock windows." This made it possible to install 200 as-new windows that were stored at the companies due to overproduction or incorrect orders and would otherwise have been discarded.

We're still very much at the start of things when it comes to really thinking of ecology and social justice in one breath. Then we would need to relegate the economy to its place as a means to an end, not an end in itself. Economic prosperity cannot be a normative social objective. The economy can only be an instrument in order to attain a socially just and ecological society.

AN At the core of the degrowth debate is the notion that things must no longer just revolve around "less is more" but around selective shrinkage—and at the same time the selective growth of specific areas of society that actually need to prosper.

ABL There is no empirical evidence to suggest that we can sever the link between our model of prosperity, on the one hand, and resource consumption and growth, on the other. Philosopher Frank Martela put it poignantly when he said that what we have instead successfully uncoupled from each other are economic growth and a satisfied life for the vast majority of the population. For this reason, the economic sectors that are especially responsible for environmental damage or social injustice need to be selectively shrunk and stripped of their privileges. What we as a society find serves life, and what is destructive, both for the social foundations of our society and for the planetary limits is both a question for academic study and also always a position in political discourse. However, who at present has what weight in this discourse? It's an illusion to believe that there is a deliberative model of politics at work, i.e., that we exist in a space that is factually power-free. For this reason, any degrowth vision with a view to what can still be repaired most definitely needs to also include democratization. We need to talk about radical, direct democracy and locally accountable democratic institutions. Furthermore, we need other indicators and stipulations. For cities, the donut model could point to the right path to take as promulgated by economist Kate Raworth. Instead of focusing on growth in gross domestic product, the donut economy seeks to adhere to planetary ecological limits and at the same time cover all basic human needs. In the shape of a donut, these two conditions designate an area in which economic activity should take place. Cities such as Amsterdam and Berlin, not to mention countries like Scotland and Wales, have for some time now been experimenting with how this could work. As mentioned above with regard to the example of Copenhagen, it is key here that the immense external costs are also integrated into the city's model of prosperity.

AN This *ARCH+* issue also includes contributions on the topic of reparations, for example an interview with political philosopher Olúfẹ́mi O. Táíwò. To what extent can a degrowth perspective be not only about turning away from growth today but also repairing the damage that the Global North has caused elsewhere through its drive for growth?

KG The issue of reparations makes immediate good sense in the context of Global North and Global South. What this means in concrete terms is a matter for experts other than myself. Until

recently, I was unable to make much sense of it in terms of energy policies or for local communities. But on an excursion to a lignite mining district near Halle and Leipzig I had a sudden realization. I was astonished to hear that the people who had been displaced and resettled due to lignite mining did not in the least have the idea that something has been taken from them for which they had a claim to reparations. Yet they had lost their homes. Instead,

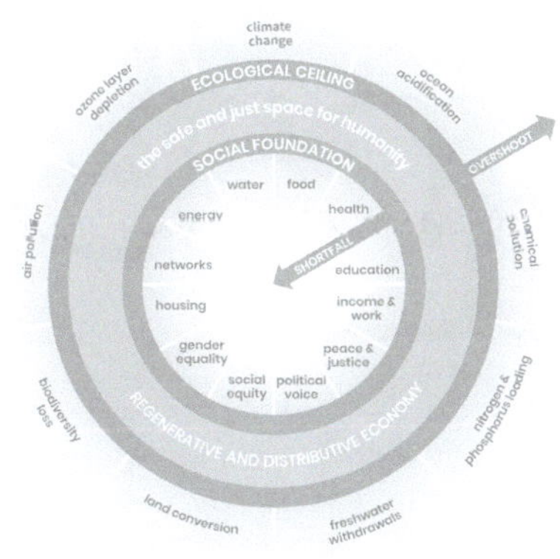

Kate Raworth's "donut model" for a regenerative and distributive economy. The aim is neither to exceed ecological limits nor to fall short of social limits.

their bond to coal and open-cast mining was a fixed point of identity. An 80-year-old man in a retirement home told me and my students: "I'm a miner. What could be better?" The locals still identified with the mining companies even if they are now in a different economic context and no longer what they had built up as engineers in the days of the GDR. The question of what fossil fuel–based industrialization has destroyed here and what that means on a global scale is anything but trivial. Yet to date, any discussion of this has simply provoked strong denial. Questions of justice arise, but they focus on the distribution of resources and recognition in the present.

ABL That's an interesting thought which would place the "just transition" debate on a new footing. As regards reparations, I think that the Global North has to provide quite a bit of material redress. However, the immaterial, namely the knowledge that was destroyed in the Global South by colonial structures, far outweighs this and is also far less tangible. The imperial mode of production and way of life, and the capitalist logic, which were exported everywhere and imposed on everyone as "progress," have caused immense damage and further stoked the flames of that destructive system.

In this context, any kind of redress must start with reflecting on one's own responsibility in this system. This discussion is something each discipline must conduct internally. I don't want to speak here at some abstract level of "we," as that already entails the question as to what privileges one enjoys. For me personally I can only conclude that I must criticize these logics, expose them, and work on alternatives. For example, in the debate on the degrowth city the focus cannot be one on developing yet another export model for the entire world, but on critically and in a spirit of self-reflection examining the social dynamics in your own country. There is a need, and an absolutely urgent need at that, for a real change in thinking and direction in the very heart of the system.

1   Thomas Sieverts, *Cities Without Cities: An Interpretation of the Zwischenstadt* (London: Spon Press, 2003), x.

longevity

Text: Florian Hertweck

The material culture of the Global North is more than ever characterized by the principle of creative destruction. Constant innovation is its primary goal. As technologies age ever more quickly, however, ever more waste is produced. Or in the words of Niko Paech: "The acceleration of innovation activities cultivates an all-encompassing throwaway-syndrome."[1] In this context, the richer societies and households are, the greater *Waste Makers* they are—the title Vance Packard gave his benchmark critique of consumerism as long ago as 1960.[2]

The World Bank projects that the volume of worldwide waste produced will grow from some two billion tons at present to 3.4 billion tons by 2050.[3] In Germany, around half the total volume is made up of construction and demolition waste.[4] According to Daniel M. Abramson, modern architectural history is a history of obsolescence.[5] In contemporary capitalism, buildings are not constructed with longevity in mind, their life span is instead based on amortization periods and

Enzo Mari, *Timor Perpetual Calendar*, 1967

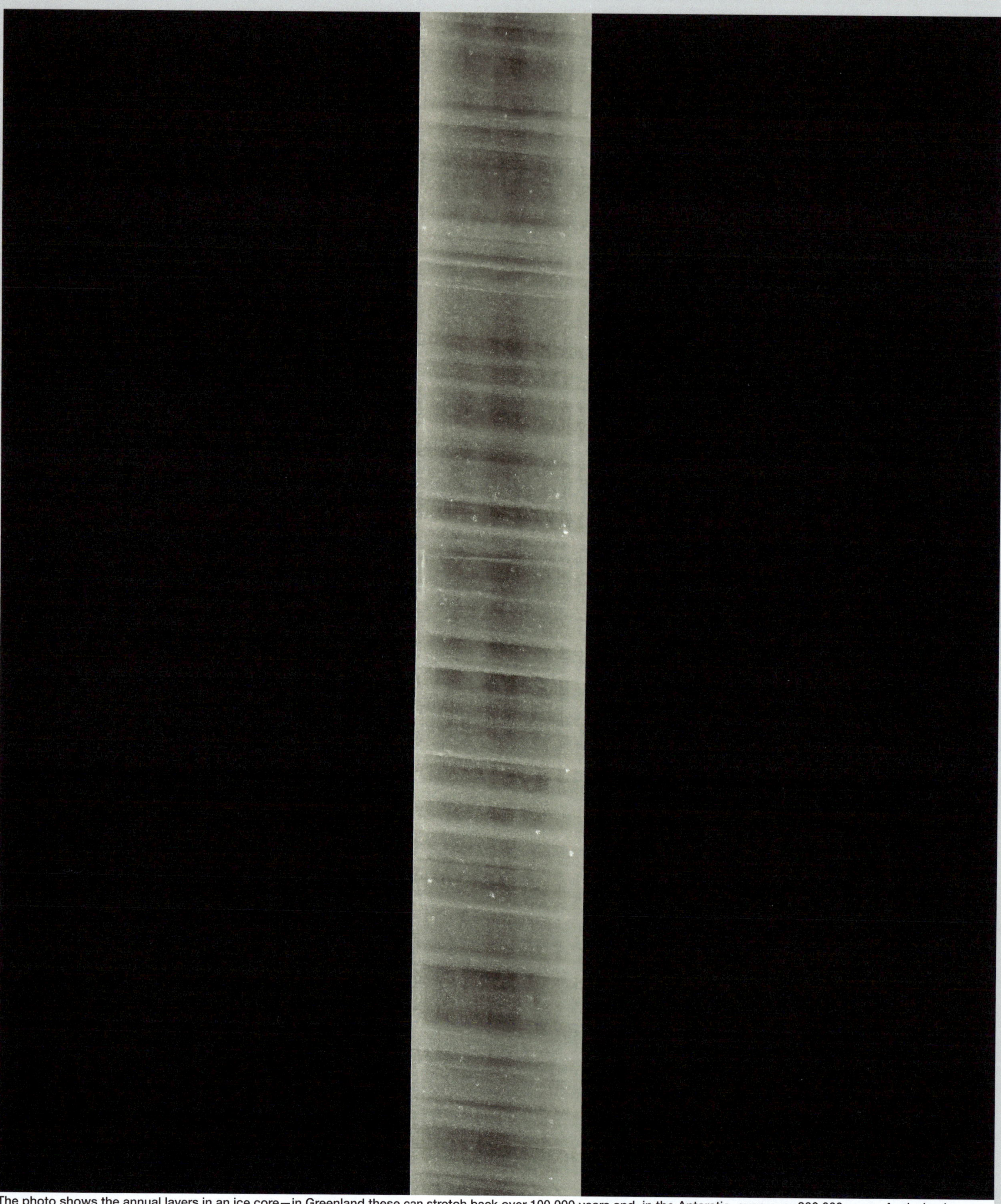

The photo shows the annual layers in an ice core—in Greenland these can stretch back over 100,000 years and, in the Antarctic, even over 800,000 years. Analyzing ice cores is one of the most important methods of studying past climate conditions.

short-term profit interests. When the renovation backlog starts to increase or the site can be more densely built on or better utilized, the decision is still too often made in favor of demolition over repair and transformation of the existing building stock.

In view of the climate crisis and dwindling resources, the question of the longevity of objects and spaces is becoming ever more pressing. In all of this, a distinction must be made between longevity and sustainability, at least as the terms are used today. While sustainability, as Pierre Caye points out, is often geared at nothing other than transposing market principles onto ecology, longevity aims at changing the system of production itself.[6] It is thus about nothing less, according to Fabio Merlini, than turning our backs on the "tragic destiny" of a future made up of nothing but an endless succession of technical innovations.[7] This makes repair the crucial counter-paradigm to obsolescence for a new material culture of longevity.[8]

1   Niko Paech, "Die Welt lässt sich nur in der Postwachstumsökologie reparieren," in *Die Welt reparieren: Open Source und Selbermachen als postkapitalistische Praxis*, eds. Andrea Bayer et al. (Bielefeld: transcript, 2016), 288.
2   Vance Packard, *The Waste Makers* (New York: David McKay, 1960).
3   Dominik Reintjes: "Diese Länder sind die größten Müllsünder," *Die Wirtschaftswoche*, September 20, 2019, accessed July 22, 2022, www.wiwo.de/politik/deutschland/studie-zum-world-cleanup-day-diese-laender-sind-die-groessten-muellsuender/25028328.html.
4   Of the approximately 413 million tons of waste generated in Germany, construction and demolition waste accounts for more than 229 million tons. Accessed July 22, 2022, www.destatis.de/DE/Themen/Gesellschaft-Umwelt/Umwelt/Abfallwirtschaft/Tabellen/liste-abfallbilanz-kurzuebersicht.html;jsessionid=C5C0D122C47D40E15C5C4AFC20DDF097.live742.

5   Daniel M. Abramson, *Obsolescence: An Architectural History* (Chicago: University of Chicago Press, 2016).
6   Pierre Caye, *Durer: Éléments pour la transformation du système productif* (Paris: Les Belles Lettres, 2020).
7   Fabio Merlini, *L'architecture inefficiente: Luigi Snozzi et Fabio Merlini* (Marseille: Cosa Mentale, 2016), 9.
8   See Manuel Nagel and Niko Paech, "Reparatur kontra Obsoleszenz: Chancen für eine Postwachstumsökonomie," in *Konsumkritische Projekte und Praktiken: Interdisziplinäre Perspektiven auf gemeinschaftlichen Konsum*, eds. Sigrid Kannengiesser and Ines Weller (Munich: oekom, 2018), 39–56; Stefan Krebs et al., eds., *Kulturen des Reparierens: Dinge, Wissen, Praktiken* (Bielefeld: transcript, 2018).

protecting the world from Depletion

Pierre Caye in conversation with Florian Hertweck and Panos Mantziaras

No less than 84 percent of the waste and about one third of greenhouse gas emissions in Switzerland are caused by the construction industry. New builds may be more efficient to operate, but erecting them releases about as much greenhouse gas emissions as operating them for 50 years. This is why, when it comes to achieving climate targets, careful modernization clearly has an edge over demolition and replacement new builds. Countdown 2030 is an association of architects and planners who champion a sustainable construction culture in Switzerland. Their medium: exhibitions, discussions, guide tours, campaigns in the urban space, and publications, including the demolition atlas produced by a participating process: the *Abriss-Atlas*.

How can our economic and production system be transformed toward sustainability and longevity? Guest editor Florian Hertweck and urban planner Panos Mantziaras speak with philosopher Pierre Caye, who looks at environmental questions from the intersection of ecology, economics, and technology, and also critically engages with architecture and urban planning.

Florian Hertweck You are calling on people not to jettison the widely criticized notion of *sustainable development*. What advantages do you see in retaining it?

Pierre Caye Let me first briefly touch on why this term is so problematic. For most governments and businesses, sustainable development simply means environmental economics, which amounts to extending market laws to apply to environmental goods. According to this logic, a price is then assigned to carbon emissions, for example. This is based on the idea that environmental pollution and destruction are ultimately due to insufficient compliance with market laws. Which is of course completely smoke and mirrors! Environmental economics inevitably lead to a dead end. I believe that in order to find an answer to the environmental question, there is no alternative but to fundamentally reshape the economy.

FH Against this background, you conceptualize sustainable development as a comprehensive economic model that takes into account all economic, ecological, and social forces. What is the basis for this model?

PC I looked at three important production factors—capital, labor, and technology—and asked myself the question: What do these factors mean for the goal of sustainability if we consider them in a temporal dimension? In short, in the service of permanence, does capital become heritage, labor become maintenance and repair, and technology become an instrument for expanding space and time, as architecture potentially does?

FH Before we look more closely at these three factors of production, let's touch on your deconstruction of the notions of growth and degrowth.

Panos Mantziaras The postulate of exiting growth still seems valid today, 50 years after the publication of the famous report to the Club of Rome on *The Limits to Growth*, in which Donella and Dennis Meadows and Jørgen Randers demonstrated the incompatibility of economic and population growth with the finite nature of resources.[1]

PC To my mind, binaries such as technophilia/technophobia or growth/degrowth are not fruitful. The term "degrowth" (*décroissance* in French) sounds off-putting at first. On the other hand, growth is something very relative that only takes into account what it wants to take into account and leaves much out: Only what is defined as valuable *a priori* is considered to have value.

Gross domestic product, for example, the most common indicator of wealth and growth, tends to be calculated in terms of flows of goods and financial assets rather than what has already been created. On the other hand, no national account systems factor in things like the losses caused by soil depletion. Certainly, there are already attempts to calculate ecosystem services, meaning the various benefits we humans derive from functioning natural cycles,[2] but what exactly are we calculating here? Is it a matter of better incorporating the natural heritage into environmental economics? If so then we run the risk, as described at the outset, of falling into a logic of weak sustainability and replacing natural capital with financial or technological capital. However, the more we try to account for ecosystem services, the more we realize that they are not quantifiable. That great economic theorist Jean-Baptiste Say, paradoxically given that he was a liberal, recognized this very early on. He also counted gravity among the "cosmological" services on which the economy depends, and this puts us in an area that defies any calculation or accounting.

FH Even if not all physical processes can be assessed economically, the calculation systems with which we can attach a price tag to production and other undertakings are becoming increasingly precise. In the balance sheet of urban development or architectural projects, however, neither the environmental damage nor the positive effects of ecological transformation are sufficiently taken into account to date.

PC If that were the case, it would be possible to determine

Tree Mountain—A Living Time Capsule—11,000 Trees, 11,000 People, 400 Years (since 1992) is a project by US artist Agnes Denes, who made an artificial hill in Finland on which 11,000 people have planted a total of 11,000 trees. The entire area has been placed under protection for the next four centuries, allowing a new forest to grow. All persons involved in the planting received a deed they can pass on to the next generation and which states they are guardians of the trees. The piece highlights the intergenerational responsibility for the future well-being of the ecological, social, and cultural life of the planet.

whether growth is actually taking place or not. Growth is nothing other than the expression of a functioning system. If we were to take as a basis a different system of production in which other criteria are benchmarked, we would be able to achieve growth on the basis of these new criteria, although it would not be identical to the growth that is calculated today. Unfortunately, the international criteria for accounting are extremely stringent and rigid. Failure to meet these criteria means you don't exist on the financial markets. The transformation of our system of production therefore inevitably requires a revolution in accounting.

pM   In addition to a revolution in accounting, you advocate speaking of *patrimoine*, patrimony or heritage, instead of capital. What advantages would that have?

pC   As mentioned earlier, I wondered how one might envision an economic model in which the most important factors of production were in the thrall of durability. After all, without durability there can be no sustainable development. Capital in the service of durability has an old name that runs throughout legal history: patrimony. We rarely perceive capital as something to which temporality is intrinsic, but private assets serve the purpose of securing the living conditions of their owners in perpetuity. What banks are allowed to do with their customers' assets is legally linked to the interests of the latter. Beyond the realm of private law, the idea of patrimony also forms the basis for the theory of public ownership. And it is also the basis for the more recent theory of the commons, i.e., essentially a heritage that belongs to humanity as a whole. Patrimony, as I use the word, can thus also become institutionalized capital. Institutionalized in this context means that the capital is assigned to a task of social or public interest, a kind of special-purpose reserve.

Stop Ecocide International (SEI) campaigns for the introduction of laws that enable ecocide—the massive damaging and destruction of eco-systems—to be penalized as crimes. Anyone who by their actions tacitly promotes the climate crisis should not only face litigation and fines, but also punishment under criminal law.

FH   Where does the term "special-purpose reserve" come from and what does it mean?

pC   The concept of special-purpose reserve or *Zweckvermögen* is specific to German law. The concept states that the asset owns itself, which is surprising. More precisely, its destiny, its purpose, is to be its owner, and such purpose must necessarily include its preservation.

pM   To what extent could this concept serve as a model for ecological transformation?

pC   Under French law, common goods serve a public function and can thus be freely used, no matter how costly to the environment that use may be. However, as soon as you consider this collective patrimony to be its own owner, its purpose becomes its own preservation and not its use by society. Making such a good its own owner is therefore an act of protection. It is then valuable in its own right because of its intrinsic value. And imbuing common goods with intrinsic value is the prerequisite for strong sustainability. I think certain environmental goods, so-called "critical natural capital," deserve to enjoy this protection because of their own intrinsic value.

For a good to be its own owner, it does not necessarily have to be a legal subject. I believe that property law, as an objective right, provides more protection to this critical natural capital than giving it legal subjecthood. After all, a tree or river does not possess the will to go to court, to take legal action, and inevitably relies on representation. Property law protects a thing much better against possible abuse by its representatives than any legal claim. The protection—similarly to the special-purpose reserve of a foundation—consists essentially in the restriction of the possibility of exchange and trade. There are, for example, perpetually inalienable common goods, which in many countries include water. Ultimately, this kind of special-purpose reserve, precisely because it is protected from the logic of profit and the excesses of exchange, is better destined to be bequeathed rather than bartered. This passing on is the absolute prerequisite for us to be able to fulfill our responsibility to future generations.

pM   If conservation and bequeathal are so important to sustainability, the question for me is whether the ecological transformation can escape conservatism?

pC   The environmental question is indeed accompanied by a renaissance of conservative ideas, with all the problems that such a development entails. This needs to be tackled critically in the face of public, politically conservative discourses based on Joseph Schumpeter's ideology of innovation, creative destruction, or disruption, which is antithetical to any truly sustainable development.[3] Something that is enlightening in this context is the excellent work by Thomas Piketty, who has meticulously compiled and analyzed income data. This has enabled him to show that social inequality has been steadily increasing for some 50 years, whereas the preceding phase from the end of World War II to 1970 had fostered a leveling of economic and social conditions unprecedented in history up to that time. That period of egalitarianism was, however, also a period of hyper-productivity with equally unprecedented growth, made possible in large part only by increased overexploitation of the environment—like a real estate owner who sells her house for an annuity and thus earns her income only by depleting her capital. Is this the price of social equality? Ultimately, it comes down to reconciling intergenerational equity and intra-generational equity in a non-productivist framework—namely by conceiving of environmental goods as patrimony.

The environmental question undoubtedly leads away from progressivism. Progressivism does not abolish property at all, but merely has a profoundly productivist view of it, which is why, for example, it exempts stocks and shares from property tax. Bidding farewell to the notions of Thine and Mine—to use Rousseau's famous formula in his *Discourse on Inequality*—is best achieved, I believe, by moving away from the subjective right to property and toward an objective approach to rights based on the idea of patrimony, such as the one I outlined earlier. This would facilitate the organization of a *bundle of rights*.[4] Since the late 19th century, this term from American jurisprudence has referred to a bundle of rights that, in addition to property rights in the narrower sense, also includes rights of use, rights of representation, and statutory regulations. In it, no right is absolute, which ultimately leads to a theory of the commons. Drawing on the work of Elinor Ostrom, I have shown that commons construed thus, based on property as a bundle of rights, necessarily presuppose an institutional framework. Yet the culture of the institution—which reached its peak at the end of the 19th and beginning of the 20th centuries when public services were developed in French and German administrative law—is on the wane. The current intellectual mood is not conducive to a theory of the institution. Indeed, the primary concern today is deinstitutionalization in order to intensify social interactions. However, the multiplication of abstract social interactions mediated by money also accelerates the depletion of the world. If, on the other hand, we want to build stability and longevity, it seems to

An alliance of Berliners from the social and cultural fields prevented the sale of the vacant Haus der Statistik to investors and the foreseeable demolition of the old GDR building with its 45,000 square meters at Alexanderplatz. With support from the public administration, it has been re-communalized and non-profit usages have moved in. Their objective: through participation to impart knowledge that is necessary for a social and sustainable future.

The now vacant former Instituto Nacional de Seguridade Social INNS in the heart of São Paulo has been occupied since 2016 by the Movimento Sem Teto do Centro (MSTC, Homeless Movement in the Center). In the context of this "Ocupação 9 de Julho," accommodation, working, and cultural spaces were established and the building restored. The artistic work *Patrimônio=Nois* (We Are the Heritage, 2019) by Erica Ferrari on the building facade is a reflection on elitist heritage politics and the construction of memory in the public space.

Already in the 19th century, British welfare reformer Octavia Hill practiced a form of social housing in existing buildings. She had John Ruskin acquire rundown houses in Freshwater Place and then modernized them as council housing. She later realized new-build projects, too, such as the Redcross Cottages in Southwark shown here. The women who handled maintenance of the buildings also acted as avant-la-lettre social workers.

FH   me to be important to take some things off the market, to make them *extra commercium*, and not to allow everything to be commodified.

FH   Now you are in the degrowth discourse after all.

pC   Certainly … at least insofar as we are talking about purely nominal growth, which is essentially based on including in the calculation of gross domestic product more and more goods and services that only a generation ago were considered *extra commercium*. But if we are talking about growth that consists in increasing productive patrimony, in building better, in making the earth more fertile, the sea richer in fish, then I am not an advocate of ending growth.

FH   Another term you are very critical of is *resilience.*

pC   Resilience is a highly ideological term used in the context of current state management of environmental crises. Since 2001 at the latest, capitalism has been constituted as an economy of systemic crisis. The crisis is no longer a more or less inevitable accident, but the very engine of growth. This is the opposite of the theory formulated by economist Walt Rostow in the 1950s, according to which sustainable, or more precisely "self-sustaining," development (and back then it had nothing to do with ecological thinking) consists of a steady growth path that cushions crises wherever possible. The carefree times of growth are behind us. These days, crises are engines that drive the creation of wealth, and they inevitably lead to greater inequality. Crises are not so much ruptures as elements of a pathological dynamic: spikes of disruption that inflame and poison the economic machine. Resilience then constitutes accepting the systemic crisis and using it to bounce back even better. We are expected to adapt and become crisis-proof without even the slightest will to reduce the crises, because in reality they are considered necessary.

pM   Ultimately, all cities that have built walls to protect themselves were trying to strengthen their resilience.

pC   What you describe is more resistance than resilience. Resilience purports that no wall can keep the crisis out! Resilience excludes protection. Protection is *ex ante* of the crisis, while resilience is *ex post*. The concept of resilience is meant to deal with crises that we cannot prevent. If we fail to introduce a new system of production based on sufficiency, if we fail to curb global warming, then we must provide the means to cope with a situation we can no longer control. The richest, the "lions," as Nietzsche would say, can certainly be persuaded by the promises of transhumanism, while the poorest, the "camels," must be prepared to endure the unstoppable crises as best they can. There are numerous scenarios like this in science fiction. Are they all just the product of fantasy? This makes it clear why the current economic system, which is based on systemic crises, is the most unequal of all: The rich possess "magical" means of coping with crises that will never be available to the poor, which thus widens the advantage of the rich over the poor to an ever greater extent.

FH   According to Patricia Espinosa Cantellano, Secretary General of the United Nations Framework Convention on Climate Change until July 2022, we are moving toward the *worst-case scenario* you describe. In fact, everyone working on strategies to reduce CO_2 emissions is pretty pessimistic. So, whether we like it or not, we will have to focus on resilience, on dealing with natural disasters, loss of biodiversity, and so on.

pC   We need life jackets, or rather rescue manuals.

pM   What form would these rescue manuals take?

pC   It can only work through institutions, an economy of maintenance, architecture as well as governance that leaves short-termism behind. The big question of the day is how we can inhabit and expand the present. Only by taking responsibility for the present will we fulfill our responsibility to future generations. Decisions must be made now; we must stop putting them off again and again. All the tortuous maneuvering over glyphosate, for example, reveals a will to do nothing, and one masked at that by the fine words of the political class.

FH   This is the ontological problem of change: Changes are postponed until later, and goals are fixed for a distant date. Previously it was the year 2000, then 2020, now 2035, 2040, 2050 …

pC   We must abolish the projections, the scenarios for the next 5, 10, or 20 years—which, by the way, are never reviewed. We need action in the present! It is true that today we feel the consequences of the actions of previous generations, but also, awareness of environmental problems is not something that has just come about today. You mentioned the report to the Club of Rome. In 1971, in France, Robert Poujade became the first ever Minister of Ecology. All the problems and many ideas were already on the table in the 1970s, but little has been done since then.

FH   That also applies to architecture and urban planning. Based on this idea of inhabiting the present, how could architecture and urban planning—where change is even slower—be incorporated?

pC   Maintenance, repair, and restoration need to gain greater importance in European cities, as you also set out in the goals of the *Great Repair* project: to repair what already exists instead of constantly tearing it down and planning new large-scale projects. This also includes a comprehensive land policy. And finally, there needs to be reterritorialization, which means taking local and regional productive cultures into account.

pM   For me, however, there is also something daunting about the repair project: The surplus value of capitalism, after all, consists in the liberation from physical labor. The abolition of physical labor amounts to evoking paradise on Earth. Repairing, maintaining, and tilling the soil, on the other hand, involve physically strenuous work.

pC   Yes, I stand by that: We will have more work because we will have to work not only to produce but also to protect the world from depletion. Your fears in this regard bring to mind the idealistic proposition André Gorz makes in his *Critique of Economic Reason*: Repair and maintenance are more alienating than other tasks, he suggests, because they do not provide for people's self-realization.[5] They become, in a kind of symbolic, intolerable inversion, slaves to the machines and objects they have conceived. I, however, consider the repair of objects and the preservation

Hortes de Baix is an ancient irrigation system in the small Catalan town of Caldes de Montbui that provided private gardens with water and fell increasingly into disrepair. In 2013–15, the practices of cíclica and CAVAA transformed the 3.7-hectare area into self-administered public space, and restored the system, which requires no mechanical pumping. The gardens on what is now common property boost the community's subsistence food resources.

of the world imposed on us as no less dignified than the creative acts of the human spirit.

Back to the question of how best to reconcile labor and human existence. I believe the two central theories of our epoch on the future of labor are unsatisfactory: on the one hand, the rule of the robots, that is, the idea that thanks to the automation of the production system we would have to work less; on the other hand, the spillover theory, the no less dangerous idea according to which technical progress favors the emergence of new production sectors in a kind of infinite increase of productive labor. In fact, the future of labor follows a third path: The more the system of production taps its potentials, the more complicated and complex it becomes; and the more complicated and complex it becomes, the more prone to failure it becomes; and the more prone to failure it becomes, the more maintenance it requires, to the point where every act of production must be compensated by an act of protection and maintenance, that is, an act of reproduction. The more that is produced, the more labor goes into repair. The future of labor lies in maintenance. The discourse of innovation, disruption, and creative destruction is pure ideology. Since time immemorial, every system of production has been based primarily on maintenance. The question then arises as to the remuneration of this very maintenance work, which in the productivist logic of growth is minimized, underpaid, or even, as Antonio Casilli puts it, made invisible.[6]

FH Because the system of production as it is structured today focuses primarily on innovation and neglects maintenance, servicing, and repair, which should actually be the main sources of innovation.

PC Exactly, but nobody says that out loud. Originally, the task of economics was to promote an optimal distribution of the factors of production. As soon as this optimum is achieved—or so the claim of John Stuart Mill, Karl Marx, and also John Maynard Keynes—people get busy with other things: leisure activities, cultural and intellectual life, hobbies. This model is dead. These days everything is economic, everything is commercial. The economy encompasses everything so that a new upturn is always possible. In the orthodoxy of economics, innovation is autonomous: Innovation begets innovation. Joseph Schumpeter, who revolutionized the ideological foundations of economics, talks about chains of innovation. He also brought another theory into play, one which is no longer a static theory of equilibrium based on the optimal distribution of production factors. It is a dynamic theory of growth, a theory of permanent disequilibrium based, in military terms, on "positional advantage": Added value exists from the moment one enjoys a positional advantage.[7] Whoever is one step ahead thanks to innovation gets everything—*winner takes all.* Innovation reinforces inequality.

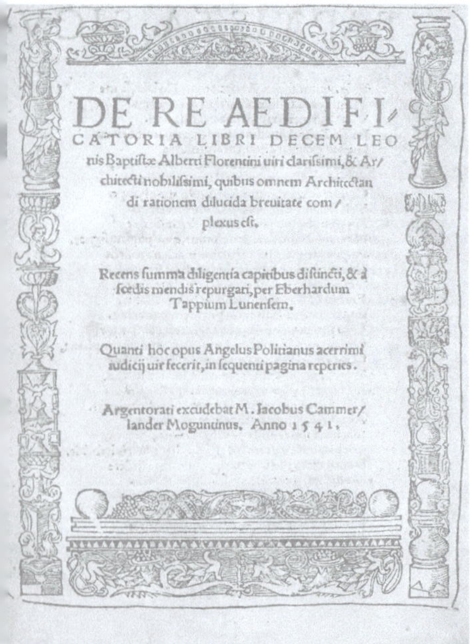
DE RE AEDIFICATORIA LIBRI DECEM LEOnis Baptistae Alberti Florentini uiri clarissimi, & Architecti nobilissimi, quibus omnem Architectandi rationem dilucida breuitate complexus est.

Recens summa diligentia capitibus distincti, & a foedis mendis repurgati, per Eberhardum Tappium Lunensem.

Quanti hoc opus Angelus Politianus acerrimi iudicij uir fecerit, in sequenti pagina reperies.

Argentorati excudebat M. Iacobus Cammerlander Moguntinus. Anno 1541.

"If the Wall is swerved from its Perpendicular, fix Planks or Timbers upright against it, and against each of these set a strong Timber by Way of Shore, with its Foot stretching at some Distance from the Wall. Then either with Levers or with Wedges, drive forwards the Feet of the Shores by degrees, so as they may press against the Wall, and so by distributing this Force equally in all Parts, you will raise the Wall again to its perpendicular."
Quoted from Leon Battista Alberti, *Ten Books on Architecture, Book Ten,* trans. C. Bartoli (London: Alex Tiranti, 1955), 283.

FH Refocusing innovation on repair, servicing, and maintenance would mean designing items that can be repaired. This also applies to infrastructure. Instead of constantly creating new infrastructure, perhaps more attention should be paid to what already exists, and in the design of new architectures, infrastructures, or urban neighborhoods, to making sure that they are repairable.

PC Yes, infrastructure is essential for the transformation of the system of production. By infrastructure, I mean not only the material infrastructure, such as arable land or power plants, but also all the conditions for the reproduction of life, both physical and symbolic, such as education or justice. The neglect of material infrastructure—and one could extend this to symbolic infrastructure—is explained by two illusions to which those administratively and technically responsible for it have fallen prey: first, the illusion that industrial infrastructures are stable and perfectly oiled automata, and then the illusion that only commodity flows create value, and that infrastructure has value only insofar as it makes these flows possible. People tell themselves that they can generate a maximum of flows with minimal maintenance costs, and when it no longer works, the time has come for something new anyway. People would rather spend money on something new than finance the maintenance of the old. That's why the Morandi Bridge in Genoa, which collapsed in 2018, was not repaired, even though the company operating the bridge had been informed of the dangers in 2016.

FH Finally, let's talk about architecture. I see three categories of potentially sustainable architecture: architecture that sees itself as classical and thus durable, especially tectonically oriented postmodernism, thus an architecture of hardness; in contrast, *bricolage* architecture, which makes do with what is already there, is easy to assemble and disassemble, and whose elements can be reused, up to and including *do-it-yourself* architecture; and finally, architecture that is organized around generous and stable structures and allows for constant change in its components as well as in its users and activities. You seem to prefer the first category?

PC I will answer you with an analogy: Hardness and flexibility in building construction are in the same relationship as light and opacity in design. I would add, though, that this constructive dialectic undoubtedly has an influence on design. Traditional Japanese architecture—I'm thinking here of *katsura* in particular—uses the interplay of hardness and flexibility to create an architecture of thresholds, vestibules, and passages. One can ask whether a new architectural rationalism is possible, based not on the physics of solids but of fluids, whether one can also develop a design starting from heat transfer, or in the tropics, *free cooling*, of which, by the way, there are numerous examples in the architecture of Antiquity, Classicism, or the Mughal Empire. One can ask whether the passive house is only a question of construction, materials, and technical equipment, or whether the design as an organization of spaces can also make a contribution. In Alberti's case, for example, light incidence, air circulation, and rainwater and wastewater drainage are important elements of the design, which find expression in the categories of openings and roof.

FH I understand this as a *low-tech* architecture that can be both solid and light, depending on the solid, liquid, and immaterial environmental influences on the place for which it is developed. If we can certainly learn from Alberti in this regard, whose Tenth Book is, after all, about repair, then we must also break away from a different conception of him: Marvin Trachtenberg, in his book *Building-in-Time: From Giotto to Alberti and Modern Oblivion*, identifies Alberti as a turning point. Previously, people built "in time" *(building-in-time)*, buildings were continuously rebuilt by many different planners and craftsmen, as a continuous construction site, so to speak. Alberti, meanwhile, coined the myth of the finished building and strong authorship *(building-outside-time).* This still resonates today, insofar as buildings are always conceived as finished and thus irreversible artifacts.[8] If, as you are calling for, we want to inhabit the present and take responsibility for it, we must also find new forms in architecture so that now we no longer build "outside" or "against" but rather "in" time.

1   Dennis Meadows et al., *The Limits to Growth: A Report for the Club of Rome's Project on the Predicament of Mankind* (New York: Universe Books, 1972).
2   Joseph Alcamo et al., *Millennium Ecosystem Assessment: Ecosystems and Human Well-Being: A Framework for Assessment* (Washington: Island Press, 2003), 3.
3   Joseph Schumpeter, *Capitalism, Socialism, and Democracy* (New York: Harper & Brothers, 1942).
4   Jean-Jacques Rousseau, *Discourse on the Origin of Inequality among Men* (1754), (Indianapolis: Hackett Publishing, 1992).
5   André Gorz, *Critique of Economic Reason* (London: Verso, 1989).
6   Antonio Casilli, "Digital Labor Studies Go Global: Toward a Digital Decolonial Turn," *International Journal of Communication* 11 (2017): 3934–54.
7   Joseph Schumpeter, *The Theory of Economic Development: An Inquiry into Profits, Capital, Credit, Interest, and the Business Cycle* (Cambridge: Harvard University Press, 1934).
8   Marvin Trachtenberg, *Building-in-Time: From Giotto to Alberti and Modern Oblivion* (New Haven: Yale University Press, 2010).

Matters

This photograph by Bas Princen shows Frank Lloyd Wright's Ennis House. Built in 1924 in Los Angeles, it fell into increasing decay as a result of an earthquake and strong rainfall. It was restored in the mid-2000s.

# of Care

Text: Sarah Nichols

We know that buildings—no matter how long they can endure as assemblages—are not made up of permanent things. The longevity of structures durable or disposable is predicated on repair. Maintaining the substance of buildings includes acts like patching a hole in a wall or replacing the silicone caulk in a curtain wall joint—acts that are small, practical, and raise no questions as to the integrity of the whole. But repair also includes acts of renovation and preservation that point to the instability of the substance in the face of the whole, from replacing the roof and joists while perhaps subbing in ceramic tiles for slate to recasting an exposed concrete facade.

Even before the repairers come in, buildings both very ephemeral and very long-lasting show that they are materially transforming. Drywall will warp if it gets wet and dent if it's bumped; vinyl flooring will scuff and peel. But so too at the other end of endurance, whether in the bowled sag of stone steps or the bright spot on a brass banister. Yet this instability is easy to forget until something goes wrong. Before and sometimes despite these traces, we tend to think of building materials as inert—possibly vulnerable to outside forces but, if left well alone, as unchanging in state. In particular, many of the materials taken on as emblematic of modernity—concrete, steel, glass, and aluminum but also finishes like chrome and ceramic glaze—are often thought of as immutable. Not only do they escape romanticized ideas of weathering or beautiful ruin, they also tend to promise complete resistance to decay. That these materials are not in fact inert is a recurrent source of disappointment, from the concrete engineers newly convinced, generation after generation, that any perceived failure can be conquered by improved technologies, to the architects visiting a project they admire only to be disappointed that it is not pristine as it was in publication photos. Assumptions of building are tied to pernicious ignorance of the fact that buildings are not "finished" when construction is over—that trying to keep them inert is itself a questionable goal that often prizes authorship over dwelling and occupation.

Moreover, materials thought of as inert also tend to be energy-intensive, with hard surfaces made under high temperatures achieved through burning fossil fuels. Often they are predicated on mining practices that disturb far more mass than needs to be extracted. As is so often the case, the ecologically and socially disastrous consequences are felt most strongly in the areas of the globe rendered most vulnerable already. To believe that strong and inorganic should be equated as inert is thus damaging twice, in that it validates harmful extractive processes and then, paradoxically, puts the longevity of those materials at risk by ignoring that their durability is predicated on protection and care.

Why does this myth of immutability persist nonetheless? Is it that the sturdy standard in highly regulated construction cultures like German-speaking Europe has a narcotizing effect on the understanding of mutability? Perhaps practical, well-built things hold together long enough that it becomes easy to forget that they are not as fixed as we think they are. Indeed, there is also a correlated tendency to blame wear on things that have gone wrong or do not follow "best practice," from cut corners or cheap substitutions to poor workmanship or even corruption. The roots, however, go deeper, into the modern dogma of predictability and control in which the culture of building is stewed, from material science that lays the framework for expected material properties like strength, to civil engineering's predictions of structural behavior, or architecture's reliance on lifecycle analysis projections. For as much as breakdown and waste are now acknowledged as both disciplinary and societal problems urgently necessitating the revaluing of repair and the rejection of a tabula rasa mentality, dissection of the problem and how we got here may still rely on similar modernist doctrines. For example, the idea of obsolescence seeks to exsanguinate breakdown and failure, making the process "planned" and thereby bringing it back into the realm of predictability and control. Pulling apart this narrative, as for example Daniel M. Abramson has done in his history of obsolescence in architecture,[1] is essential to finding our way to less harmful building cultures.

As Jane Bennett argues in *Vibrant Matter*, viewing matter as dead legitimizes environmentally detrimental cycles of consumption and destruction.[2] It also delegitimizes maintenance and care, practices that the thoroughly modern professions of architecture and engineering have often either ignored or disdained. Largely, the building professions have viewed maintenance with suspicion—as a threat to codified systems of knowledge enclosure and social hierarchy inscribed through formal training, norms and standards, and industrialized building. And yet of course, buildings and building professions rely on maintenance, both seen and unseen. Some care is called "monitoring," and in doing so is placed comfortably back under the umbrella of empiricism. Yet it can reveal that materials and buildings are doing far more than we think. Take reinforced concrete structures for example, which are constantly though imperceptibly deforming under different climatic and loading conditions. Over decades, they continue to hydrate, thereby gaining strength in one way, yet as they undergo carbonation the reinforcement is threatened with corrosion. But the surface of the concrete is becoming a CO_2 sink—a complex and multidirectional process of transformation.

Other forms of care propagate the myth of immutability. When something displeasing appears in exposed concrete, the *Betonkosmetiker* (lit.: concrete cosmetician) can be called in to fix the surface, repairing it but doing so in a way that hides the traces of their own work, and with it, the evidence that the material was ever vulnerable. Similar to the function of other cosmetics, these often superficial interventions perpetuate the appearance of inertness without necessarily changing the substance of the material to which they are applied, protecting the false notion that maintenance is not needed or projecting an ease of solidity that is not real.

Much is lost with this. As architect Anna Heringer has argued and shown in her practice, maintenance as cycles of renewal—whether thatching, rammed earth, stucco, or similar techniques—produces and reproduces tacit knowledge, itself a call for making maintenance more integral.[3] While Heringer focuses on natural and traditional materials in a way that can be limiting in their reproducing of pastoral ideals, inorganic and industrialized materials also need to be thought of as benefitting from maintenance and renewal. Unlike the *Betonkosmetiker* who disappears their own work, how can hard materials be maintained in ways that leave traces, or even allow maintenance to be thought of as an ongoing process of refinement and working in? More broadly, how would our disciplinary understanding of materiality and maintenance change if we took seriously that materials, but also buildings, are mutable? While such ideas have been put forward to understand metabolic flows and material stores, it is possible also to use this as a starting point to better recognize the relationality of materials and buildings. Mutability is an ideal way of once again dragging architecture out of its objecthood. Taking it seriously means considering buildings in deep relation to their context geologically, hydrologically, and ecologically as the materials of the building are in sometimes profound interaction with all of these systems, from local to global scales. It means denaturalizing the idea of weathering (and in doing so probably renaming it), in that weather itself is no longer understood as something natural, but also finding new value in the complex relations it can produce. The beginning and end of a project as well as the list of actors involved all become longer and less defined or perhaps more cyborgian or tentacular from this perspective. Articulating an idea of care and repair based on the mutability of the material world could begin with explorations in reconfiguring aesthetics and ethics, but would perhaps end up with a different idea about what constitutes the "design process" entirely. Driving the inertness out of materials could also shake up the inertia of our professional roles and routines, loosening them up and making them more subtle and open to interaction. Repair can be more than an alternative to planned obsolescence and more than a fix of the harm done to things by an external force. It can be a future-oriented material practice which at once acknowledges the damages done and resists the temptation of the new and pristine.

1   Daniel M. Abramson, *Obsolescence: An Architectural History* (Chicago: University of Chicago Press, 2016).
2   Jane Bennett, *Vibrant Matter: A Political Ecology of Things* (Durham: Duke University Press, 2010).
3   See for example Anna Heringer, "Re-Materializing Construction," Holcim roundtable in Einsiedeln, Switzerland, summer 2015.

"Maintenance, Care, and Repair Are Today's Key Values"

In 2017, Portland Anarchist Road Care was founded in response to the deteriorating state of roads that made driving cars or riding bicycles unsafe and left vehicle owners facing a financial burden for repairs.

What are the consequences when novelty and innovation take precedence over all else? How can we raise awareness of the importance of repair and care instead? The science and technology historians Andrew L. Russell and Stefan Krebs discussed these questions and more with guest editors Florian Hertweck and Marija Marić.

Andrew L. Russell and Stefan Krebs in conversation with Florian Hertweck and Marija Marić

Florian Hertweck The narrative that technological innovation will solve climate change and resource scarcity dominates the public debate. You deconstruct this innovation-focused, technofix-narrative in your book *The Innovation Delusion* (2020), which you wrote together with Lee Vinsel. What's wrong with innovation?

Andrew L. Russell In our book, we distinguish between two uses of the term "innovation": on the one hand, there is actual innovation, which happens incrementally over a long period of time and contributes to improvement both in material and societal aspects. On the other hand, there is what we call "innovation-speak," which is all the bluster and promotional language around supposed innovation with the purpose of attracting investors and customers. That distinction is important because we're neither against innovation nor anti-modern reactionaries. Rather, we wanted to document how much damage innovation-speak does to societies at large, to specific organizations, and to individuals who get caught up in this impulse to change and are captivated by these violent metaphors to disrupt and destroy, fail fast, and break things. We wanted to provide a more positive vision and profile people and initiatives who already understand that maintenance, care, and repair are today's key values.

FH When did this gap between innovation and innovation-speak emerge? You criticize Silicon Valley, but doesn't this start even further in the past?

Stefan Krebs In the history of technology, the interwar period is often seen as a turning point, at least in the United States. One prominent example is the car manufacturer General Motors, which introduced its yearly model change at that time, not because there were so many radical innovations in automobile technology but to increase sales. Because of the rapid growth of the economy and the saturation of entire market segments, marketing and innovation-speak soon became an important way to keep customers buying products. In Europe, this development only started in the 1960s and 1970s once the continent had recovered from the Second World War.

ALR Indeed, the 1920s are very important: Advertising, public relations, new model changes, and planned obsolescence come from that era. In the postwar period, there was tremendous growth in the mass production of consumer products. These developments flattened out in the 1970s with successive political and material crises. But it was only in the 1980s and 90s that people started talking about innovation in noticeable ways. Ironically, the changes taking place then were not as transformational

Vehicle assembly at General Motors, Upper Hutt, New Zealand, 1974

as in earlier periods. In 1880, Americans rode a horse to town to get their mail, drew water with hand pumps, and plowed their fields by hand. Forty years later, there were tractors and telephones—a complete transformation of society. Whereas between 1970 and 2000, or even today, we are saturated by innovation-speak, although we still live in cities, fly in airplanes, and drive cars. Our interpretation is that innovation-speak masks an underlying staleness in societal development that lurks beneath the surface of our now-ubiquitous digital interfaces.

SK That innovation-speak became more popular in the 1980s also has to do with the economic crisis of the 1970s. In a capitalist society, the economy is based on growth, so there were also fears on the part of politicians and economists. How can we save our economic model? All hope was placed on the next big technological disruption that would boost economic growth again.

Marija Marić Andrew, in your book, you challenge us "to think about not only *what* technology is, but also *when* it is." What's your take on the relationship between technology, temporality, and, more specifically, longevity?

ALR The spectacle of invention or discovery attracts a lot of interest from the public as well as scholars. But after that comes the process of selling and using these technologies. In the history of technology, there has been more attention and perhaps even fixation over the last decades on the technologies in use and their appropriation by users. But then there also is a period of senescence. Architectural historians have done a better job than historians of technology at paying attention to how things fade and fail, fall apart, and finally cease to exist—maybe because it's more fun to look at babies than funerals.

SK David Edgerton's book *The Shock of the Old* (2006) was quite influential in the history of technology in reminding us of how much old technology is present in infrastructure and large technological systems, even in innovative technological sectors like airplanes and automobiles. Shortly before this conversation, we vis-

In Burkina Faso, small repair shops get defective mobile phones from Europe going again and sell them under the brand "Au revoir France." To this end, often parts of different devices are combined, and provider blocks are circumvented by special software.

ited Metzeschmelz, an old ironworks in Esch-sur-Alzette in Luxembourg, where even highly innovative companies still rely on very old technology for their buildings. The foundry halls, which were built in 1871 at the very beginning of the ironworks, for example, were still in use when the factory closed in 2016; the buildings had been adapted several times over the years. But we should not only focus on the act of repair and maintenance; we should also consider what happens to technology after repair. It does not simply vanish, even if we do not maintain it. Built structures in particular can be very durable. Blast Furnace C was shipped to China. On the other hand, the concrete foundation is so massive that it is almost impossible, or unprofitable, to remove it, which is why it is still there. Some technologies, not only in the nuclear sector, will last almost forever.

MM Histories, including those of architecture and cities, are usually organized around innovations, events, and ruptures. How can we write histories grounded in continuities instead, such as the histories of repair? I feel this would require challenging existing structures of knowledge production and raising questions of authorship and archive, for example.

ALR Our colleague Gabriele Balbi, who is a communication historian, recently organized a workshop on the *longue durée* in the history of communication technology. *Longue durée* was a concept of the French Annales school of historiography, which never really caught on in the US. For a long time, North America was considered a blank slate from the perspective of historians and ethnologists. The US defined itself by the moment of its "discovery," then by the near extinction of the Indigenous peoples, and then by revolution after revolution. The persistent theme in American history has been the frontier. First expansion and conquest across the continent, then empire in the Pacific, then space exploration—American history is dominated by stories about heroic white men, and that has seeped into how we think about technology. I hope that if we as a society place more value on maintenance and repair, historians will also pay more attention to questions of how things and social arrangements persist and what makes them so resistant to change—for better and worse. This requires different sources, which sometimes might not exist because archival materials traditionally focus on moments of creation, discovery, or transformation. But sometimes, it is a matter of looking at existing sources in a different way. And as we get closer to the present, we can take advantage of different tools from other disciplines, like oral history and embedded ethnography. We don't have to write all of these histories today, but if we create good records, then maybe 50 years from now, someone else will be able to take advantage of it.

SK *Longue durée* also means to write a multilayered history. One of its most prominent proponents, Fernand Braudel, conceptualized three layers of historical development. The *longue durée* perspective first aims to analyze how geography and climate have a slow, long-term impact on how societies develop. Second, there is a meso-level of macropolitical and macroeconomic developments shaping society. Third, there are short-term events. If we only look at the surface layer, the short-term events, we may forget that there are underlying layers that also profoundly shape societies. This also applies to the history of technology: Some aspects of a technological system last a long time, while new technologies are introduced at other layers. In history writing in general, there is an increasing awareness that we must go beyond this fixation on the ruptures. However—and this explains why Fernand Braudel's approach failed in a way—our innovation-centric academic system is not conducive to investigations of so many sources spanning several centuries.

I have to publish my next paper in three months, not in ten years. In Braudel's time in the 1970s, academia was slower and allowed more reflection. We might have lost some of the self-reflexivity we once had in the discipline.

FH   Andrew, when it comes to longevity and the opposition between the pursuit of innovation vs. maintenance, one of the main protagonists in your book is Charles Marohn and the Strong Towns movement. Who is he?

ALR   Charles "Chuck" Marohn was born in 1973. He is a civil engineer from Minnesota who identifies as a libertarian, so center-right, with a "get big government out of my business" approach. In the course of his life, he had a series of "Aha!" moments. One of them was when he was walking through a village in Italy and thought how silly it was that Italian construction workers were replacing broken paving stones, repairing the street instead of asphalting it. But then he realized that these streets had been around for centuries, so there must be something to it. He eventually saw his own profession as propagating some of its deepest problems because it was obsessed with building and expansion. For example, Marohn was contracted by a small Minnesota municipality to repair a leaking sewer pipe under a highway. Since the town couldn't afford the cost of repair, Marohn decided to apply for a federal grant. For the project to be eligible, he had to make it larger than necessary. A few years later, he realized he had left the city with an unfunded liability because no one had factored in the maintenance costs for the far too large infrastructure. Such problems are not uncommon. In fact, this form of shortsighted funding afflicts almost every discipline. You get a burst of money up front to do something, and then the funding ends. And then what happens to the finished project, whether it's a museum exhibit, a highway, or a lab? There's no funding and no plan to ensure its longevity. Marohn sensed the ridiculousness of this in his field and changed gears. He started a group called Strong Towns, a membership-driven organization to familiarize people with its principles so they could then build Strong Town movements in their own cities. The goal is to counteract the unsustainable infrastructure, social alienation, and geographic sprawl that suburbanization has produced since the 1920s. Instead, the movement advocates for safe, welcoming cities and seeks to empower citizens to take local collective action in collaboration with the authorities.

FH   It is certainly not unique to the US to discount future costs in light of present gains. The French philosopher Pierre Caye (see our interview in this issue) calls for an accounting revolution to introduce longevity into our socioeconomic system. This would be particularly true when it comes to the realm of infrastructure, right?

ALR   Yes, what really blew my mind was when Marohn pointed out the 30-year depreciation that investors can claim in accounting for a new property. You finance a building and pay it off over 30 years. At the end of that term, you owe nothing to your bank anymore, but you actually owe a ton to the building. Over the years, the cost of maintaining and operating the building has accumulated enormously and typically remains invisible on the balance sheets. If money drives everything, as it does in this neoliberal moment, then a change in accounting practices might also change behavior.

SK   At the same time, companies do have accounting systems for maintenance costs; it's not that they are not aware of it. Nevertheless, we have limited resources in our systems, be it city governments or companies. We investigated the maintenance practice of Post Luxembourg with regard to the telephone system.

State Route 40 in Baltimore, dubbed the "Road to Nowhere" by residents, illustrates not only the decay of large infrastructure investments that rely on individual transportation because communities cannot shoulder the maintenance costs. It is also an example of how state-funded growth projects have been used as a pretext for the socio-spatial exclusion of marginalized groups by cutting through neighborhoods perceived as "slums" by white planners.

In its 140-year-long history since being founded in 1880, its management has constantly renegotiated priorities in terms of different modes of maintenance. First, the maintenance of technology: If a landline breaks, it needs to be repaired. Then, with the growth of the telephone system, capacity had to adapt to user demand. Even early on, when the telephone was introduced in 1886, a veritable race began with neighboring countries for technological leadership. To maintain these different aspects, you need resources: people, money, and technology. And if all three are limited, you must decide what is more important. The organization knew that spending less on daily maintenance would eventually cause new problems and more costs. Accounting couldn't save them.

FH   This reminds me of a key sentence in your book, Andrew: "If governments, organizations, and individuals build and buy systems without providing for their future care, we end up facing a stress-inducing mountain of deferred maintenance and infrastructure debt, which is precisely what we see in many parts of society today." Indeed, there is such a massive backlog of deferred maintenance in buildings and infrastructure that we have a specific word for it in German: *Renovierungsstau* (literally "renovation congestion").

ALR   This is why there is such enthusiasm for things like geoengineering and the colonization of Mars. Sometimes it seems the easiest thing to do is to run away from a problem because there is nothing left to save. Or saving something means making sacrifices people don't want to make, or doing work so difficult that thinking the absurd—like the colonization of Mars—becomes a conceivable option.

FH   You also discuss the "illusion of a maintenance-free future." This reminds me of many discussions with clients who dream of an architectural object that can keep its original state forever. You mentioned this illusion in relation to the Morandi Bridge in Genova.

ALR   When it was finished in 1967, the Morandi Bridge, designed by civil engineer Riccardo Morandi, was celebrated for being so high-tech that it would not require maintenance. The architects and Italian press joined together in perpetuating this illusion, and they were so successful that parts of the bridge were not maintained for decades. The illusion had tragic consequences when the bridge collapsed in 2018, killing 43 people. Unfortunately, this logic and sleight-of-hand are also present in consumer products, partly enabled by a software mentality and, specifically, the logic of the auto-update. These principles have infected construction and fields of technology outside of software. It is relatively easy to change software, and the costs of failure are low. Companies can roll products out, and if they are buggy, they simply patch them. The success of Silicon Valley relies on the model of software. But this success has been enabled by infrastructure funded in the US by investments by the Department of Defense and the monopoly telephone system over a hundred years. People have forgotten that they are only shown the success, which allows software developers to rest on their laurels. And other industries try to imitate that success. But of course, you can't auto-update a bridge or a building.

SK   The idea of maintenance-free objects has been around at least since the 1960s and 1970s. Before, companies advertised their good customer service: If something needed maintenance,

Demolition of the pylons of the Morandi Bridge that had survived the collapse, in Genoa in August 2019

there would be someone to help. But that changed in the 1960s as companies started advertising that their products required less maintenance. Then companies realized that many of the technologies they used themselves—especially IT technologies—came with huge maintenance costs. After a few years, it becomes difficult to repair computers and update their software. So it's easier, at least in the books, to just throw them away and buy new ones.

MM Where does recycling fit in this discussion? Is recycling merely an industrial compromise to deal with the waste we produce a bit more efficiently without challenging obsolescence and consumption?

FH Isn't recycling even an enemy of repair? Recycling consumes energy, and promises of climate-neutral recycling processes are misleading—at least given our current energy sources. Moreover, repair is about sufficiency, whereas recycling is more about consistency and supposedly green technologies. In our discipline, for example, there is pressure to create housing and social infrastructure. Many argue that we need to tear down smaller buildings in particular because it's cheaper and more efficient to rebuild bigger to meet the demand instead of transforming what already exists. Since we can recycle steel and other metals, even concrete, we're told not to worry because it's all part of the circular economy. But our conviction is that we have enough spaces and surfaces that can be repurposed without demolition. Ultimately, recycling competes with repair by implying you can skip the often tedious practice of continuous maintenance.

SK I think we have to differentiate here. There are some materials that totally make sense to recycle, and where recycling has a long tradition. Take glass, which can be recycled over and over. Breweries introduced recycling systems long ago, not because they cared about the environment, but out of economic interests: Bottles are costly to produce. In many other cases, it's more downcycling than recycling. Like plastic, for example. Or paper, which can be recycled, but after several cycles, you can only make cardboard out of it. There are also some absurd ideas, like waste-to-energy—in which burning household waste to produce electricity is touted as a form of recycling when it's more like greenwashing. Recycling sounds green and environmentally friendly, but of course, it's not environmentally friendly to burn household waste, plastic, etc. At the same time, we cannot maintain and repair everything forever. It makes sense to first extend the lifespan through maintenance and repair. But we also need solutions for the end of the lifespan of specific technologies.

MM Recycling and repair also have to be distinguished in the sense that they engage with the individual or the community differently. While recycling in a way offloads the work and responsibility to the individual, or more precisely—the individual consumer—repair, even when it's a personal act, relies on collective knowledge and shared resources.

ALR It also raises the question of labor. Sometimes it's easier just to send something away and have someone else take care of it. The externalities and energy that go into the recycling plant remain invisible. Nor do we see those things in certain forms of repair. But repair is generally more visible and more local than recycling.

FH Real estate projects are inscribed in a capitalistic cycle of demolition and new builds. Even if they could last 150 years, they are considered out-of-date and torn down after 25 to 50 years. Innovation-speak is an instrument of this massive destruction. However, I also see a critical point, a lesson from the Arts and Crafts movement: Objects that last longer are often handmade and are therefore expensive, whereas industrial, mass-produced objects with a shorter life span are cheaper. How can we extend the longevity of material culture and ensure social equity at the same time? The warranty is undoubtedly one tool to do so; the German construction sector has a legal ten-year warranty. But we could also imagine a warranty of 100 years or more that would include a whole process of maintenance and care. Or we protect all buildings—no more demolition—which would also promote maintenance and care. Could these be efficient measures for a sustainable material culture?

SK Yes and no. Companies first introduced warranties as a marketing ploy: If you buy our products, we will provide after-sale services. Legal warranties are relatively new. Only in the past 30 or 40 years have they become more important. What you mentioned is not easy to fix by warranty: Some consumer products might be made to last longer, but they would be much more expensive because they would have to be manufactured differently, with different materials, etc. Is that where we want to go? So only a few can afford to own a mobile phone or car? Consumer and company logic come together on this point. In the 1960s and 1970s, some car companies, like Porsche, investigated more durable cars that would last at least 20 years or 180,000 miles, much longer than the average lifespan of a car at that time. But although engineers figured out how to produce them, manufacturers argued that the product would be about 30 percent more expensive so that consumers would not buy them.

FH What about the Right to Repair? Where did that come from, and could it be an effective measure to ensure longevity?

ALR Demands for a right to repair emerged in the 2000s from protests about monopoly control on repairing automobiles. Auto dealers have higher prices than independent repair shops. On the other hand, some independent car mechanics lack the information or tools to perform the work that customers request. In the US, the movement operates mostly on a state level. Despite opposition from car manufacturers and their lobbyists, the first motor vehicle owner's right-to-repair bill was passed in Massachusetts in 2012. In subsequent years, state legislatures have been the focus of a concerted consumer awareness and lobbying movement. The movement spread to consumer electronics at the same time, leading to the birth of the advocacy-focused Repair Association (repair.org) and the growth of iFixit.org, which offers consumers instructions and parts so they can fix things on their own. Internationally there have been successes in the EU. To some extent, it is a very individualistic approach to say you should have the right to repair the appliances you own. It can be empowering for people who enjoy it and have the skill and confidence to do so. But that's not everybody, of course. So another aspect of the Right to Repair movement is the support of independent repair shops for electronics and other products. There is a broader ethos that has emerged in the wake of that.

MM When we talk about warranties, we take for granted the company and the consumer as the central subjects. Questions of maintenance and repair seem to need another kind of vocabulary to help us imagine other kinds of relationships, subjectivities, and practices. This brings me to what you describe in your book as "maintenance mindset." Could a new mindset be the first step toward a new language of maintenance and repair?

SK There is also innovation-speak within the Right to Repair. The focus often is on the individual consumer, which fits nicely with our individualistic, neoliberal time. If I want to repair my phone, I often need special tools. I use them once and then discard them. It would make much more sense to go to a local repair shop, where these tools can be used hundreds of times. There's also greenwashing from the consumer perspective: It makes

Todd McLellan, *Disassembled Jig Saw*, 2012. From the series *Things Come Apart*, 2012–ongoing

1. Make your products live longer!
Repairing means taking the opportunity to give your product a second life. Don't ditch it, stitch it! Don't end it, mend it! Repairing is not anti-consumption. It is anti- needlessly throwing things away.

2. Things should be designed so that they can be repaired.
Product designers: Make your products repairable. Share clear, understandable information about DIY repairs.
Consumers: Buy things you know can be repaired, or else find out why they don't exist. Be critical and inquisitive.

3. Repair is not replacement.
Replacement is throwing away the broken bit. This is NOT the kind of repair that we're talking about.

4. What doesn't kill it makes it stronger.
Every time we repair something, we add to its potential, its history, its soul and its inherent beauty.

5. Repairing is a creative challenge.
Making repairs is good for the imagination. Using new techniques, tools and materials ushers in possibility rather than dead ends.

6. Repair survives fashion.
Repair is not about styling or trends. There are no due-dates for repairable items.

7. To repair is to discover.
As you fix objects, you'll learn amazing things about how they actually work. Or don't work.

8. Repair – even in good times!
If you think this manifesto has to do with the recession, forget it. This isn't about money, it's about a mentality.

9. Repaired things are unique.
Even fakes become originals when you repair them.

10. Repairing is about independence.
Don't be a slave to technology – be its master. If it's broken, fix it and make it better. And if you're a master, empower others.

11. You can repair anything, even a plastic bag.
But we'd recommend getting a bag that will last longer, and then repairing it if necessary.

Stop Recycling. Start Repairing.   www.platform21.nl

The *Repair Manifesto* by Platform21 rejects throwaway culture and calls for repair instead of recycling.

me feel better if I can use my phone a year or two longer through maintenance and repair. But we tend to forget that the portable telephone itself is a very unsustainable product. Many of its materials are mined under catastrophic ecological and social conditions in the Global South. The best and most sustainable solution would be not to have a cell phone at all.

FH How can the Great Repair be a political project that goes beyond just creating more repair shops?

ALR The path that seems most promising for me is the language, politics, and ethics of care coming from feminist philosophy. An infrastructure bill in the US was recently debated for months. In the end, the bill was divided into two parts, one focused on "hard" infrastructure like roads and bridges, and the other on "soft" infrastructure, meaning the human side of things, including healthcare and family leave. It was a heavily gendered split: The hard stuff passed, and the soft stuff did not, or it got watered down. It's discouraging to see people refuse to acknowledge that education and healthcare are also infrastructure. But from a science and technology studies perspective, it was fascinating to see senators debating the definition of infrastructure. We are not moving quite at the pace and direction that I would like, but at least there's movement around terms like infrastructure, care, and repair.

MM Andrew, not only do you research these topics, you also co-founded the initiative The Maintainers. What I particularly like about that project is that it does not focus on the objects but on the people, the maintainers. It centers around networks of solidarity, shared knowledge, labor, and the politics these relationships entail. Tell us more about what and who The Maintainers are.

ALR The group started as an informal academic workshop in 2016, which turned out more successful than Lee Vinsel and I had expected. So we held it again, and it grew even more. Since then, we have experimented with different ways of organizing and scaling up. We want to bring together people in similar occupations to exchange information and ideas and create a community around maintenance, repair, and preservation. We quickly learned that people who worked in such different areas like digital preservation, healthcare, or repair cafés kept saying the same things about their maintenance work: That it wasn't valued enough, that the people with the new ideas would always get all the funding and status, that burnout was a major problem, and that tacit knowledge was an important feature. It became overwhelming to hear this again and again. We saw a need to both support people within their own domains, and help practitioners make connections across different fields and realize the value in their own work. Thanks to support from foundations, we were able to recruit fellows, specifically also from outside academia and outside North America. This year, we have a second cohort of five fellows who are pursuing their own individual projects as well as a communal project for which they have settled on two concepts: degrowth and solidarity. Even though innovators, software guys, and crypto bros are getting a lot of attention these days, we understand that "essential workers" are crucial for society—that term and those people helped us immensely over the last couple of years. It's progress because it is a consciousness, not exactly a class consciousness, although class has a lot to do with it. That's where we are at the moment. And we're eager to connect with like-minded individuals and groups to grow solidarity in the global movement to build and sustain a well-maintained world.

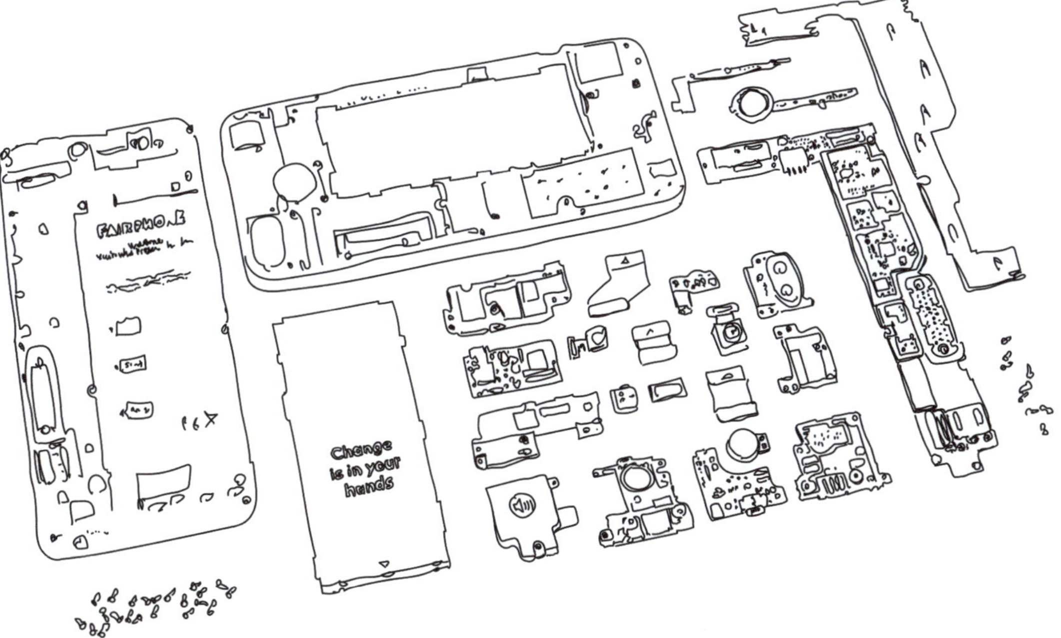

Drawing of a Fairphone broken down into its individual elements, from the entry on the new Right-to-Repair EU Guidelines in the maintenance manual of the Brussels spatial-planning collective MAMA.

 Care

Text: Alex Nehmer

The capitalist logic of turning all social relations into commodities has led to a deep crisis in the reproduction of life.[1] What is required by way of a response is a practice of care, which for Joan C. Tronto and Berenice Fisher "includes everything that we do to maintain, continue, and repair our 'world' so that we can live in it as well as possible." According to the two feminist theorists and activists, this world encompasses "our bodies, our selves, and our environment," all of which we need to "interweave in a complex, life-sustaining 'web'."[2]

Care as a political category is a practice of resistance. It must oppose the fact that reproductive work—both the care work more often than not imposed upon women as well as the work done by nature—is rendered invisible in order to enable its exploitation as a cheap resource.[3] At the same time, it must resist the assimilation of care work into the logic of the accumulation of capital. Care is not concerned with a notion of healing that in capitalism is "in reality, only the restoration of

Mierle Laderman Ukeles, *Washing, June 13, 1974*   Performance in front of the A.I.R. Gallery, New York, 1974

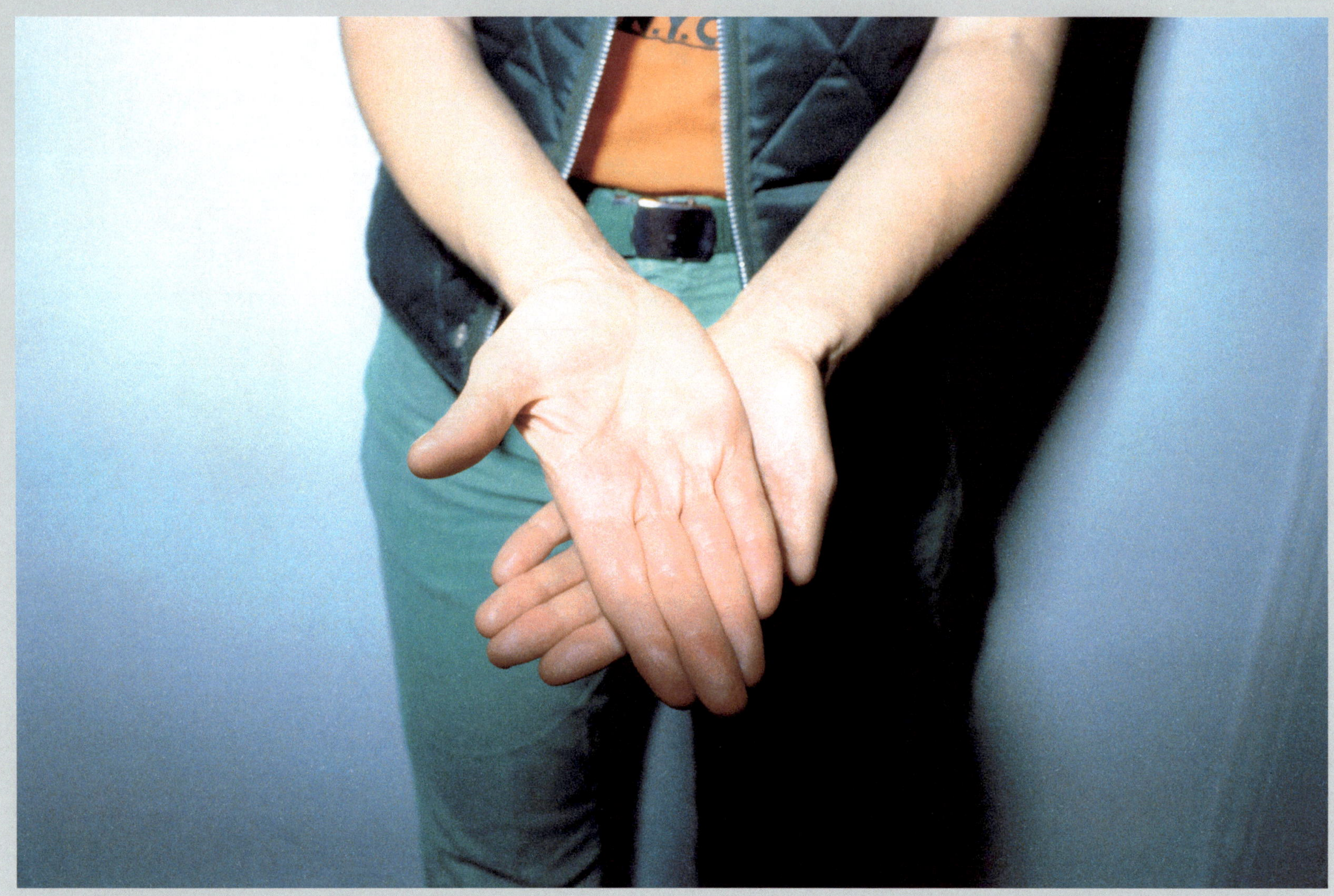

Mierle Laderman Ukeles, *Touch Sanitation Performance*, 1979–80
Sweep 4, end of day in Artist's office, DSNY, November 20, 1979

In the performance, which lasted over 11 months, the artist visited all 8,500-plus employees of New York Sanitation Department for *Touch Sanitation*, where she thanked each and every one of them with a handshake and the words: "Thank you for keeping New York City alive."

one's capability to work,"[4] but with a practice directed in solidarity against the organized abandonment, the systematic neglect of the marginalized.[5]

Neither may the "unequal extent to which bodies are made vulnerable and wounded differently [by the prevailing conditions]" be concealed, nor may certain people be marked as per se vulnerable and thus *othered*. We instead need practices of care that assume vulnerability as a shared "condition of life."[6] However, this insight must not lead to an individualization of risk. Instead, "this feeling of vulnerability [has] to translate into collective rather than individual care and self-defense"[7] in order for us to establish a society based on solidarity in which care relationships play a central role.[8]

1   See Silvia Federici, "The Common Is Us: Principles of Health Autonomy," foreword to *For Health Autonomy: Horizons of Care Beyond Austerity*, ed. CareNotes Collective (New York: Common Notions, 2020), ix–xvi.

2   Joan C. Tronto and Berenice Fisher, "Toward a Feminist Theory of Caring," in *Circles of Care: Work and Identity in Women's Lives*, eds. Emily K. Abel and Margaret K. Nelson (New York: SUNY Press, 1990), 40.

3   See Carolyn Merchant, *Earthcare: Women and the Environment* (New York: Routledge, 1996).

4   Jean-Paul Sartre, preface to *Turn Illness into a Weapon*, Sozialistisches Patientenkollektiv (Socialist Patients' Collective) (Hamburg, 1972), revised and expanded online edition 2021, accessed November 24, 2022, www.spkpfh.de/Preface_Sartre.htm#Sarte_Facsimile.

5   Ruth Wilson Gilmore, *Golden Gulag: Prisons, Surplus, Crisis, and Opposition in Globalizing California* (Berkeley: University of California Press, 2007).

6   Jule Govrin, *Politische Körper: Von Sorge und Solidarität* (Berlin: Matthes & Seitz, 2022), 10.

7   Manuela Zechner, "Commoning Vulnerability? Towards a Radical Politics of Earthcare," contribution to the text series *After Extractivism* by *Berliner Gazette*, September 8, 2022, accessed November 24, 2022, blogs.mediapart.fr/berliner-gazette/blog/080922/commoning-vulnerability-towards-radical-politics-earthcare.

8   Gabriele Winker, *Solidarische Care-Ökonomie: Revolutionäre Realpolitik für Care und Klima*, with Matthias Neumann (Bielefeld: transcript, 2021), 186.

Meditations on Natural Worlds, Disabled Bodies,

Elke Marhöfer's film and research project on the southern Russian steppe highlights the contradictory, overlapping stories of environmental protection, "renaturing" of eco-systems, and the persistence of racist and colonial violence. Like the North American bison, the European wild horse, the tarpan, was systematically hunted and killed, which in this case led to the animal's extinction.

Elke Marhöfer, *Becoming Extinct (Wild Grass)*, 2017; 16mm film, color/sound, 23 min.

and a Politics

Text: Eli Clare

# of Cure

prairie

You and I walk in the summer rain through a thirty-acre pocket of tallgrass prairie that was, not so long ago, one big cornfield. We follow the path mowed as a firebreak. You carry a big pink umbrella. Water droplets hang on the grasses. Spiderwebs glint. The bee balm hasn't blossomed yet. You point to numerous patches of birch and goldenrod; they belong here but not in this plenty. The thistle, on the other hand, simply shouldn't be here. The Canada wild rye waves, the big bluestem almost open. Sunflowers cluster, spots of yellow orange amid the gray green of a rainy day. The songbirds and butterflies have taken shelter. For the moment the prairie is quiet. Soon my jeans are sopping wet from the knees down. Not an ocean of grasses but a start, this little piece of prairie is utterly different from row upon row of corn.

With the help of the Department of Natural Resources, you mowed and burned the corn, broadcast the seed—bluestem, wild rye, bee balm, cornflower, sunflower, aster—sack upon sack of just the right mix that might replicate the tallgrass prairie that was once here. Only remnants of the original ecosystem remain in the Midwest, isolated pockets of leadplants, milkweed, burr oaks, and switchgrass growing in cemeteries, along railroad beds, on remote bluffs, somehow miraculously surviving.

You burn; you plant; you root out thistle and prickly ash. You tend, save money for more seed, burn again. Over the past decade and a half of labor, you've worked to undo the two centuries of damage wrought by plows, pesticides, monoculture farming, and fire suppression. The state of Wisconsin partners in this work precisely because the damage is so great. Without the massive web of prairie roots to anchor the earth; bison to turn, fertilize, and aerate the earth; and lightning-strike fire to burn and renew the earth, the land now known as Wisconsin is literally draining away. Rain catches the topsoil, washing it from field to creek to river to ocean. Prairie restoration reverses this process, both stabilizing and creating soil. So you work hard to restore this eight-thousand-year-old ecosystem, all the while remembering that the land isn't yours or the dairy farmer's down the road, but rather stolen a mere century and a half ago from the Dakota people. The histories of dirt, grass, genocide, bison massacre float here.

We have taken this walk a dozen times over the past fifteen years—at noon with the sun blazing, at dusk with fireflies lacing the grasses, at dawn with finches and warblers greeting the day. My feet still feel the old corn furrows. As we walk, I think about the words *natural* and *unnatural, normal* and *abnormal*. Does this fragment of land in transition from cornfield to tallgrass prairie define what *natural* is? If so, how do we name the overabundance of birch and goldenrod, the absence of bison? What was once normal here; what can we consider *normal* now? *Normal* and *natural* dance together, while *unnatural* and *abnormal* bully, threaten, patrol the boundaries. Of course, it's an inscrutable dance. How does *unnatural* technology repair so-called *abnormal* bodies to their *natural* ways of being? Dismissing the distinctions between *normal* and *abnormal, natural* and *unnatural,* as meaningless would be lovely, except they wield extraordinary power.

Abnormal, Unnatural

It is not an exaggeration to say that the words *unnatural* and *abnormal* haunt me as a disabled person. Or maybe more accurately, they pummel me. Complete strangers ask me, "What's your defect?" Their intent is mostly benign. To them, my body simply doesn't work right, *defect* being another variation of broken, supposedly neutral. But think of the things called defective—the boom box that won't play a CD, the car that never started reliably, the calf born with three legs. They end up in the back closet, trash heap, scrap yard, slaughterhouse. Defects are disposable and *abnormal*, bodies to eradicate.[1]

Or complete strangers yell at me down the road, across the playground, "Hey, retard!" Their intent is often malicious. Sometimes they have thrown rocks, sand, rubber erasers. Once on a camping trip with my family, I joined a whole crowd of kids playing tag in and around the picnic shelter. A slow and clumsy nine-year-old, I quickly became "it." I chased and chased but caught no one. The game turned. Kids came close, ducked away, yelling *defect, retard*. Frustrated, I yelled back for a while. *Retard* became *monkey*; became a circle around me; became a torrent, *monkey defect retard you're a monkey monkey monkey*; became huge gulping sobs of rage, frustration, humiliation, shame; became not knowing who I was. My body crumpled. It lasted two minutes or two hours until my father appeared and the circle scattered. Even as the word *monkey* connected to me the nonhuman *natural* world, I became supremely *unnatural*.

Or complete strangers pat me on the head. They whisper platitudes in my ear, clichés about courage and inspiration. They enthuse about how remarkable I am. They declare me special. Once a woman wearing dream-catcher earrings, a big turquoise necklace, and a fringed leather tunic with a medicine wheel painted on its back confided that I was, like all people who tremor, a *natural* shaman. She grabbed me in a long hug and advised that if I were trained, I could become a great healer. Before this woman, sporting a mishmash of First Nations' symbols, jewelry, and clothing, released me from her grip, she directed me never to forget my specialness. Oh, how *special* disabled people are: We have *special* education, *special* needs, *special* restrooms, *special* parking spots. That word drips condescension. It's no better than being defective. As *special* people, we are still *abnormal* and disposable.

Or complete strangers offer me Christian prayer or crystals and vitamins, always with the same intent—to touch me, fix me, mend my cerebral palsy, if only I will comply. They cry over me, wrap their arms around my shoulders, kiss my cheek. Even now, after four decades of these kinds of interactions, I still don't know how to rebuff their pity, how to tell them the simple truth that I'm not broken. Even if there were a cure for brain cells that died at birth, I'd refuse. I have no idea who I'd be without my specific tremoring, slurring, tense body.

Those strangers assume my body *unnatural,* want to make me *normal,* take for granted the need and desire for cure. *Unnatural* and *abnormal* pummel me every day.

Restoration

As an ideology seeped into every corner of Western thought and culture, cure rides on the back of *normal* and *natural*. Insidious and pervasive, it impacts many, many bodies. In response, we need a politics of cure: not a simple or reactive belief system, not an anticure stance in the face of the endless assumptions about bodily difference, but rather a broad-based politics mirroring the complexity of all our bodies and minds.

The American Heritage Dictionary defines *cure* as "restoration of health." In developing a politics of cure based upon this definition, it would be all too easy to get mired in an argument about health, trying to determine who's healthy and who's not, as if there's one objective standard. As an alternative, I want to bypass the questions of who defines health and for what purposes. So many folks are working to redefine health, struggling toward a theory and practice that will contribute to the well-being of entire communities. But I won't be joining them with a redefinition of my own. Instead, I want a politics of cure that speaks from inside the intense contradictions presented by the multiple meanings of health.

Today in the white Western world dominated by allopathic medicine, the meanings of health range from individual and communal bodily comfort to profound social control. Between these two poles, a myriad of permutations exist. Health is both the well-being sustained by good food and the products sold by the multimillion-dollar diet industry. It is both effective pain management for folks who live with chronic pain and the policed refusal to prescribe narcotic-based pain relief to people perceived as drug seeking. It is both the saving of lives and the aggressive marketing of synthetic growth hormone to children whose only bodily "problem" is being short.

Rather than offer a resolution to this whole range of contradictory, overlapping, and confused meanings of *health,* I want to follow the word *restoration*. To restore an object or an ecosystem is to return it to an earlier, and often better, condition. We restore a house that's falling down, a prairie that's been decimated by generations of monoculture farming and fire suppression. In this return, we try to undo the harm, wishing the harm had never happened. Talk to anyone who does restoration work—a carpenter who rebuilds 150-year-old neglected houses, a conservation biologist who turns cornfields back to prairie—and she'll say it's a complex undertaking. A fluid, responsive process, restoration requires digging into the past, stretching toward the future, working hard in the present. And the end results rarely, if ever, match the original state.

Restoring an ecosystem means rebuilding a dynamic system that has somehow been interrupted or broken—devastated by strip mining or clear-cut logging, taken over by invasive species, unbalanced by the loss of predators, crushed by pollution. The work is not about recreating a static landscape somehow frozen in time, but rather about encouraging and reshaping dynamic ecological interdependencies, ranging from clods of dirt to towering thunderheads, tiny microbes to herds of bison, into a self-sustaining system of constant flux. This reshaping mirrors the original or historical ecosystem as closely as possible, but inevitably some element is missing or different. The return may be close but never complete. The process of restoration is simpler with a static object—an antique chair or old house. Still, if the carpenters aren't using ax-hewn timbers of assorted and quirky sizes, mixing the plaster with horse hair, building at least a few walls with chicken wire, and using newspaper, rags, or nothing at all for insulation, then the return will be incomplete, possibly sturdier and definitely more energy efficient, but different from the original house. Even though restoration as a process is never complete, it always requires an original or historical state in which to root itself, a belief that this state is better than what currently exists, and a desire to return to the original.

Thinking about the framework of restoration, I circle back to the folks who offer disabled and chronically ill people prayers, crystals, and vitamins, believing deeply in the necessity of cure. A simple one-to-one correspondence between ecological restoration and bodily restoration reveals cure's mandate of returning damaged bodies to some former, and nondisabled, state of being. This mandate clearly locates the problem, or damage, of disability within individual disabled or chronically ill bodies.

To resist the ableism in this framing, a disability politics has emerged in the past forty years. It asserts that disability is lodged not in paralysis but rather in the stairs without an accompanying ramp, not in blindness but rather in the lack of Braille. Disability itself does not live in depression or anxiety but rather exists in a whole host of stereotypes, not in dyslexia but in teaching methods unwilling to flex, not in lupus or multiple sclerosis but in the belief that certain bodily conditions are a fate worse than death. In short, disability politics establishes that the problem of disability is not about individual bodies but about social injustice.

But for some of us, even if we accept disability as harm to individual bodies, restoration still does not make sense, because an original nondisabled body does not exist. How would I, or the medical establishment, go about restoring my body? The vision of me without tremoring hands and slurred speech, with more balance and coordination, does not originate from my body's history. Rather, it arises from an imagination of what my body should be like, some definition of *normal* and *natural*.

Not Simple

To reflect the multilayered relationships between disabled and chronically ill bodies and restoration, a politics of cure needs to be as messy and visceral as our bodies. To reach into this messiness, I turn to story.

You and I know each other through a loose national network of queer disability activists, made possible by the internet. Online one evening, I receive a message from you containing the cyber equivalent to a long, anguished moan of physical pain. You explain that you're having a bad pain day, and it helps just to acknowledge the need to howl. Before I log off, I type a good night to you, wish you a little less pain for the morning. The next day you thank me for not wishing you a pain-free day. You say: The question isn't whether I'm in pain but rather how much. *Later as I get to know you in person, you tell me:* I read medical journals hoping for a breakthrough in pain treatment that might make a difference. *You wait, trying to get doctors to believe your pain, and once you get the appropriate scripts, working to find the right balance of narcotics. The rhetoric of many disability activists declares:* There's nothing wrong with disabled bodies and minds, even as they differ from what's considered normal. I have used this line myself more than once, to which you respond:* Not assuming our bodies are wrong makes sense, but the chronic fatiguing hell pain I live with is not a healthy variation, not a *natural* bodily difference.

I pause, thinking hard about natural. In disability community we sometimes half-sarcastically call nondisabled people *temporar-*

ily able-bodied, or *TABs,* precisely because of the one instant that can disable any of us. Are these moments and locations of disability and chronic illness *natural* as our fragile, resilient human bodies interact with the world? Is it *natural* when a spine snaps after being flung from a car; when a brain processes information in fragmented ways after being exposed to lead, mercury, pesticides, uranium tailings; when a body or mind assumes its own shape with withered muscles or foreshortened limbs, brittle bones or ears that do not hear sound, after genes settle into their own particular patterns soon after conception? And when are those moments and locations of disability and chronic illness *unnatural*—as *unnatural* as war, toxic landfills, and poverty? Who, pray tell, determines *natural* and *unnatural*? I'm searching for a politics of cure that grapples both with the pain, brokenness, and limitation contained within disabled bodies and with the encompassing damage of ableism.

I return to story. *You and I sit in a roomful of disabled people, slowly inching our way toward enough familiarity to start telling bone-deep truths. And when we arrive there, you say:* If I could wake up tomorrow and not have diabetes, I'd choose that day in a heartbeat. *I can almost hear the stream of memory: the daily insulin; the tracking of blood sugar level; the shame; the endless doctors judging your weight, your food, your numbers; the seizures; the long-term unknowns. You don't hate your body or equate diabetes with misery. You're not waiting desperate, half panicked. All the time and money spent on research, rather than universal health care, a genuine social safety net, an end to poverty and hunger, pisses you off. At the same time, you're weary of all the analogies: the hope that one day AIDS will become as treatable and manageable as diabetes, the equating of transsexual hormone replacement therapy with insulin. You want to stamp your feet:* Pay attention to this specific experience of Type I diabetes—my daily dependence on a synthesized hormone, my life balanced on this chemical, the maintenance that marks every meal. *You'd take a cure tomorrow, and at the same time you relish sitting in this room.*

In creating a politics of cure, we need to hold both the desire to restore a pancreas to its typical functioning and the value of bodily difference, knowing all the while that we will never live in a world where disability does not exist. How do we embrace the brilliant imperfection of disability and what it has to offer the world while knowing that very few of us would actively choose it to begin with?[2] [...]

I turn yet again to story in disability community. *You and I meet at a disability cultural event. I've given a presentation about body shame and body love, how bodies are stolen and reclaimed. Afterward, you find me. Military pollution in the groundwater in your childhood neighborhood shaped your disabled body, toxins molding neurons and muscles as you floated in utero. Most of the time when you talk about the military dumping of trichloroethylene (TCE) and its connection to you, folks look at your body with pity.[3] As you tell me this story, I think of all the ways disabled bodies are used as cautionary tales: the arguments against drunk driving, drug use, air pollution, lead paint, asbestos, vaccines, and on and on. So many public campaigns use the cultural fear and hatred of disability to make the case against environmental degradation. You want to know how to express your hatred of military dumping without feeding the assumption that your body is bad, wrong,* unnatural. *No easy answers exist. You and I talk intensely; both the emotions and the ideas are dense. We arrive at a slogan for you:* I hate the military and love my body.

As simplified and incomplete as it is, this slogan is also profound. How do we witness, name, and resist the injustices that reshape and damage all kinds of bodies—plant and animal, organic and inorganic, nonhuman and human? And alongside our resistance, how do we make peace with the reshaped and damaged bodies themselves, cultivate love and respect for them? Inside this work, these stories, the concepts of *unnatural* and *abnormal* stop being useful.

The recultivation of the Loess Plateau in China was one of the world's largest ever projects to restore the agricultural productivity of a piece of the countryside eroded by over-exploitation. The project cost a total of 500 million US dollars and was financed with assistance from the World Bank. It was realized by state-ordained mass mobilization to build dams to retain sediments, create terraces on the steep slopes, and plant new trees, orchards, bushes, and grasses and was accompanied by an educational program on agricultural practices.

At the beginning of the 19th century, around 30 million Bison roamed the prairies of the Great Plains in the American Midwest. A century later there were hardly any left to be seen. White settlers had hunted the wild animals down and thus robbed the Native Americans of the basis of their livelihoods. This 1892 photo portrays a mountain of bison skulls that were destined to be processed into glue, fertilizer, or paints by the Michigan Carbon Works.

LOSS

The desire for restoration is bound to bodily loss and yearning—the sheer loss of bodies and bodily functions, whether it be human, bison, dirt, or an entire ecosystem. For many disabled and chronically ill people, there is a time before our particular bodily impairments, differences, dysfunctions existed.

What we remember about our bodies is seductive. We yearn; we wish; we regret; we make deals. We desire to return to the days before immobilizing exhaustion or impending death; to the nights thirty years ago when we spun across the dance floor; to the years before depression descended, a thick, unrelenting fog; to the long afternoons curled up with a book before the stroke, before the ability to read vanished in a heartbeat. We feel grief, bitterness, regret. We remain tethered to the past. We compare our bodies to those of neighbors, friends, lovers, models in *Glamour* and *Men's Health,* and we come up lacking. We feel inadequate, ashamed, envious. We remain tethered to images outside ourselves, to Photoshopped versions of the human body. Tethered to the gym, the diet plan, the miracle cure. But can any of us move our bodies back in time, undo the lessons learned, the knowledge gained, the scars acquired? The desire for restoration, the return to a bodily past—whether shaped by actual history, imagination, or the vice grip of *normal* and *natural*—is complex.

Even those of us who live with disability or chronic illness as familiar and ordinary and have settled into our bodies with a measure of self-love, even those of us who have no nondisabled past, deal with yearning. Sometimes I wish I could throw my body into the powerful grace of a gymnast, rock climber, cliff diver, but that wish is distant, dissolving into echo almost as soon as I recognize it. Sometimes the frustration of not being able to do some task right in front of me roars up, and I have to turn away again from bitterness and simply ask for help. But the real yearning for me centers upon bodily change. As my wrists, elbows, and shoulders grow chronically painful, I miss kayaking, miss gliding on the rippling surface of a lake, miss the rhythm of a paddle dipping in and out of the water. Restoration can be a powerful way of dealing with loss. Cure—when desired, possible, and successful—offers the return some of us sometimes yearn for.

* * *

Of course, the connections among loss, yearning, and restoration are not only about human bodies. Many of us mourn the swamp, once a childhood playground, now a parking lot. We fear the wide-reaching impacts of global warming as hurricanes grow more frequent, glaciers melt, and deserts expand. We yearn back to the days when bison roamed the Great Plains in the millions and Chinook salmon swam upstream so numerous that rivers churned frothy white. We yearn for a return, and so we broadcast just the right mix of tallgrass prairie seeds, raise and release wolves, bison, whooping cranes. We tear up drainage tiles and reroute water back into what used to be wetlands. We pick up trash, blow up dams, root out loosestrife, tansy ragwort, gorse, scotch broom, bamboo, and a multitude of other invasive species. Sometimes we can return a place to some semblance of its former self before the white colonialist, capitalist, industrial damage was done. And in doing so, we sometimes return ourselves as human animals into the *natural* world, moving from domination to collaboration. When it works, restoration can be a powerful resolution to grief, fear, despair.

Restoration's possibilities grow even more inviting as loss extends beyond individual bodies and places to entire communities and ecosystems. I remember bison herds hunted to near extinction, carcasses left to rot. White hunters sold bison tongue and skin, returned later to collect bone. Then ranchers with cattle and farmers with plows tore up the grasslands; beef animals, wheat, corn, and soybeans replaced prairie. In a photo from the 1870s, a man stands atop an immense pile of bison skulls waiting to be ground up for fertilizer. The immensity of this mountain of bone is irrevocable. I remember whole forests of towering Douglas fir, western red cedar, Sitka spruce, and redwoods leveled. Loggers left slash piles, clear-cuts, and washouts in their wake. In a photo from the late 1800s, fourteen men stand, sit, and lounge in the deep cross-cut of a single redwood tree in the process of being felled. The breadth of this stump provides a window into the forests demolished. I remember mountaintops removed wholesale in Kentucky. Miners cleared, blasted, dug, and blasted some more in the southern Appalachian Mountains, extracting layer upon layer of coal, creating huge, open gashes. In a photo from 2003, the mountaintop has been leveled into a pit that stretches out toward the horizon, the scale large enough that I can't quite make sense of what I see.[4]

As evidence of ecosystems destroyed, all three of these photos measure magnitudes of loss, a sheer loss of bodies—animal, grass, tree, earth, mountain. This devastation includes, of course, human bodies. The mass slaying of bison interweaves with the genocide of First Nations peoples who depended on those big shaggy animals and open prairie for material and cultural sustenance. So many loggers broke their backs, lost their limbs, damaged their hearing as they cut down the titan trees. The bulldozers displaced and relocated working-class and poor folks from their generational homes, turning both people and mountaintops into rubble to push over the edge.

* * *

But how do we deal with bodily and ecological loss when restoration in its various manifestations is not the answer? Sometimes viable restoration is not possible. Sometimes restoration is a bandage trying to mend a gaping wound. Sometimes restoration is an ungrounded hope

In the mid-19th century, settlers discovered "red gold" on California's Pacific coast—the wood of the sequoia tree, which could be as much as 2,000 years old. This developed into a huge industry that supplied hardwood to the construction industry that was booming as the settlers arrived in the West. The forests were ruthlessly chopped down and exploited for profit. In 1918, the Save the Redwoods League was established, which set out to protect the surviving old trees. At the end of the 1960s, the region was declared a National Park.

Elke Marhöfer, *Becoming Extinct (Wild Grass),* 2017; 16mm film, color/sound, 23 min.

motivated by the shadows of *natural* and *normal*. Sometimes restoration is pure social control. I want us to tend the unrestorable places and ecosystems that are ugly, stripped down, full of toxins, rather than considering them *unnatural* and abandoning them. I want us to respect and embrace the bodies disabled through environmental destruction, age, war, genocide, abysmal working conditions, hunger, poverty, and twists of fate, rather than deeming them *abnormal* bodies to isolate, fear, hate, and dispose of. How can bodily and ecological loss become an integral conundrum of both the human and nonhuman world, accepted in a variety of ways, cure and restoration only a single response among many? When the woman whose body has been shaped by military pollution declares, "I hate the military and love my body," she is saying something brand new and deeply complex. […]

prairie

   I return in early fall to the thirty acres of restored tallgrass prairie in Wisconsin. I walk, thinking not of concepts but of bodies. The grasses swish against my legs. A few swallowtail butterflies still hover. Coyote scat appears next to the path. The white-throated sparrows sing. The grasses rustle, and I imagine a white-footed mouse scurrying and a red fox pouncing. Above vultures circle on the thermals. A red-tailed hawk cries not so far away. I am one body—a tremoring, slurring human body—among many different kinds of bodies. Could it all be this complexly woven yet simple? The answer comes back an inevitable yes and no.

   Right now in this moment, the prairie both contains and is made up of a myriad of bodies. But just over the rise, another cornfield turns brown and brittle. Just over the rise are a barbed-wire fence, a two-lane dirt road, and an absence of bison. […] Just over the rise, we grapple with loss and desire, with damaged bodies and deep social and ecological injustices. Just over the rise are the bullies with their rocks and fists, the words *monkey* and *retard*. Just over the rise, we need to choose between monocultures, on one hand, and bio- and cultural diversities, on the other, between eradication and uncontainable flourishing. In so many ways, the prairie cannot be a retreat but the ground upon which we ask all these questions.

1   The white Western drive to eradicate *unnatural* and *abnormal* bodies and cultures has never targeted disability alone. Patriarchy, white supremacy, and capitalism have twined together in ever-changing combinations to make eradication through genocide, incarceration, institutionalization, sterilization, and wholesale assimilation a reality in many marginalized communities.
2   The idea of brilliant imperfection as a way of knowing, understanding, and living disability or chronic illness is one of hundreds of things I have learned in disability communities. In particular I want to thank Sebastian Margaret for this phrase.
3   Sunaura Taylor, *Beasts of Burden: Animal and Disability Liberation* (New York: The New Press, 2017).
4   Photo series by Vivian Stockman in *Ohio Valley Environmental Coalition*, October 19, 2003, accessed October 20, 2022, ohvec.org/high-resolution-mountaintop-removal-pictures.

The Tree we

To harvest the mastic trees and obtain the aromatic resin, its bark has to be hurt by a metal tool.
Film still from Tokomburu, *The Chios Mastic Museum*, 2018, for the Piraeus Bank Group Cultural Foundation

Hurt

Text: Metaxia Markaki

Under the short mastiha tree, they caress the ground: a mother, wrapped in fabrics, and her young son, their bodies bent low as if in prayer or a kowtow. Their hands move in circles around the trunk. Rhythmically, they touch, flatten, and smooth as they spread a white cleansing powder. White fingers, white soil. Arms and twigs bend and twist. Figures fuse in this bodily encounter between humans and a tree. We see the preparation of the ground for mastiha (also called mastic), the aromatic resin of the tree, to fall after its trunk is pierced with cuts from a blade. In this way, the film *The Tree We Hurt* by Dimos Avdeliodis (1986) captures the mastiha landscapes of Chios in the 1960s as well as its practices of care and harvesting as they still exist and are performed today.

On the map of the Mediterranean island of Chios in the northern Aegean Sea, there is a specific mental line, the "natural and mysterious borderline," as the linguist Hubert Pernot named it, dividing the mountainous and arid island in two.[1] North of this line, every effort ever made to cultivate the mastiha shrub has failed. To the south, the terrain slopes smoothly from 600 meters to the sea. It is only and uniquely here, in this specific ground and climate, where mastiha flourishes, shaping the mastiha regions, cultivation, and the 24 mastiha villages. The aromatic resin is unique and valued for its healing and cosmetic features. It is used as an ingredient for food and medicinal products, as well as for fine varnishes and adhesives. Yet the dioecious evergreen shrub *Pistacia lentiscus* is common to all dry and rocky Mediterranean landscapes. Resistant to wind, winter, and salt, growing in a variety of soils, it is a native species that grows from Morocco and the Iberian Peninsula in the west to Iraq and Iran in the east, covering semi-mountainous areas that are otherwise hostile to agriculture or forest. Short in stature, two to five meters high, with deep green leaves, small flowers, and a tart red drupe fruit, the shrub presents similar features along different geographies. Although so common in Mediterranean regions, it is exclusively in southern Chios that its trunk produces the aromatic mastiha resin. The reason? On the one hand, there are particular climatic and geotopographic conditions. On the other hand, a centuries-long process of intensive care and human interaction with the tree has created the ideal environment for a uniquely fertile shrub variety to flourish. In the entanglement of ecological specificity and systematic human care, contemporary botany has distinguished a new subspecies: *Pistacia lentiscus var. Chia.*

As concerns intensify about the climate emergency, the socioecological crisis, and the extreme loss of Earth's biocultural diversity, the question of humanity's relationship with the "rest of nature" becomes more relevant than ever. Humanity, in its abstraction as a species, is frequently perceived as a force external to nature, either dominant, destructive, and exploiting, or in the duty of protecting it. Nature, positioned at the other end, is often represented as a separate entity, "outside" human life, either as an endless resource for humanity to extract from for capitalist development and the colonial project, the subject of anthropogenic environmental destruction, or idealized as a pristine, paradisiac remnant for humans to conserve intact and protect from human destruction itself. In mastiha fields, the bodily encounters that occur between humans and trees exude a different narrative about this human–nonhuman relationship: one of care and repair. A narrative that starts with an act of injuring and continues with an act of healing.

Kentos—an act of injury

A few months after preparing the ground, the woman and her son will return to the field to cut the shrub. In the film *The Tree We Hurt*, the two human bodies will blend again with the trees. Using a sharp metallic tool, they will bleed the bark, causing the aromatic transparent mastiha resin to ooze from the scars in the shape of teardrops. The resin will fall on the prepared ground, where hands, fingers, and sieves will distill and collect it. The act of injury creates unity between humans and nature.

The practice of harvesting the mastiha tree is called *kentos*. The word derives from the Greek verb *kentáō (κεντάω)*, meaning *to sting*—an act of inflicting injury and pain, but also meaning *to embroider*—an act of crafting and creation, both mediated through the same sharp surface of the metallic tool, *kentitiri*. In the word *kentos* dwells the human consciousness of a harvest that requires a necessary act of injury, the hurting of the tree to extract its resource. Aren't all harvests, all extractions and agricultural practices based on this principle of care that starts with injury: hurting the soil, hurting the forest, hurting the animal? And yet, in the practice of *kentos* also dwells the consciousness of an injury that must be performed carefully, as an act of art and craft. Reaching the moment of *kentos* requires a year-long preparation and care for the tree and the ground, manual precision and sensitivity in opening the scars to productively harvest while protecting the tree from exhaustion, and respect for the tree and its fruits to ensure its health and longevity.

Today, 1,800 mastiha growers cultivate around 1,350,000 trees on the island, harvesting 150 tons of resin annually. Each year, 150,000 trees among those remain *akentia*—un-stung, un-embroidered, un-harvested. Those trees, as bodies, too, need to rest. In this time of repose dwells the consciousness of healing as vital for the trees to become productive again. Thus, the injury that lies in *kentos* harvesting is coupled with counter-acts: acts of healing and a ritual of domestication and comforting that follows.

Bathing—an act of healing

After the harvest, the resin is transported to the villages, where it is diligently washed. Water will be poured abundantly; hands will take the time to not only rinse the "tears of the tree" from leaves, soils, and dust but also to bathe the fruit. Bathing a body is an act of profound cultural and ritual significance, extend-

This family photo from the 1910s was taken in the village of Bounos on the Greek island of Chios.

ing beyond the necessity of cleansing. It is an act of comforting and healing. It fosters relating and community. It shapes a space of care, interaction, and knowledge sharing between bodies. From this perspective, bathing the mastic resin can be understood as a form of care work that strengthens the connection between the aromatic harvest and the human community.

"Then it will enter our homes. Mastiha will fill living rooms and bedrooms. Tables, sofas, and beds will be moved aside for the fruit to dry and to rest," reads an oral testimony in the Chios Mastic Museum.[2] For a while, domestic spaces will be shared with smells, dust, and tools, extending and blurring the borders of households and productive spheres. Cohabitation is performed between humans, and the fruit and everyday life adapt to embrace the life of mastiha, its cleaning and resting. Could one go as far as to claim that the nuclear family extends and a collective is formed to include the resin? In the historic archives of the Chios Koraes Library, a picture from the 1910s depicts a family from the mastic village of Bounos. A man—probably the father—holds a newborn baby in his arms, while three women—presumably the mother, grandmother and young daughter—surround a bronze disk full of mastic tears to be cleaned. The resin, in this family picture, poses domesticated, almost as a member of the family. Equal to if not more important than the newborn, it has attracted female care. Cleaning and distilling the resin is time-consuming, requiring manual precision and undivided attention. Hosted in the domestic sphere, it has been a labor traditionally attributed to women. And it has traditionally been a social activity. From autumn to spring, village women form companionships, referred to as *syntrofisses* (female comrades), to collectively clean the resin in their homes, courtyards, and public spaces in their villages.[3] "We sit here (in the street) for hours. We tell stories, we laugh, we gossip sometimes," recounts one of the women.[4] Taking care of the mastic and sharing domestic and public spaces has shaped communities. Social roles and relations, but also material artifacts, tools, and spaces, as well as immaterial culture, songs, and customs—temporalities—emerged from the engagement of human bodies with the resin. In many senses, this community extended to include the fruit. In those entanglements and interrelations, we suspect a different kind of relationship between humans and their "natural other" and the formation of a *more-than-human collective* that articulates around care, healing, and comforting. In this amalgamation, "natureculture,"[5] the human body extends to comfort the fruit, the family extends to include it, the productive and domestic spheres extend into each other, and care takes on different meanings. Maybe here, I should seek another definition of care, one based on acts of bodily extension, perhaps a *haptic* definition of care.

On a hill on the outskirts of Ramallah is Sakiya, founded by architect Sahar Qawasmi and artist Nida Sinnokrot as a "progressive academy, a field for experimental knowledge production and sharing." Local agrarian traditions of self-sufficiency, permaculture, contemporary art, and the repair of the existing buildings are combined here to form a practice that takes its cue from Silvia Federici's *Re-enchanting the World*.

Body and tree are superimposed during the work in the countryside.
Film still from Tokomburu, *The Chios Mastic Museum*, 2018, for the Piraeus Bank Group Cultural Foundation

A haptic definition of care

"*To care* means to feel concern, and *care* is attention given"—a sentiment of responsibility, protection, covering needs, the act of maintenance, a cure. Often used to describe the relationship that someone stronger, a caregiver, has with someone more vulnerable, fragile, or endangered, as in healthcare, childcare, or environmental care. The word *care* derives from the old English word *caru*, meaning "sorrow, anxiety, an internal grief," and said to be linked to the root *gar—"to cry," the ancient Greek word γῆρυς meaning "voice, speech." "Take care," "give care"—care is an act. To *caress* derives from the root *ka—"to love," meaning an endearment, a tender touch.

In the encounter between humans and mastiha trees, *care* and *caress* fuse. Hands injuring, hands healing, entanglements of bodies and trees, caressing the ground, the haptic bathing of the resin… In these bodily conversations, borders blur between species. The tree, its roots, branches, and resin are humanized and domesticated, receiving treatment and touch almost as if a human body. The tactility involved hints at a way of relating through touch, an embodied knowledge transferred through touch; bonds and attachments enabled through hands that are laboring. They reveal a *haptic definition of care*. Which now calls for other, less linear, less hierarchical, less common conceptions of care: care as a shared bond, a community, as in "ecologies of care,"[6] a shared tactic of healing and survival.[7] Through the laboring hands, through the touch, through the bridges and relations between beings that this touch triggers, I may now understand care as a condition of mutuality and reciprocity, a reciprocal concern, a bond that enables bodily extensions and interspecies encounters. And in this mutuality, as I slowly reverse my gaze, I now wonder: *Who takes care of whom?* Do the human bodies take care of the trees? Or maybe it is the trees that take care of the human bodies?

Entanglements with an operationalized land

The uniqueness of the Chios shrub has been known since antiquity. Used over the last 2,500 years by local populations, mastiha was valued for its cosmetic and healing capacities as traditional gastrointestinal medicine. Valorized as a preindustrial commodity, it was traded as a spice in the Near and Middle East and even used as pure currency because of its high exchange value with traders from China. Different ruling regimes, driven by the wish to profit from the prized aromatic resin, saw mastiha as a commodity and its territory as a land to be operationalized. At the same time, they recognized the resource as dependent on specific local conditions and labor as an indispensable counterpart to the resource itself. The acknowledgment of situated skill and the sharing of this knowledge over generations "protected" the inhabitants throughout history from those who sought to profit from the precious resource. Thus special privileges were offered to the island for the tree to flourish, along with the community that harvested it.

In the 14th century, the Republic of Genoa systematized cultivation. As part of this process, the mastiha villages were designed as fortresses that served both the exploitation and protec-

Sometimes called "floating gardens," chinampas are an indigenous, highly productive agriculture system that promotes biodiversity. In fragments, it has survived Mexico's colonization. The islands artificially created in a lake are held in place by wooden posts made from a local type of willow (*Salix bonplandiana*), of which some then grow into trees. They call for the construction of a complex drainage system made of ditches, dikes, lock gates, and filtering plants that by means of its hydraulic effect regulates the water inflow. The presence of fish and other animals (such as the threatened axolotl) keeps the fields supplied with nutrients. Chinampas were an element of the major Aztec cities such as Tenochtitlan and to this day constitute a form of urban farming in Mexico City.

Packaging the resin in the rooms of the Chios Gum Mastic Growers Association.
Film still from Tokomburu, *The Chios Mastic Museum*, 2018, for the Piraeus Bank Group Cultural Foundation

tion of the resource and the inhabitants as workers. Second, the landscape was designed as agricultural land to cultivate mastiha trees for export. Later, mastiha became one of the successful monopolies of the Ottoman Empire. Mastiha was especially adored by the sultan's harem as a breath freshener and a skincare ingredient. To ensure production, a regime of protection and freedom was offered to the inhabitants of Chios, their only obligation being the turnover of the entire mastic harvest as a fee to the sultan. Worth its weight in gold, the penalty for stealing mastic was execution. Historical sources mention that in the Chios Massacre of 1822, when tens of thousands of Greeks were killed by Ottoman troops during the Greek War of Independence, the mastiha village inhabitants were spared in order to guarantee the continuation of cultivation.[8]

In 1912, when Chios gained independence from the Ottoman Empire as part of Greece, the mastic commerce collapsed, with dire economic consequences for the island. Prices fell radically, and the economic crash of 1929 only intensified the socioeconomic crisis. In response to the financial pressure and precarity, the Mastic Gum Growers Association, an obligatory union of cooperatives of mastic producers was formed in 1938 (State Law 1390). Following the motto "Above all the cooperatives," the union's purpose was to protect producers from intermediaries, collectivize the means of production, and stabilize market prices and thus growers' incomes. Recommercializing mastiha,[9] it gradually addressed globalization and industrializing markets by introducing standardized mastiha products crafted locally by the union (among them an alcoholic beverage and a new chewing gum, ELMA). The union further extended its tasks to include the branding, circulation, and direct sale of its products globally (under the label *Mastihashop*, launched in 2006). It managed to revalorize mastiha, on the one hand certifying its therapeutic, medical value for pharmaceutical use,[10] and, on the other hand, reinventing it as a contemporary luxury commodity for bodily care. In addition to commodifying mastiha for capitalist markets, the union also intervened to protect the growers and the resource from price dumping. This enabled the social ecology of mastiha to survive, its traditional, non-industrialized mode of harvesting to persist, and processes of care to remain ingrained in an otherwise operationalized landscape.

The present landscapes of Chios have been shaped over centuries by making the soil productive.[11] And care for the tree, the fruit, and the social ecology of mastiha production was always at the center of the operationalization. Thus, the territorial and economic architecture of the island emerged not only from the wish to operationalize but also from the consensus on the need for the care work that this entailed. The one motive doesn't exclude the other, and care remains nested in spaces and relations of production in the commodity itself. It allows reconceptualizing and revalorizing mastiha as a product fabricated within relations of social and ecological care, as a product capable of offering back bodily care and healing.

The fruitful subspecies itself, *Pistacia lentiscus var. Chia,* took shape out of a systematic engagement with the tree and centuries of methodical human care and treatment. The reproduction, or *eugonismós,* of the mastiha shrub is undertaken through a specific process of selective cultivation. The strongest and most fertile trees are chosen each year. They are treated with special attention and reproduced. *Eugonismós* literally means eugenism, which seeks to improve or preserve the best hereditary qualities through reproduction. As a social and political practice, this principle has caused enormous harm in human history linked to discrimination, racism, ableism, and colonialism. Yet, for agriculture, the selection and reproduction of the strongest, most abundant species is a common practice, if not its very principle. And this leads me to a doubt: *In the end, is the mastiha territory of Chios shaped by acts of care, or are we witnessing the architecture of a monoculture?*

An ecology of care

On Chios, the mastiha shrub still grows in an ancient cultivated landscape. Semi-mountainous land—elsewhere standing fallow with only bush and thorns—here slopes smoothly towards the sea, divided into small fields, fragmented and dispersed properties resulting from centuries of inheritances and dowries. Ownership is small and cultivating, and harvesting is a family business. The shrub rests comfortably in rows three to four meters apart, enjoying ideal ventilation and sun exposure. *Pezoules,* dry-stone walls, prevent soil erosion and retain rainwater so that it can slowly percolate into the soil and provide moisture during the dry summer months. The walls are an ideal habitat for lizards and insects; the place is full of life. The ground is cleaned through human acts or seasonal grazing by sheep and goats. With the aid of the human grower, the lemniscus of the shrub grows to form a dense crown of leaves. *Kentos*, the injuring and healing of the trunk, does not interfere with the life of the tree's crown, roots, and soil. And thus, caring for the tree also means care for its ecological neighbors, allowing a livelihood that further extends to the social ecology that flourishes around the shrub. The anthropologist Vasiliki Galani-Moutafi, who has done extensive fieldwork on socioeconomic transformation in Aegean island societies, reports: "The life histories I collected from old growers reveal that property transmission does not comprise a market-like transaction; it often incorporates the desires and concerns that elders pass on to the younger generation. Family interest is not confined to narrow economic terms but is mostly linked to sentiments, revealing affective values formed over time in complex and continuous relations with the land."[12] In this productive landscape, economic reproduction is interwoven with and depends on social and ecologic values. The reproduction of the resource relies on the reproduction of other structures, which are not necessarily capitalist or profit-driven: affective structures, social structures, and reproductive structures, as the food system sociologist Harriet Friedmann explains elsewhere.[13] These reproductive relationships prevent ruthless exploitation and bind all elements in a web of life, a web of relations of care. Unlike a monoculture, on the large geological body of Chios island, we encounter a thin layer of operationalization entangled with and dependent on social and ecological interrelations: an *ecology of care*.

Field

I return to the field. As the mother and her young son merge with the trees to harvest them, my gaze shifts. What I see now is not separate bodies but the space in between: fluid, moving shapes taking shape through touch, between branches and arms, bodies, and trunks. In their entanglement, a space is contoured, the space of their relationship, a continuous, uninterrupted circle that needs all bodies to be complete. And I shift from an ontology that looks at divides to one that sees relations between species.[14] In the mastiha field, in its bodily extensions and conversations, it is rendered visible to me—material and haptic, the space of relations between human and tree, a circle of care extending between bodies in space and time. And I wonder: *What harm has been done by the modern Western conception of humans as separate from the rest of nature, the "other"?*

It is July 2022. As I write this piece, the temperature in Europe is unusually high, and wildfires are spreading again uncontrollably through fields and forests—Chios, in 2012, lost many of her oldest mastiha trees to fire. Climate change threatens the ecological balance of the region. Although the price of mastiha is rising, the recent demographic census indicates that Chios is experiencing a dramatic loss of its population,[15] as are all agricultural peripheries in Greece. As original communities empty out they often become seasonal destinations. "Tourist ruinification, vanishing utopias," wrote a friend.[16] This social drainage of the productive land has immediate ecological implications, as processes of care are interrupted and local ecologies are rendered vulnerable. And the question presents itself with renewed

"We sit here (in the street) for hours. We tell stories, we laugh, we gossip sometimes."
Film still from Tokomburu, *The Chios Mastic Museum*, 2018, for the Piraeus Bank Group Cultural Foundation

urgency: *What is the role of human presence for this "rest of nature"? For the care, repair, and survival of those landscapes?*

The mastiha field casts doubt on narratives of the Anthropocene, which separates the Anthropos, seen as a homogeneous disruptive force, from an idealized "nature without humans" with its landscapes "intact" from human intervention. Reproducing this human/nature dichotomy is not only illusory but destructive in understanding and dealing with the planetary environmental crisis. In the mastiha field, a different narrative emerges: Proximities form relations and community; acts of injury coexist with acts of healing; and operationalized land relies on an ecology of care. It is in these contradicting coexistences that care and repair take shape: not as one-sided "human" acts for the correction of a "natural" other, but rather as an interaction transcending divides between human and nonhuman counterparts in a circle of self-care and self-repair within a socioecological community. Looking at this space between species, the role of humans is nuanced and reframed relationally as one of many ecological agents, part of a community with conflicting interests and in negotiation within other complex, multiscale processes and pressures such as climate change and urbanization. In decoupling the human from the tree, one can see "the ethical and aesthetic tragedy of industrial agriculture and capitalist extraction, of an injury, inflicted decoupled of the consciousness of hurting or healing"[17] and the fallacy of idealizing, operationalizing "nature" as external to humans, othered and voided of its social relations. In recoupling them, we can find the space latent between species, the richness and knowledge that we encounter there. A space of relations that recounts uncommon narratives of humans and trees, anthropos and nature, apart from domination and exploitation; of bodily dialogues and encounters, of circles of care, of contradictory coexistences; of how to extend oneself, of how to reach, to touch and be touched, to lend a hand and be helped by each other.[18]

1   Hubert Pernot, *En pays turc: L'île de Chio* (Paris: J. Maisonneuve, 1903), 135.
2   Oral testimony from the film *Chios Mastic Museum* by Tokomburu, 2018.
3   Valadis Pagoudis and Christos Kurios, Ενωση Μαστιχοπαραγωγών Χίου, E.M.X (Association of Chios Mastiha Farmers (Mesolongi: Technological Educational Institute of Western Greece, 2015).
4   Oral testimony from the film *Chios Mastic Museum* by Tokomburu (see note 2).
5   Donna Haraway, *The Companion Species Manifesto: Dogs, People, and Significant Otherness* (Chicago: Prickly Paradigm Press, 2003), 1. See also Bruno Latour, *We Have Never Been Modern*, trans. Catherine Porter (Cambridge: Harvard University Press, 1993), 104: "How can one not establish a radical difference between universal Nature and relative culture? But *the very notion of culture is an artifact created by bracketing Nature off.* Cultures—different or universal—do not exist, any more than Nature does. There are only natures-cultures, and these offer the only possible basis for comparison."
6   Kim Satchell, "Ecologies of Care: Belonging in Un/Australia," *UNAUSTRALIA*, The Cultural Studies Association of Australasia's Annual Conference, December 2006.
7   Tom Hall and Robin James Smith, "Care and Repair and the Politics of Urban Kindness," *Sociology* 49, no. 1 (2015): 3–18.
8   Dimitris Ierapetritis, "The Geography of the Chios Mastic Trade from the 17th through to the 19th Century," *Ethnobotany Research and Applications* 8 (2010): 153–67.
9   In 1958, international demand reached the amount of yearly production (183,000 kg) and production continued to increase, reaching 241,000 kg in 1968. Pagoudis and Kurios, Ενωση Μαστιχοπαραγωγών (see note 3).
10   "More than 120 chemical compounds have been identified in the resin plant extracts, revealing its therapeutic potential, the antibacterial, anti-inflammatory, antioxidant, anti-ulcer, anti-diabetic, cardioprotective, and anti-cancer properties." In 2015, *Pistacia lentiscus* L. resin (mastiha) was officially recognized as a herbal medicinal product with traditional use by the European Medicines Agency (EMA). Mastiha has since been increasingly used in medicinal products, food supplements, and cosmetics and become an object of study, including in the field of pharmacotechnology. See Vasiliki K. Pachi et al., "Traditional Uses, Phytochemistry and Pharmacology of Chios Mastic Gum (Pistacia Lentiscus Var. Chia, Anacardiaceae): A Review," *Journal of Ethnopharmacology* 254 (2020), article 112485.
11   Nikos Katsikis, "The Operationalization of the US Soy and Corn Belt," in *Extended Urbanisation: Tracing Planetary Struggles*, eds. Christian Schmid and Milica Topalović (Basel: Birkhäuser, forthcoming).
12   Vasiliki Galani-Moutafi, "Rural Space (Re)Produced. Practices, Performances and Visions: A Case Study from an Aegean Island," *Journal of Rural Studies* 32 (2013): 103–13.
13   Harriet Friedmann, "Household Production and the National Economy: Concepts for the Analysis of Agrarian Formations," *The Journal of Peasant Studies* 7, no. 2 (1980): 158–84.
14   Iván Darío Vargas Roncancio et al., "From the Anthropocene to Mutual Thriving: An Agenda for Higher Education in the Ecozoic," *Sustainability* 11, no. 12 (2019): 3312.
15   The Hellenic Statistical Authority of Greece (ELSTAT), 2022.
16   Yiannis Mylonas, Instagram post, August 5, 2022.
17   Milica Topalović, personal correspondence with the author, 2022.
18   AbdouMaliq Simone, "When extended urbanization becomes extensive urbanization," in Schmid and Topalović, eds., *Extended Urbanisation* (see note 11).

ReapproPriation

Text: Nazlı Tümerdem

(Re)appropriation is a troubled word. It carries the baggage of what has been appropriated throughout history: lands, peoples, animals, plants, knowledges, resources. Yet, it is this fraught relationship with the past that makes it a gesture of resistance, reclamation, empowerment, decolonialization, and reparation.

Reappropriation is a powerful tool to radically rewire and rewrite seemingly immutable sociopolitical narratives. This starts with language: For instance, certain words used as disparaging terms for non-normative sexual and gender identities (e. g., dyke, queer, fag) have been linguistically reappropriated by the LGBTQ+ community.[1] Likewise, during the Gezi Park protests, after the then Turkish prime minister Erdoğan called the activists *çapulcus*, meaning looters, the activists embraced the insulting term and coined the neologism *chapuling* as an English verb.[2] In the face of the destruction caused by endless capitalist accumulation, Silvia Federici goes even further. She calls for a reappropriation of the commons, which are central to women's struggles worldwide and the reproductive work they do.[3] Similarly, Indigenous

This photograph by Donna Svennevik shows Agnes Denes's work *Wheatfield – A Confrontation: Battery Park Landfill, Downtown Manhattan*. In the summer of 1982, the artist planted wheat on two hectares of wasteland at the southern end of Manhattan, which she then harvested four months later.

Kader Attia, *Satellite Dishes*, 2010
Photograph

peoples have strived to reverse and resist the processes of colonial modernization, extraction, and exploitation of their lands, bodies, intellectual properties, and tangible and intangible heritages.[4] Across various instances and in diverse geographies—from the Arab Spring to Occupy Wallstreet, from the Gezi Park protests to the protests against coal mining near the German town of Hambach—contested space is reoccupied, reclaimed, and transformed. According to Henri Lefebvre, reappropriating space becomes a productive act that reorders social relations.[5]

Nevertheless, reappropriation is always bound to remain somewhat incomplete. Since appropriations occur incessantly, the quest for reappropriation never ends. First of all, who gets to decide when and what to reappropriate? Who has the right to reappropriate, and in what form? And what happens after a word, a narrative, or a space has been reappropriated? Slavoj Žižek warns us against momentary mass mobilizations and reminds us that "the morning after" is more important than the day of the revolution.[6] In this respect, we must be farsighted in finding meaningful ways to maintain what has been reappropriated but also intuitive in understanding when it is time to make space for new reappropriations.

1   Judith Butler, *Gender Trouble: Feminism and the Subversion of Identity* (New York: Routledge, 1999).
2   Luke Harding, "Turkish protestors embrace Erdoğan insult and start 'capuling' craze," *The Guardian*, June 10, 2013, accessed November 17, 2022, www.theguardian.com/world/2013/jun/10/turkish-protesters-capuling-erdogan.
3   Silvia Federici, *Re-Enchanting the World: Feminism and the Politics of the Commons* (Oakland: PM Press, 2018).
4   Sócrates Vasquez and Avexnim Cojtí, "Cultural Appropriation: Another Form of Extractivism of Indigenous Communities," *Cultural Survival*, December 7, 2020, accessed November 17, 2022, www.culturalsurvival.org/news/cultural-appropriation-another-form-extractivism-indigenous-communities.
5   Henri Lefebvre, *Writings on Cities* (Oxford: Blackwell Publishers, 1996).
6   Círculo de Bellas Artes, "¿Qué es la revolución? Lxs conferenciantes de 'El Gran Río. 4R' contestan," March 2020, YouTube video, 43:20, accessed November 17, 2022, youtu.be/9AvHP6UhgCo?t=5.

"Repair cannot only Be a Metaphor

Kader Attia in conversation with Charlotte Grace and Dubravka Sekulić

It Thrives on Action"

Kader Attia, *Kasbah,* 2008
Installation view, 17th Biennale of Sydney, 2010, on Cockatoo Island

The extensive installation *Kasbah* is a roof world made up of corrugated iron, pallets, car tires, satellite dishes, and other waste materials of globalization. The contrast between the title, which evokes a traditional Arab old town, and the ubiquitous aesthetic of a slum in the Global South raises any number of questions that relate to the economic and social externalization costs of colonization and globalization.

The themes of repair and reparation have long been a focus of Kader Attia's artistic and curatorial work. As curator of the Berlin Biennale 2022, he gave special emphasis to repair as a form of agency and means for decolonial resistance. In conversation with architects Charlotte Grace and Dubravka Sekulić, he discusses how we can repair the wounds that modernity has inflicted on the world.

Charlotte Grace Repair and reparation are a key focus of your practice. To contextualize your work within architectural discourse, we want to situate it in what we might call the "space of repair." We could grasp this space broadly—and apolitically—as the space where inputs and outputs and different states meet. But we could also bring into this idea the space of reparation, which can come in forms like the riot, the revolution, or in structures of redistribution or retribution. In this sense, space would not be a static set of definitive coordinates, then, but a spatial relation, active and ongoing.

Kader Attia Repair defines a space through time. In other words, there is no way to understand repair without the wounds that were inflicted in the past. Repair is actually an oxymoron. When we think: repair, we actually think: injury. The injuries are always somewhere, they cannot be evacuated. The reason that we focus on the repair instead of the injuries—I say "we" in the sense of the Global North and its postmodern society—is because we have been brainwashed by a conceptualization of repair that is very European, modern, and colonial. This notion derives from the Latin "reparare," which means to restore, that is to return to the original state of the thing or idea. In reality you never return something to an original state. You return only to the idea of an original state. Yet modernity has sold us the incredible illusion that if we repair something, we do return it to an original state. That the conservator, or the *reparator*, has, by magic, got rid of the cracks, the fault, the accident.

Pre-modern societies, however, have always kept the injuries of the object explicit as they were repairing them. I made this observation initially in Africa when I lived in Congo in the 1990s, but it is just as true for China, Japan, or other cultures around the world. Until the Middle Ages, this practice was also common in the West. In a medieval cemetery in Bergamo, for instance, you can still see broken marble grave plates that have been repaired with large metal brackets, which is also the way sculptures and calabashes are repaired in Africa. This means a lot. This means that there is another relation to the past, namely one of continuity. Yet in the West, with modernity, we lost this sense of the need to keep the imprint of time on our environment visible.

For me, the question of repair as a space is defined by this extremely narrow, almost imperceptible space in which the injury and the repair follow each other forever. There is a movement from the accident, or the injury, to the repair. These two states—of the injured object and of the repaired object—are likewise defined by time. Time is space, for without a movement through time we would not move through space either. This may sound very philosophical, but there is no denying it. However, repair, particularly for an artist, creates an interstitial space in which we can elaborate a new and deeper understanding of the object and the world in which we live. I am deeply convinced that repair can help us understand the blind spots of modernity. This understanding that repairing an object isn't meant to erase the damage or injury is not an invention of art, but, as I said, deeply rooted in pre-modern societies.

Dubravka Sekulić It's instructive to think this through the case of Diocletian's Palace in Split, Croatia. The palace was designed to house a Roman emperor and grew into a city of thousands of people. Instead of falling into ruin, it survived through the Middle Ages and into the present, as a result of constant inhabitation, adaptation, and repair by way of supporting the needs of everyday life, without obsessing that much over the authenticity of the original image. Although the palace-qua-town is a structure that has evolved through history, today all maintenance is geared towards preservation, towards freezing its history in the present. While everything is being done to keep its structures in "pristine" condition, unsurprisingly the community itself is falling apart. This reveals a profound misunderstanding of what has kept the palace flourishing for centuries and filled it with life.

KA Yes, it is an illustrative case of how much we are guided by modernity's paradigm that things can be planned: That principle seeks to control the unpredictable, the accident, and therefore to control time and history. At the same time, modernity denies all responsibility for the chaos it has produced. In fact, the present world is the way it is because it bears all the wounds accumulated throughout the history of Western modernity. This world of wounds is based on the extraordinary crimes committed by modernity—from slavery to colonialism, with racism an ideological lever to establish the certainty of the West's supremacy over subjugated peoples. The West based modern capitalism on brutalizing others and in this process also destroyed the natural environment. These wounds continue to

Kader Attia, *Modern Genealogy*, 2012

Taking the example of Le Corbusier's buildings, the series highlights the appropriation of vernacular architectural idioms by modernism in the West, which thus profited from the asymmetrical power relationships of colonialism. When searching for an "eternal Mediterranean architecture" Le Corbusier traveled through colonized Algeria and was strongly influenced by the M'zab architecture in Ghardaïa, as Attia highlights in his essay "Signs of Reappropriation."

haunt our societies. Repairing them may seem like a never-ending task. But we must not let this discourage us.

CG I find the idea interesting that modernity, in its obsession with planning, sees the unpredictable as an "accident," as a mistake. Colonized societies are often portrayed as having strayed from a supposedly universal process of civilization through mistake, as if there was something corrupted in their essence that needs to be corrected so they can be put on the supposedly inevitable track of "neutral" modernity. Speaking of modernity, you have in the past discussed French architects Le Corbusier and Fernand Pouillon as being integral to the colonization process in Algeria. Could you elaborate on that?

KA I have been working on the question of architecture as a field of research for years. After the Berlin Biennale, I will continue working on a project on the vernacular adobe architectures that have been built by First Nations in many places in the world, in Algeria, Mali, Mexico, and the United States, for example. I am interested in the continuity between what precedes these architectures, how they have become part of modernism, and how they persist to this day.

There are many striking aspects in the way that Le Corbusier went into the world and was inspired, for want of a better word, by the architectures of the colonized. In architectural history, there is a total denial of their influence on him. But he appropriated the forms and elements he found, for example in the oasis town of Ghardaïa in Algeria, and supposedly "rationalized" them in his own work. Corbusier was obsessed with an aesthetic of austerity. The "rationalization" of vernacular architectures by Corbusier can be seen as a process of, I would say, *whitening* this architecture, of fetishizing and "fascizing" it. Later, Le Corbusier actually turned to fascism. For example, he assured Marshal Pétain of his support for the new, fascist Vichy government.

This reveals one of modernity's blind spots. I think that we have completely misunderstood how fascism functions. Since World War II, we have believed the Allies who sold us the idea that Europe and the West were rid of fascism. No, fascism has never disappeared, it is always around, and the seeds of fascism were sown by modernity. As the Martinican poet and one of the founders of the Négritude movement Aimé Césaire argued concisely, "fascism is the homecoming of colonialism."[1] In other words, the outwardly directed categorization and hierarchization of people for the construction of the "other" which was constitutive for colonialism, came back to the West via the detour of the colonies, as it were, and became effective internally in fascism.

DS Your work fundamentally deals with the reappropriation, the repossession after this process of *whitening. Re-possession* was also the title of an international lecture series at the Royal College of Art in London, which we co-curated.[2] Throughout the series we explored the repossession of selves and spaces in both material and ethereal form. We chose the title because we wanted to highlight that repossession challenges the notion of property. What are your thoughts on the relationship between property and repair?

KA I think the problem of property is crucial because the entire process of coloniality begins with it. We have to understand how the modernization of the West has impacted our relationship to the Earth through the tension between *owing* and *owning.* Europeans arrived in lands where the Indigenous population had no notion of property in the sense of owning the land. The colonialists "negotiated" the acquisition of land with natives who often had no clue about what that implied. And then the colonialists started wars, telling them, "You have to leave, you are on my property." On this basis, colonialism appropri-

ated wealth through extraction: from the body through slavery, from the soil with the imposition of Western modern technologies, from the imaginary with the extraction of concepts from occupied societies as in the case of modern art, which was profoundly influenced by African and Oceanic art and culture. This is admittedly a crude summary of what I elaborated in my essay "Repair: Architecture, Reappropriation, and The Body Repaired" (2013).[3] As the title suggests, for me the theme of repair is deeply related to the concept of reappropriation that I have been developing for many years now. The use of the word "reappropriation" dates back to the second half of the 19th century in France where the word was taken up by anarchist theorists such as Proudhon and Fourier. Its use was inspired by the concept of property, which it aimed to redefine. "What is property? Property is theft," Proudhon declared. In his vision, the concept of property was to be redefined and shifted from the single owner to the community as a whole. From socialism to anarchism, from modernism to colonialism, from Karl Marx to Franz Fanon, dispossession has always sown the seeds of reappropriation, and it still does so today. Reappropriation, for me, is a process of repair.

CG This aligns with a core mantra for *Re-possession* which came from the Zapatistas, "The land belongs to the tiller." This emancipatory practice connects ownership to those who do the labor. Thus, there is no contractual or static definition, but a constant reproduction of ownership. We see a connection here to your ideas around repair and decoloniality. In your approach, you show different kinds of repair as work. For example, many of the projects you have assembled at the Berlin Biennale critically engage with the colonial origins of museum collections and seek new forms of preservation and shared responsibility for cultural heritage. The decolonization of these institutions must go beyond the material gesture of returning looted artifacts; restitution, you have argued in this context, must make the confrontation with one's own colonial past productive for the present.

KA The most difficult task of the decolonial conversation is probably to clarify the continuity of colonialism today. For years now there has been a misunderstanding of decolonization, because people, particularly in the West, keep thinking that colonialism is over: All those colonized countries got their independence, so why should we still talk about this? What such commentators don't understand is that what we are talking about is the decolonization of the *West* and its organs of power. This is what normalizes systemic racism, for instance. Labor is another field where the continuity of this process of exploitation still binds us to colonialism, but today within a much more complex neoliberal society.

CG Something that connects Dubravka's and my work is a consideration of reproductive labor—care, maintenance, sustenance of spaces and selves—with and through space, especially in the context of social movements or political struggles. However, reproductive labor becomes more complicated when we consider it against the background of colonizing and colonized societies. Colonialism overturned previous labor roles and enforced new ones. Today's gendered and racialized divisions of labor are thus also the result of colonization processes. How can we take this into account when we think about the work of repair?

KA In calls for a decolonization of the world, one point often goes unmentioned: In the conceptualization of the decolonial, the fact remains unspoken and thus invisible that feminism as a political struggle comes from both parts of the world, from the white West and from the Global South. I hope that we will be able to go beyond this terminology. In fact, I find the term "decolonial" isn't that relevant any longer, I think much more about de-modernizing the world. In an effort to add feminism to the decolonial discourse, to the extent that I could, it was important to me to invite many different voices from the Global South and many different feminist voices to the Berlin Biennial, like Françoise Vergès, who wrote *Un féminisme Décolonial* (2019).[4] But I don't see the gender question as being that inherent to the concept of repair in the way I was defining it before, because, to be honest, I think that such repair is asexual in a very physical sense. Years ago, I read a fantastic book by physicist Leonard Susskind. There he proposes a view of black holes completely contrary to that of Stephen Hawking. While Hawking describes them as destroyers of the universe, Susskind argues that the extraordinary gravitational powers of black holes of course swallow stars but at the same time they re-eject billions of galactic dust particles, gamma rays, electromagnetic fields which will create new galaxies. In other words, black holes in fact contribute to the repair of the universe.

I think that is a beautiful metaphor which takes the notion of repair far beyond questions of gender to something that has also to be thought of metaphysically. But repair cannot only be a metaphor, it thrives on action. The reason that I'm fascinated by repair is that it is really polysemous as a concept and can also include the notion of reparation in a political sense, such as in relation to colonialism. I think the fact that repair is agender is what makes the concept, paradoxically, useful for feminist claims because it can be appropriated by anyone as it is not solely connected to the male.

CG I was thinking more in terms of the specific forms of gendering of labor imposed through colonialism. Hortense Spillers describes how gender was suspended in the hold of the slave ships, that in the "theft of bodies" for the exploitation of labor, gender became illegible. But in other instances, whenever violence was enacted for example, gender came hurtling back into the frame. We have to think about this tension when we ask when and how we regard labor as gendered and what the liberational potential of that might be.

KA That's a very interesting point. In the colonial process, there was a de- and re-genderization of the colonized subject. This played a role in many contexts, for instance in practices of "slave breeding," whereby slaveholders systematically forced the enslaved to reproduce, or on the slave ships. In order to survive on the boat, many women had to find another, supposedly more powerful person so that they could be protected and not raped and harmed, or rather be raped by only one man instead of many.

This reminds me of stories that I heard a couple of years ago from a psychologist who worked with refugees in Lausanne. The accounts told me that the same thing happens among refugees fleeing across the Mediterranean. When there are hundreds of people in one single boat, the few women on board have no choice but to find a companion for protection. As soon as they arrive in Europe, the problem often is that the companion doesn't understand that the woman is not interested in him anymore. Ecological engineer and political philosopher Malcolm Ferdinand called this the "hold politics,"[5] and it extends beyond the slave ships to the present in the sense that ultra-violence occurs amongst

Kader Attia, *Signs of Reappropriation as Repair*, 2017
The slide projection shows 80 images of traditional Berber jewelry into which the coins of the former colonial powers of Belgium and France have been integrated in an act of cultural reappropriation.

subaltern subjects. I experienced this myself when I was growing up in a banlieue. There is violence within your own community which you are confronted with at a very young age and which you have to survive. The weakest get hounded into addiction, the strong hounded into criminality, jail. There are many girls in the suburbs who wear the hijab, not necessarily because they want to, but because they know that then they won't be harassed by other kids. This is another blind spot of coloniality that we have to keep in mind.

DS Colonialism has violently erased relations between things. Modernity likewise negates the relational. It's as if it were fighting against the work of time, but the violence it uses to commit these erasures is enacted through space and through time. Thinking through the space of repair is precisely insisting that one has to think relationally and not through separation; about the connection between time and space, between the past and the present, and the past and the future. It's also about *presence*—as is the title of your Biennale, *Still Present!*

KA Yes, my curatorial statement for the Biennale[6] goes very much in the direction of what you have just described. And you're right, for me care for the present is crucial, in the sense that probably the worst misconception of our times is that we think we act in the present. An everyday example is the pseudo-present in social media: posting, tweeting, giving ourselves the illusion that we are in the present while we are actually constantly projecting ourselves onto the future or the past.

We believe that we control our present when in fact the present no longer belongs to us. The omnipresence of computational governance, its spread into our everyday lives, means that now capitalism has not only colonized other lands, it has colonized time. Our private time, our everyday lifetime now belongs to processes of data extraction. We are constantly, endlessly, even in our sleep, tracked and traced. Algorithms extract our behavioral data in order to predict—and colonize—our future behavior. And while we might almost immediately forget about the information we share, algorithmic governance never forgets. On the contrary, as philosopher and media theorist Bernard Stiegler argues, algorithmic governance duplicates us by exteriorizing our memory and thus dispossesses us of it. All this data is sold at the speed of light in markets of behavior, and they are the markets of the future.

DS How can we resist becoming, both individually and collectively, reduced to data?

KA What is important here is that the whole process of extraction is possible because our attention is hijacked by this algorithmic governance. In other words, to reclaim our present we need to reclaim our attention. Your attention is present, it cannot be turned on in the future or the past. An important method to attract attention is emotion. Emotionally, too, you cannot live in the future or the past. You are emotionally present.

What is emotion? Just a small history lesson: Two things are crucial. The first thinker who understood the power of emotion is Aristotle, when he defined catharsis and connected it to the identification the audience experiences with the action on the theater stage. Aristotle described the cathartic experience of the theater as repairing the wounds of its audience.

The second, extremely important aspect is that this concept of emotion was actually used for the first time in France in the 13th century in connection with the peasant revolts. The historians of that time wrote that the rioting peasants moved as if they were "outside themselves," *ex movere.* The Latin term describes a movement from inside of the body, as if the soul were leaving the body. Here we are back to the question of space. Emotion is presence but it's also space because it is movement.

Kader Attia, *Indépendance Tchao*, 2014

The sculpture is a replica of the Hôtel de l'Indépendance which was erected in the Senegalese capital Dakar after its liberation from French colonial rule. The piece consists of stacked index-card boxes in which the French colonial police collected information on the resistance during the Algerian War of Independence.

Kader Attia, *Traditional Repair, Immaterial Injury*, 2014
Exhibition view, *The Field of Emotion*, The Power Plant, Toronto, 2018

Kader Attia's concept of repair is manifest in *Traditional Repair, Immaterial Injury*—an approach common in non-Western cultures. Tears and ruptures are mended but remain visible—just as the wounds of history can never be unmade but as such must form an essential part of the work of reparation.

Probably the only way we can actually stand up to this appropriation of emotion through algorithmic governance by politics and capitalism is by the field of emotion. Nothing else can unleash such a powerful pull and capture the attention of a whole crowd. They create the space for collective catharsis. As media theorist Marshall McLuhan said, in the final analysis artists are thieves. They create artworks to steal the audience's attention for a moment. Artists have the incredible capacity to draw our attention to the present, this imperceptible slice of presence that assures you that you are alive, you feel alive. This makes art a highly effective instrument to stand against computational governance. "If humanity has only ever invented machines to speed up," maybe artworks are machines to slow down time, as communications expert Daniel Bougnoux argues.[7]

DS　This brings us to the question of how claiming space can slow time. In this context we've been fascinated by your project *La Colonie* as the establishing of space, a "claiming" of an institution and maintaining it as a space. You founded *La Colonie* in Paris together with Zico Selloum in 2016 as an independent exhibition space, but also as a space for meeting, discussion, and new forms of knowledge. We see this almost as a way of scaling up the space of the repair.

KA　As I emphasized earlier, repair cannot be only a metaphor, it must be turned into actions. When we created *La Colonie*, for me, it was really an act, the idea of acting. We all act in different ways, by writing, by taking part, sometimes also by being activists, but we also need to create spaces for encounter, for conversation, and care for these spaces. To create a room for so many different fields of research and conversation. The emotional aspect, the field of emotion we discussed, also means that we cannot work only through texts but need to meet and interact and listen. This unpredictable moment that you live when we come together also creates space for individuation, that is, collective individuation—the creation of a meaning that can be shared between individuals and groups of individuals, thus stepping from an individual dream to its collective realization. It's like with us in this moment, I don't feel like this is an interview, it is a conversation. In the process, we are allowing a collective individual to emerge.

However, I have always also been very realistic about this. The theoretical conversations that we enjoy also reproduce the bourgeoisie. This is why in creating *La Colonie* it was important to us to also create a space for people who were not the usual audience of art, people who are not "supposed" to participate in our discourse. They would gather in the space because it had a bar where you could come just for coffee or drink with friends. This provided an unpredictable moment; it added another layer. At *La Colonie* we had a lot of activists, particularly from the banlieue where I grew up, Arabs and Blacks, who were not the usual graduate teachers or students, instead they were locals, on the ground. They are the ones who are getting the truncheons from the police.

La Colonie was an open art and culture space in a neighborhood of Paris with a primarily migrant population; it was intended to impart postcolonial knowledge and forms of action. Devised as an agora, it was founded in 2016 by Kader Attia, Zico Selloum, and their families, and existed until 2020.

Their experience of systemic racism, for instance immensely helped other people who've never had to live through that to understand these problems conceptually and develop counterstrategies. This is what I call the individuation.

But to go back to art, and what I was saying before about the vanishing process of collective individuation: I think exhibitions are very important in this process. We need spaces where we can go physically to visit, to see, to listen, to experience, even in a form of silence between each other. You don't go to an exhibition to talk with other people. Still, it's an experience that prompts you to, as it were, edit the narrative that has been provided by the curator or the artist. I think this is so important because, again, you are present, you are alive, you are thinking through and editing what you see. Particularly today, where the intellectual, theoretical, and emotional landscape is completely polluted by a governance that is faster, wealthier, and much more powerful than us, we urgently need spaces to counter the hegemony of digital colonialism that is taking over the power of our interpretation of the world. Human society has become automated to such an extent that the collective individuation is reduced to an instinctual and narcissistic individualization dependent upon its own technological alienation. Creating shared physical and intellectual spaces, and that was the idea with *La Colonie*, is thus an absolute necessity for, I would go as far as to say, the struggle against fascism.

1　Aimé Césaire, "Culture and Colonization," *Social Text* 28, no. 2 (2010): 127–44.
2　Charlotte Grace and Dubravka Sekulić, *Re-possession*, RCA International Lecture Series 2021–22, accessed October 25, 2022, editions.rca-architecture.com/re-possession.
3　Kader Attia, "Repair: Architecture, Reappropriation, and The Body Repaired," 2013, accessed October 25, 2022, kaderattia.de/repair-architecture-reappropriation-and-the-body-repaired.
4　The book is translated into English as François Vergès, *A Decolonial Feminism* (London: Pluto Press, 2021).
5　Malcom Ferdinand, *Decolonial Ecology: Thinking from the Caribbean World* (Cambridge: Polity Press, 2021).
6　Kader Attia, "Still Present!," Curatorial Statement for the 12th Berlin Biennale, 2022, accessed January 19, 2023, 12.berlinbiennale.de/wp-content/uploads/2022/08/BB12_Kuratorisches-Statement_EN.pdf?x16932.
7　Daniel Bougnoux, *La communication contre l'information* (Paris: Hachette, 1995), 35, trans. Kader Attia.

How to Blow Up a Pipeline

Text: Andreas Malm

Action by the climate justice movement Ende Gelände in 2017 in the Hambach open-cast mine on the occasion of the COP23 UN Climate Conference in Bonn

Tim Wagner, from the series *Ende-Gelände,* 2015–ongoing

We find ourselves between two scissor blades: on the one hand, unbending business-as-usual, taking emissions ever higher and confounding hopes for mitigation; on the other, delicate ecosystems crashing down—the extraordinary inertia of the capitalist mode of production meeting the reactivity of the earth. This is the temporal predicament in which the climate movement has to devise meaningful strategies. "Even under optimistic assumptions," the pathways to a "tolerable future" are "rapidly narrowing," in the words of the umpteenth scientific supplication for "immediate global action."[1] Using models with incomplete representation of positive feedback mechanisms, writing in 2019— another year of rising emissions— Dan Tong and his colleagues concluded that 1.5°C still remained "technically possible" on two conditions. First, to have "a reasonable chance" of respecting the limit, human societies would have to institute *a global prohibition of all new CO$_2$-emitting devices.*[2] Now the likelihood of the ruling classes implementing a global prohibition of all new CO$_2$-emitting devices because scientists tell them to, or because billions of people would otherwise suffer grievous harm, or because the planet could spin into a hothouse, is about the same as them lining up at the summit of the steepest mountain and meekly proceeding to throw themselves off the edge.

So here is what this movement of millions should do for a start: announce and enforce the prohibition. Damage and destroy new CO$_2$-emitting devices. Put them out of commission, pick them apart, demolish them, burn them, blow them up. Let the capitalists who keep on investing in the fire know that their properties will be trashed. "We are the investment risk," runs a slogan from Ende Gelände, but the risk clearly needs to be higher than one or two days of interrupted production per year. "If we can't get a serious carbon tax from a corrupted Congress, we can impose a de facto one with our bodies," Bill McKibben has argued, but a carbon tax is so 2004.[3] If we can't get a prohibition, we can impose a de facto one with

our bodies and any other means necessary.

That, however, would only be a start, for the second condition for staying below 1.5°C—or indeed any other boundary between a tolerable and an intolerable future— would be "substantial reductions in the historical lifetimes" of fossil fuel infrastructure. Not only new but existing, young and old CO$_2$-emitting devices would have to be deactivated. The science is eminently clear on this point. Because so much valuable, irretrievable time has been lost—as a matter of fact, not much time is left—assets have to be stranded. Investments must be written off too early for capitalist taste; on one estimate, the instant suspension of every project in the pipeline would make 2°C achievable only if accompanied by the decommissioning of one-fifth of all power plants running on fossil fuels (this estimate is as of 2018—more years or decades of business-as-usual would raise the requirement).[4] That is a lot of already sunk capital. Now one reason why climate stabilization appears such a frightfully daunting challenge is that no state seems prepared to even float this idea because capitalist property has the status of the ultimate sacred realm. Who dares to throw it on the scrapheap? […] And so there must be someone who breaks the spell: "Sabotage," writes Rebecca H. Lossin, one of the finest contemporary scholars in the field, "is a sort of prefigurative, if temporary, seizure of property. It is"—in reference to the climate emergency—"both a logical, justifiable and effective form of resistance and a direct affront to the sanctity of capitalist ownership."[5] A refinery deprived of electricity, a digger in pieces: The stranding of assets is possible, after all. Property does not stand above the earth; there is no technical or natural or divine law that makes it inviolable in this emergency. If states cannot on their own initiative open up the fences, others will have to do it for them. Or property will cost us the Earth.

The immediate purpose of such a campaign against CO$_2$-emitting property, then, would be twofold: establishing a disincentive to invest in more of it and demonstrating that it can be put out of business. The first would not require that all new

devices be disabled or dismantled, only enough to credibly communicate the risk. Strict selectivity would need to be observed. [At the beginning of the 20th century the suffragettes employed militant action in their fight to obtain the vote for women. But] there was a randomness to the property destruction undertaken by the suffragettes, which wouldn't do now; if activists from the climate movement were to attack post offices and tea shops and theaters, investors would not be dissuaded from anything in particular. It would have to be coal wharfs and steam yachts only this time. But just as the suffragettes sought to twist the arm of the state—on their own, they could not legislate any voting rights—the aim would be to force states to proclaim the prohibition and begin retiring the stock. "The current global energy system is the largest network of infrastructure ever built, reflecting tens of trillions of dollars of assets and two centuries of technological evolution," 80 percent of which energy still comes from fossil fuels.[6] No one in his or her right mind would think that bands of activists could burn all or one fifth of that to the ground (or that such a tertiary fire would be unequivocally desirable). At the end of the day, it will be states that ram through the transition or no one will.

But the states have fully proven that they will not be the prime movers. The question is not if sabotage from a militant wing of the climate movement will solve the crisis on its own—clearly a pipe dream—but if the disruptive commotion necessary for shaking business-as-usual out of the ruts can come about without it. It would seem foolhardy to trust in its absence and stick to tactics for normal times. Recognizing the direness of the situation, it is high time for the movement to more decisively shift from protest to resistance: "Protest is when I say I don't like this. Resistance is when I put an end to what I don't like. Protest is when I say I refuse to go along with this anymore. Resistance is when I make sure everybody else stops going along too," as one West German columnist wrote in 1968, relaying the words of a visiting Black Power activist.[7] […]

It is not entirely correct to say that the [climate] movement has [so far] refrained from damaging and destroying property. On the night when Donald Trump was elected president, [for example,] two members of the Des Moines Catholic Worker movement, Jessica Reznicek and Ruby Montoya, trespassed onto a site for construction of the Dakota Access Pipeline in Iowa.[8] They brought coffee canisters filled with rags and motor oil, placed them on the seats of six pieces of heavy machinery and lit matches; five of the six were burnt out in the attack. Autodidacts in the field, Reznicek and Montoya then learned to use welding-torches with oxygen and acetylene to burn through the steel in the pipes. Protective gear on, they raided the pipeline up and down the state in the spring of 2017 and pierced holes in it, compressing each hit-and-run strike into the span of seven minutes. Then they returned to arson. Equipment at multiple sites was set on fire with parcels soaked in gasoline. The property they attacked belonged to Energy Transfer, a conglomerate of pipeline companies on whose boards one could find Rick Perry, secretary of energy under Trump.

Reznicek and Montoya had immersed themselves in the movement against the Dakota Access Pipeline centered on Standing Rock;[9] they reacted to defeat not by capitulating, but by moving on to the next phase. As the two Catholic workers explained in their communiqué.

After exploring and exhausting all avenues of process, including attending public commentary hearings, gathering signatures for valid requests for Environmental Impact Statements, participating in civil disobedience, hunger strikes, marches and rallies, boycotts and encampments, we saw the clear deficiencies of our government to hear the people's demands.[10]

Eventually they resolved to come out and confess. "We are speaking publicly to empower others to act boldly, with purity of heart, to dismantle the infrastructure which deny us our rights to water, land, and liberty," Reznicek and Montoya announced at a press conference. Their sabotage delayed construction of the pipeline for an uncertain number of months, but no matter how frequently they perforated it, two individuals, of course, could not on their own bring down the juggernaut. That would have required organized upscaling. […]

Another few cases notwithstanding, the movement [for climate justice] has by and large left property destruction an untried tactic. What if it became more than a one-off occurrence? What if hundreds or thousands followed in the footsteps of Reznicek and Montoya? […] One might argue that it would open the dams of violence, or even ad lib terrorism. […] [But] Reznicek and Montoya hotly dispute that their actions fell into that category: "The oil being taken out of the ground and the machinery that does it and the infrastructure which supports it—this is violent," Reznicek stated in an interview.[11] "We never at all threatened human life. We're acting in an effort to save human life, to save our planet, to save our resources. And nothing was ever done by Ruby or me outside of peaceful, deliberate, and steady loving hands." […]

No one knows exactly how this crisis will end. No scientist, no activist, no novelist, no modeler, or soothsayer knows it, because too many variables of human action determine the outcome. […] [C]onsider a hypothetical case of torture. Someone is wired to a torture machine with 1,000 switches […]. When no switch is flipped, there is no current in the machine and the victim feels nothing; when all are flipped, she screams in unbearable pain. Between 0 and 1,000, very many switches can be flipped, each in itself of tiny consequence, adding up to a current that must at some point cross the threshold of pain. […] If collectives throw themselves against the switches with sufficient force, there will be no more flipping towards peak torture; the pain might be ameliorated. Within these parameters, one acts or one does not. Like each grain of sand in the pile, an individual joining the counter-collective could boost its capacity on the margin, and the counter-collective could get the better of the enemy. No more is required to maintain a minimum of hope: Success is neither certain nor probable, but *possible*. "The context for hope is radical uncertainty," writes [climate philosopher Catriona] McKinnon;[12] "anything could happen, and whether we act or not has everything to do with it," Rebecca Solnit. "Hope is not a door, but a sense that there might be a door somewhere." Or, more poignantly still, "hope is an axe you break down doors with in an emergency."[13]

Excerpt from:
Andreas Malm, How to Blow Up a Pipeline: Learning to Fight in a World of Fire *(London: Verso, 2021). © Andreas Malm 2021. Reproduced with permission of Verso through PLSclear.*

In 2016, Ende Gelände occupied a bucket-wheel excavator at the Welzow-Süd open-cast mine in Lusatia, north of Dresden, Germany.

Tim Wagner, from the series *Ende-Gelände*, 2015–ongoing

1   Jonathan R. Lamontagne et al., "Robust Abatement Pathways to Tolerable Climate Futures Require Immediate Global Action," *Nature Climate Change* 9, no. 4 (2019): 290.
2   Dan Tong et al., "Committed Emissions from Existing Energy Infrastructure Jeopardize 1.5°C Climate Target," *Nature* 572 (2019): 376, emphasis added by the author. Cf. e.g. the call for a moratorium "on investments in fossil fuel assets" in Filip Johnsson et al., "The Threat to Climate Change Mitigation Posed by the Abundance of Fossil Fuels," *Climate Policy* 19, no. 2 (2019): 269.
3   Bill McKibben, *Falter: Has the Human Game Begun to Play Itself Out?* (London: Headline, 2019), 222. McKibben here quotes Naomi Klein (without specific source).
4   Alexander Pfeiffer et al., "Committed Emissions from Existing and Planned Power Plants and Asset Stranding Required to Meet the Paris Agreement," *Environmental Research Letters* 13, no. 5 (2018): 1–11.
5   Rebecca H. Lossin, "Sabotage as Environmental Activism," *Public Seminar*, July 3, 2018, accessed September 15, 2022, publicseminar.org/essays/sabotage-as-environmental-activism. Cf. Jeff Diamanti and Mark Simpson, "Five Theses on Sabotage in the Shadow of Fossil Capital," *Radical Philosophy* 202 (2018): 3–12.
6   Karen C. Seto et al., "Carbon Lock-In: Types, Causes, and Policy Implications," *Annual Review of Environment and Resources* 41 (2016), 426.
7   Ulrike Meinhof, "From Protest to Resistance," in *Everybody Talks About the Weather … We Don't: The Writings of Ulrike Meinhof* (New York: Seven Stories Press, 2008), 239.

8   This follows the account provided by Reznicek and Montoya themselves in their press release. Ruby Montoya and Jessica Reznicek: "DAPL Ecosabotage Press Release," *Stop Fossil Fuels*, accessed February 20, 2023, stopfossilfuels.org. Cf. e.g. Anna Spoerre, "Women Who 'Sabotaged' Dakota Access Pipeline Charged Almost 3 Years after Damages First Reported," *Des Moines Register*, October 1, 2019, accessed February 20, 2023, eu.desmoinesregister.com/story/news/crime-and-courts/2019/10/01/dakota-access-pipeline-iowa-sabotage-federal-charges-jessica-reznicek-ruby-montoya-trial-activist-ia/3833320002/.
9   See e.g. Alleen Brown, "Dakota`Access Pipeline Activists Face 110 Years in Prison, Two Years after Confessing Sabotage," *The Intercept*, October 4, 2019, accessed September 15, 2022, theintercept.com/ 2019/10/04/dakota-access-pipeline-sabotage.
10   Montoya and Reznicek, "DAPL Ecosabotage" (see note 8).
11   "Meet the Two Catholic Workers Who Secretly Sabotaged the Dakota Access Pipeline to Halt Construction," *Democracy Now!*, July 28, 2017, accessed September 15, 2022, www.democracynow.org/2017/7/28/meet_the_two_catholic_workers_who.
12   Catriona McKinnon, "Climate Change: Against Despair," *Ethics and the Environment* 19, no. 1 (2014): 40.
13   Rebecca Solnit, *Hope in the Dark: Untold Histories, Wild Possibilities* (Edinburgh: Canongate, 2016), 4, 22.

solidarity

Text: Alex Nehmer

According to Émile Durkheim, capitalism not only destroyed earlier ties and relationships, but precisely through the division of labor in modern industrialized societies also created "a new sense of interdependence": "Increasing differentiation and individualization, on the one hand, and growing solidarity, on the other, […] thus did not contradict but conditioned each other."[1]

Today the planetary ecological crisis once more brings home our mutual dependency in a new and drastic way. Yet while for Durkheim solidarity necessarily followed on from social progress, the current crisis also shows that solidarity does not come about automatically but must be fought for again and again. All too often, our solidarity is unequally distributed due to power imbalances and racism. The devastating floods of 2022 in Pakistan and Nigeria, for example, received little attention in the Global North.[2] The fact that millions of people had to leave their homes as a result of these floods[3] points to a further danger: With

Pamela Singh, *Chipko Treehuggers of the Himalayas #4* (detail), 1994

The Chipko movement was a movement led by women in the Indian Himalayan region that from the 1970s onwards protested with peaceful actions against the logging and privatization of the forests.

Raul Walch, *Azimut*, 2016

The kites in Raul Walch's series were created in collaboration with refugees in camps on the EU border. Their materials—tent poles and fabrics, plastic from boats, and reflectors from life jackets—bear witness to the realities of displacement, but they also point to the hope of a world without borders.

the climate crisis, existing regimes of exclusion could become entrenched and solidarity could become even more nationalist at its core.

However, real "solidarity does not take equality as a prerequisite, but as its goal."[4] We must continually expand the boundaries of solidarity anew and overcome the exclusions inscribed into it. Unlike state aid, which at best softens existing conditions and at worst cements them, solidarity aims to change conditions.[5] And unlike paternalist charity that serves to perpetuate the hierarchies between those helping and those in need, solidarity is based on equality and reciprocity.[6] In many cases, it is the communities most threatened by ecological destruction themselves that are at the forefront of the fight against it and, with it, for social justice.[7] We must learn to join these struggles in solidarity. At the same time, Ananya Roy warns us not to use the term lightly. Solidarity, according to Roy, means "taking the same risks as those we want to be in solidarity with."[8] Only then can solidarity, as the revolutionary Kurt Eisner was convinced, become an "architect" of a better world order.[9]

1   After Dietmar Süß and Cornelius Torp, *Solidarität: Vom 19. Jahrhundert bis zur Corona-Krise* (Bonn: Dietz Verlag, 2021), 16 f.

2   Fatima Bhutto, "The West is ignoring Pakistan's super-floods. Heed this warning: Tomorrow it will be you," *The Guardian*, September 9, 2022, accessed November 22, 2022, www.theguardian.com/commentisfree/2022/sep/08/pakistan-floods-climate-crisis.

3   Solomon Odeniyi and Adeyinka Adedipe, "Flood Affected 3.2 Million Nigerians, 1.4 Million Displaced. UN," *The Punch*, November 14, 2022, accessed November 22, 2022, punchng.com/flood-affected-3-2million-nigerians-1-4million-displaced-un.

4   "Wovon wir reden, wenn wir von Solidarität reden," Bini Adamczak in conversation with Jan Ole Arps, *ak – analyse & kritik* 641 (2018).

5   Alexander Behr, *Globale Solidarität: Wie wir die imperiale Lebensweise überwinden und die sozial-ökologische Transformation umsetzen* (Munich: oekom, 2022).

6   Dean Spade, *Mutual Aid: Building Solidarity During This Crisis (and the Next)* (London: Verso, 2020).

7   Joan Martínez Alier, *The Environmentalism of the Poor: A Study of Ecological Conflicts and Valuation* (Cheltenham: Edward Elgar, 2002).

8   Contribution by Ananya Roy at the event *10 Questions. Centennial Edition: What Is Community?* held at the University of California Los Angeles, November 19, 2019, accessed November 22, 2022, www.youtube.com/watch?v=B-zAHUQj9xI.

9   Kurt Eisner, "Sieben Briefe, An eine Freundin: IV. Solidarität," in *Gesammelte Schriften*, vol. 2 (Berlin: Paul Cassirer, 1919), 55.

From

Paulo Tavares in conversation
with Markus Krieger and Alex Nehmer

planning to

WAI Think Tank, *A Post-Colonial Mural: Propaganda for Acts of Repair*, 2021

Poster for the Preston Thomas Memorial Symposium at the Cornell AAP Department of Architecture in Ithaca, NY, in 2021, curated by Paulo Tavares and Sean Anderson

Architecture and planning have long been instruments of colonial capitalist exploitation of people and land, argues Paulo Tavares. With Markus Krieger and Alex Nehmer, he discusses how the disciplines can begin to decolonize and align themselves with the struggles of Indigenous communities to repair the Earth.

Planting

Markus Krieger You have worked on territories whose ecological and social fabric was systematically damaged through extractivism and colonial expansion, for example the oil-and-mining frontier in the Ecuadorian Amazon. How can repair be conceived in these spaces without evoking reactionary ideas of an unbroken "original state"?

Paulo Tavares When we think of repair today, it is crucial to start by acknowledging that the work of repair has been done for years, even centuries, by communities who have suffered the damages caused by the extractive logic of colonial racial capitalism. These communities built institutions and organized themselves and others for repair, even when it was not always named as such. The idea of repair that stems from movements within the African diaspora and from Indigenous peoples is inherently forward-looking. Rather than trying to return to an "unbroken original state," the question here is to reestablish the links and connections that have been violently severed. Addressing acts, policies, and designs of repair deals with questions of the past, of course. But many of the same questions remain highly relevant because colonialism operates on a continuum. Repair must therefore include reparations that address this history as well as the future. Take the climate crisis as an example: Without reparations, there will be no process of restoring the Earth because the ecological crisis is, to a great extent, a product of the colonial logics that drove industrialization in the Global North in the first place. The powers that be must come to terms with the wrongs committed in the past if we are to conceive more livable and sustainable environments for future generations, both for human and nonhuman communities.

As architects, designers, cultural practitioners, and visual artists who engage with repair, we should add in solidarity to the social struggles ongoing today. I consider my work to be a type of "militant" design that I call *design as advocacy.* This means asking how the tools of design—material, visual, legal, cartographic, and curatorial—can be mobilized to join forces with the politics of these communities, building alliances with them in defense of their rights and territory. Thanks to various projects I was privileged to do with Indigenous communities, I believe they are at the forefront of our most important struggles today with their movements. Their political philosophy and the ways in which they frame spatial and land politics is a true avant-garde of political action in that they are fighting for the Earth, a biopolitics in the name of us all as living beings, a true universalism in that sense.

Alex Nehmer If architects and designers want to contribute in solidarity to the work of repair, they also have to challenge and overcome the colonial legacies within their own disciplines. How can those disciplines repair this legacy?

PT Architecture and planning, specifically modernism and its canons, have a long history of being operationalized to carry out damages and commit violence against land and people in various dimensions, whether they were a means to expropriate and colonize territories in the Global South or, for example, the "negative planning" in the territories occupied by Israel in Palestine, which Rafi Segal, David Tartakover, and Eyal Weizman have pointed out.[1] Design has often been and still is a means of disempowering, disfranchising, and bringing poverty to marginalized communities. It claims to drive modernization and civilization, especially in the Global South, but often leaves ruins in its wake—of communities, of land, of nature. Yet from the internal point of view of the discipline and its pedagogy, architecture is conveyed as something inherently positive. In history, and still today, you will find a whole vocabulary around notions of "development," "progress," and "betterment"—notions whose roots can be found in colonialism—used to define architecture, planning, and design, giving the discipline an almost messianic character. Architecture is built on the premise that everything it does is ethical in the sense that it purportedly aims to improve people's lives. This foundational ideological veil of design has prevented designers from seeing the evil they create and reinforce. Discarding this ideology would be a first step towards decolonizing the discipline.

Then, of course, it is also crucial to challenge syllabuses and curriculums because architectural history and architectural education in general have been instrumentalized to reinforce ideas and imaginaries that sustained colonialism and racism. This is not only a question of challenging the content of what is studied and taught but also of rethinking the power structures within the institutions that design architectural education, from academies to museums and archives. Recently we have

Paulo Tavares, *Settler-Modernism*, 2021

witnessed setbacks, but we have also seen remarkable moves in that regard, such as the project *Unlearning Whiteness* at the Graduate School of Architecture, Planning and Preservation of Columbia University, and notably the creation of the African Futures Institute in Accra, Ghana, by Lesley Lokko.

MK Your work specifically confronts the colonial legacy of modernism in architecture. *Des-Habitat* (2019), for instance, addressed the appropriation of Indigenous cultures in architecture.

PT The extraction of knowledge, the arts, and cultures is at the core of colonialism. If you look at archival records, the origins of much of the scientific knowledge attributed to the modern Western world have been extracted from Indigenous knowledge by colonial processes. In my practice, I aim for an awareness of this history and its current implications. In that respect, I particularly question how architecture has historically supported these colonial processes of expropriation. Modernism's appropriation of Indigenous motives, objects, and crafts goes back to the idea of "primitivism" developed by the early European avant-gardes. As we know, this aesthetic appropriation was a product of imperialism, of looting Indigenous artifacts and transporting them to museums in the metropolitan centers of imperial powers in Europe so they could be consumed by a cultural elite eager to relate to "exotic" non-Western cultures. That is another reason why reparations are deeply related to the field of art and culture, including, of course, architecture.

A similar process, with its own specificities, happened at the surge of the modernist vanguard in Brazil, who appropriated the "primitive" as signifiers of modernity, but a very specific type of modernity in the sense that it was distinctively national. *Des-Habitat* engages in critical dialogue with this history through the imaginary and discursive archive of modern architecture. The project focuses on the famous modernist magazine *Habitat* developed by architect and designer Lina Bo Bardi, as part of the curatorial program of the Museu de Arte de São Paulo (MASP), one of the most important modern art museums in the Americas. I tried to show how in *Habitat* specifically, and in Brazilian modernism more broadly, there was an appropriation of Indigenous symbols, images, and objects, claiming them for a nationalist modernism. The publication of Indigenous arts and crafts in *Habitat* served as an ideological veil to the violent process of colonial expropriation of Indigenous lands that was going on at that time and escalated with the US-backed military dictatorship in the 1960s and 1970s. In many ways, modernism was therefore complicit, even if not declared as such, with new forms of colonialism. Another such example is Brasília, the modernist capital built at the center of the national territory in the late 1950s, which was conceived as a means of advancing the colonial frontier of national expansion. As Lúcio Costa, the creator of Brasília's master plan wrote, the city was born from "a deliberate act of possession […] a gesture still in the sense of the pioneers, along the lines of the colonial tradition."[2] I call this "settler-modernism," in an inversion of the concept of "settler-colonialism."

MK But there are also tools and strategies for repair found within design. In the context of the project *Trees, Vines, Palms and Other Architectural Monuments* (2013–ongoing), you have argued that the Amazonian forests can be seen as the architectural and artistic heritage of non-Western forms of design. What strategy was behind using the notion of heritage to describe these artifacts?

PT The starting point for this understanding was an extensive survey undertaken with the Xavante people of central Brazil, who had been forcibly removed from their territory by the military dictatorship in the 1960s. We were asked to conduct a forensic architecture investigation of the villages that had been displaced or destroyed. As we worked on the mapping using various media and field surveys, we noticed that those abandoned sites were marked by singular forest formations, which at first glance may appear "natural," but which the elders who guided us recognized as ancient settlements. We began to ask ourselves whether we could read those forests as ruins of the architectural remains of those villages rather than simply as part of nature, and what this would imply in legal, political, and architectural terms. Could we understand them as a form of cultural, architectural heritage? What memories and histories could they register and recount? What kind of lessons do they teach contemporary design? After all, ruins are one of the main epistemic resources in architectural practice, history, and theory.

In other projects as well, I have had the privilege to do advocacy work with different Indigenous groups in Brazil and Latin America at large. Working with them, one learns how the forest configures a cultural and historic entity to which Indigenous folks attach various symbolic, memorial, and social connotations—just as Western culture does with architectural monuments and cities. In that respect, I was also deeply influenced by the thought and practice of writer and activist Ailton Krenak and anthropologists Pierre Clastres and Eduardo Viveiros de Castro. Furthermore, I had the privilege of conversing and working with some of the most prominent Amazonian archaeologists and botanists, people like William Balée, Eduardo Góes Neves, and Michael Heckenberger, who have been arguing since the 1980s that the forest is largely the product of Indigenous forms of inhabitation and land management systems. As more research is being undertaken, we are better understanding that the forest is the product of very sophisticated ways of seeing, organizing, managing, and designing the land developed by Indigenous communities across the Amazon. In that sense, the forest is a kind of architecture, an invaluable architectural heritage that Indigenous forms of knowledge and design gave to us all and to the life of the planet. The "primeval forest"—the quintessential representation of nature in colonial-modern Western epistemology—is, in fact, constructed and planted. We could explore a whole new dimension of landscape design by learning

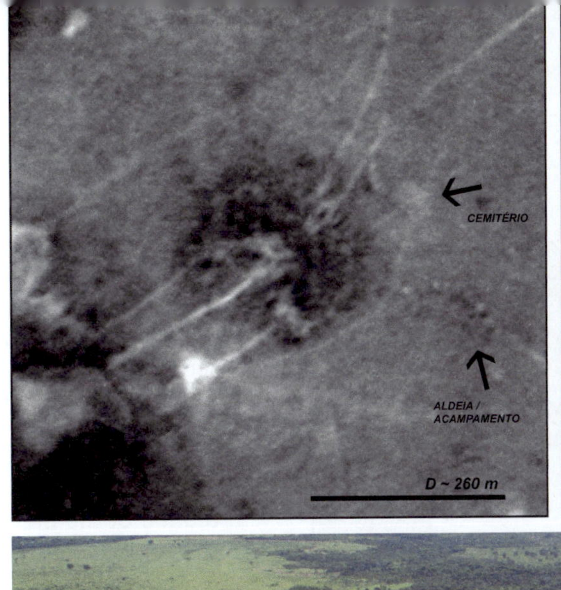

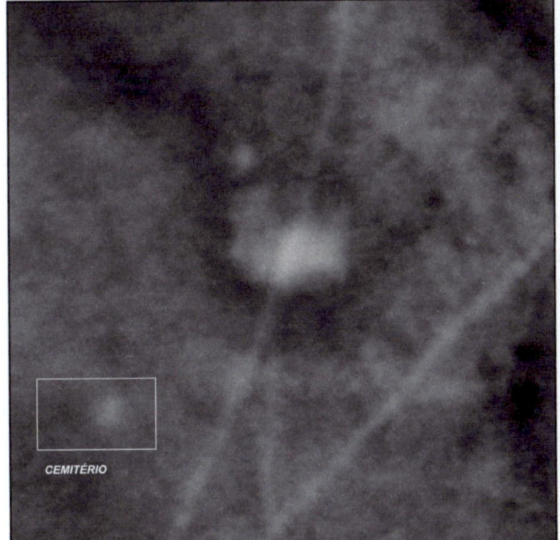

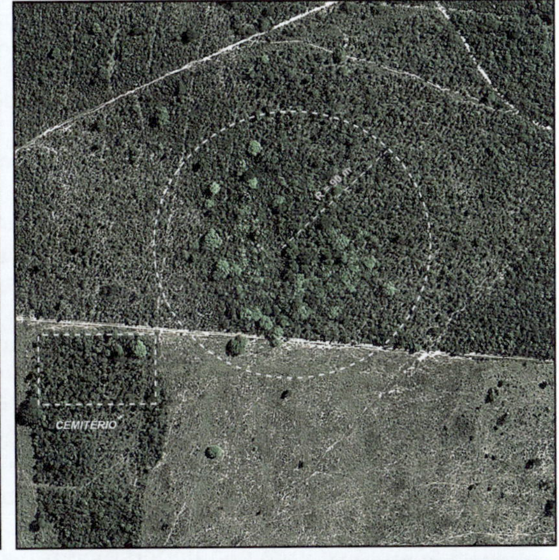

Paulo Tavares, *Trees, Vines, Palms and Other Architectural Monuments* (excerpt), since 2013
Identification of the Xavante village of Bö'u. The dense formation of the rainforest has preserved the original, circular footprint of the old village. The region is known as Bö'umoahö (place of production), alluding to its wealth of natural resources and the prosperity of the village in former times.

Paulo Tavares, *An Architectural Botany* (excerpt), since 2018
What does it mean to say that an environment that is considered the quintessence of nature is actually a cultural artifact? In the center of the project is a visual archive that ethnobotanist William Balée set up in the 1980s during his pioneering research with the Ka'apor. Can the archive be understood as an architectural inventory?

from these forest ruins and the knowledge embedded within them.

AN   What are the consequences for the work of repair or reparation if we understand these sites as heritage?

PT   This leads us to think about reparation in two ways. First, as epistemological decolonization: To legitimize itself, colonialism needed to develop a system of knowledge that identified nature as an object of mastery while at the same time racializing communities as primitive, under-civilized, and underdeveloped. Reparation necessarily requires dismantling this epistemic construction, which is at the core of colonial racial capitalism. Indigenous fights are fights for reparations for this epistemic violence that enabled colonialism to take place. And architecture, its history, and its teachings are strongly rooted in that history.

The second way we can understand repair through these "forest monuments" relates to architecture, its practices, and public manifestations. We are currently witnessing cities exploding in contestations of monuments that celebrate the history of colonial racism. Heritage and public architecture are at the center of a decolonial battle for reparations. But it is not enough to list the monuments to be dismantled. We need to work towards building new memorial landscapes to care for, sites that can enable other histories to be told while at the same time healing the Earth.

AN   If we start from the point of acknowledging nature as designed, what does this mean for design practices going forward? In your text "In the Forest Ruins," published in *e-flux* in 2016, you argue we should shift from *planning* the planet to *planting* the planet. What does this vision mean for you?

PT   As Bruno Latour and others taught us, the basis of modern knowledge—and here I should add *colonial*-modern knowl-

edge—is a fundamental distinction between nature and culture, where "man," more precisely the white man, appears as the master of the world of beings. It is important to understand the ways in which design, in its canonic Western forms, has been among the most effective means of materializing and operationalizing this dichotomy on the ground. Architecture as a knowledge system defines nature as an object of possession, mastery, domestication, and control. At the same time as architecture and urbanization have heavily impacted the ecological balance of the planet, technology has reached the capacity of operating on a planetary level. Geoengineering, which is largely based on technologies derived from environmental warfare tactics developed during the Cold War,[3] is presented as a new stage of technological evolution in which design becomes the ultimate form of planetary management. But this reproduces the same anthropocentric and evolutionary principles of Western thought and the image of "man" as the master planner that led us here in the first place. This presents a crucible paradox, which in my view is as much political as it is existential: We cannot solve the environmental crisis using the same concepts, means, and tools of design. Design needs to abandon ideas about planning and governing nature. It really bothers me to see how designers use the ecological catastrophe we are living through to promote ideas of innovation as "planning the planet" in very uncritical, depoliticized terms.

I am of course not arguing that we don't need future-oriented thinking and projects—on the contrary. But we do need to forge a different conception of design altogether. In the essay you mentioned, I make a conceptual shift from planning to planting. Planning implies hierarchy and control, a top-down approach. Such ideas are rooted in colonial views and class divisions between intellectual and practical labor. Planting—planting gardens and forests, not plantations, I should be clear—is a form of design that implies an intimate relationship with the soil, the land, and which is cultivated collectively through generations. Planting and cultivating the earth is a form of knowledge that comes from folk, Indigenous, and peasant traditions, a bottom-up approach that, as the "forest ruins" of Amazonia teach us, plays concrete roles in regulating the planet's ecological balance. Planting is, by definition, a form of planning, but one that needs to be fine-tuned to the agency of numerous nonhuman agents that are part of the environment—climate, soil, animals, bees, insects, etc. In that sense, one may think about how the concept of planting may lead us to a form of design that displaces the imperial power and anthropocentrism that historically have been embedded within design. In the text, I call this "design beyond the human." We need to be humbler and understand that we are just one piece in a larger extended network, and that design is a form of cooperation between different human and nonhuman entities and forces.

MK   Another path to overcoming anthropocentrism could be granting nature rights, i.e., recognizing nonhuman entities as legal subjects—a theme you have repeatedly come back to, for example, in your works *Forest Law* (2014) with Ursula Biemann and *Non-Human Rights* (2012). In your view, what are the possibilities and limits of employing legal means as a tool for restorative justice?

PT   *Forest Law* and *Non-Human Rights* deal with the question of the rights of nature in Latin America, and more specifically, the Ecuadorian Amazon. The rights of nature—the "rights of Pachamama," as they are known in Ecuador and Bolivia—legally came into being through the constitutional reforms in Ecuador in 2008 and in Bolivia in 2009. This represented a "new constitutionalism" in Latin America, in which nature figures as a subject of rights in similar ways as humans do. It is important to acknowledge that the rights of nature are not the outcome of some form of pure environmentalism. It emerged from years of Indigenous uprisings against neocolonial policies, neoliberal austerity, and the racial structures that define post-colonies in Latin America.

Rights like these are always the result of political struggles. Throughout history, rights have been implemented to address, or indeed to repair, forms of structural violence. For example, the Maria da Penha Law *(Lei Maria da Penha)*, implemented in Brazil in 2006, seeks to protect the rights of women against misogynist violence. It came into being as a recognition and remediation of the structural violence against women that shapes society. This necessitated specific rights that at the same time expanded the concept of universal rights. In a similar vein, the rights of nature acknowledge that within the social systems inherited from colonial-modernity, there is structural violence against nature because nature is treated as an object of appropriation and mastery, reduced to property instead of being seen as a living being. Therefore, a system of rights is needed that tries to fundamentally transform—or repair—this structure that permeates economic, political, and legal systems.

MK The Western understanding of property seems to lie at the heart of many of the struggles we have talked about.

PT The moment that nature can only be conceived as property, you are not only putting up a fence against land as commons and a resource for all but also putting up an epistemic fence against the very idea of nature itself, reducing life to an object subservient and subaltern to humans. When we claim that nature has rights, it implies that nature can not only be thought of as property. This has implications for economic equality and wealth distribution, and also our understanding of what nature is and the role it plays in our cultural, political, economic, and legal systems.

Enshrining the rights of nature into constitutional law has a cultural and educational dimension as well. Courtrooms, laws, legislations, conventions, etc., are public forums through which different relations between society and nature can be communicated. These rights offer a new political tool of struggle to the communities who do activism on behalf of the environment in very pragmatic terms: They can argue on constitutional grounds and raise their voice in the name of rights. Effectively, the rights of nature are one possible way of enacting reparations across various domains, not only environmental but also cultural, allowing us to define our societies beyond the predatory logics of capitalism and its colonial and racial structures. They are a step of "epistemic decolonization" toward a world where nature will occupy a different position within our cultural, legal, and political systems—an existential topic for humanity in the face of global climate change.

But of course, legal systems and systems of rights have limitations: They are important but not neutral. They can be turned upside down and used to enforce new forms of violence and colonization. There are many episodes, and indeed very recent ones, where the idea of human rights has been instrumentalized to wage war and impose new forms of domination. In a similar vein, we are also seeing this in how ecological discourses are being instrumentalized on behalf of global sustainability: for example, for militarized technologies of geoengineering, or new forms of land grabbing such as "carbon colonialism," in which compensation areas created for CO_2 certificate trading are withdrawn from use by the local population.

AN As part of our 2021 exhibition *Cohabitation,* we showed the documentary film *Habitat 2190* (2019) by Hanna Rullmann and Faiza Ahmad Khan, which traces the installation of a new nature protection zone on the site of a former refugee camp in Calais. It is an instance where nature protection becomes a tool of the European border regime directed against racialized people. How can we ensure that the rights of nature and humans are not pitted against each other?

PT The history of Western thought about the environment since the 18th century is, in many ways, a history of continued dispossession of colonized communities. There are various examples in history where environmental practices and discourses have been used by colonizing powers to enforce control and rule across the Global South. As historian Alfred W. Crosby famously analyzed in *Ecological Imperialism*, colonialism is also an environmental force. Today there still exist many instances in which environmental discourses and practices are instrumentalized as a means to enforce power over communities and people. The specific case in Calais you mentioned reminds me of the work of artist Ayesha Hameed, who explores the ways in which images of the "jungle" in Calais are used to criminalize migrants. I also have to think of the advocacy work by Lorenzo Pezzanni and Charles Heller against the border regime of Fortress Europe, which they define as a politics of "hostile environments"—a complex set of spatial and legal elements that include nature as a means to govern migrants. At the same time, the protection of nature is deeply connected with emancipatory struggles throughout history.

AN In what sense?

PT When studying decolonial movements, we find that there is always an environmental dimension attached to them, because racial colonialism is a system that operates against people and land, against communities and their territories. Struggles against colonial rule and slavery are fundamentally related to the dismantlement of the plantation system, which is a system of environmental destruction par excellence in the sense that it diminishes biodiversity through homogenization, treating nature as a pure commodity. Similarly, we can find deep-rooted environmental strands within the civil rights movement in the US, as exemplified in Robert Bullard's seminal work on environmental justice. That is why, when dealing with the environment, it is important that we always start off grounded in the political struggles of the communities who are at the frontlines, those who care, nurture, and defend those environments.

In that respect, one of the most influential thinkers and activists for me is the forest defender Chico Mendes. A rubber tapper in Amazonia, Mendes started his struggle against the development projects implemented by the military regime in the 1970s and early 1980s. Those projects were destroying the rubber and nut trees that ensured the livelihood of local communities. Mendes led one of the most representative movements calling for

The publication series *pumflet* was founded in 2016 by the collective pumfleteers (Ilze Wolff and Kemang Wa Lehulere). The issue on Summer Flowers (2021) is dedicated to the "Rainclouds" house which author, activist, and gardener Bessie Head had built in 1969 with the proceeds from her first novel *When Rain Clouds Gather.* Bessie Head saw her work as a continuation of that of Sol Plaatje, a South African journalist and author who documented the impact of the Land Act in his book *Native Life in South Africa* (1914). Today, the house is part of Botswana's national cultural heritage.

radical land reform that would have given common property to rubber tapper communities, stopping deforestation. Shot in a political murder in 1988, he became known worldwide for his environmental fight against the destruction of the Amazon Forest. But besides being an environmentalist, Chico Mendes was the leader of the rubber tappers labor union; he was associated with the Brazilian Workers' Party, and his practice and thought were influenced by socialist thinking. He was a community organizer and political mobilizer against the repressive, fascist-like regime implemented by the US-backed military dictatorship in Brazil. He fought for human rights and for the forest, for democracy, liberties, and freedom of speech, for workers' rights and nature's rights, as those things are all entangled. The ecocide committed by the military government in the Amazon rainforest first had to dismantle any type of political resistance and democratic means of decision-making. It had to ban the right of free association with political parties and unionists and censored free speech. This was what Mendes was fighting against; it was an intersectional politics.[4] He showed that we cannot separate politics and the environment.

We can still see this today. The neofascist government of Brazilian president Jair Bolsonaro was openly anti-Indigenous and anti-environmental. It systematically dismantled legal protections for the environment and Indigenous lands and promoted land grab policies against forest communities of Amazonia, foremost illegal mining, which led to numerous cases of violence against Indigenous communities.[5] At the same time, Bolsonaro's government was deeply authoritarian. He attempted to block every possible democratic avenue that would allow social movements to discuss those policies within traditional democratic and political arenas. For that reason, we must always look at environmental protection intersectionally and build alliances between different struggles. Environmental repair is never only about physically repairing the environment but also always about making historical reparations for historical injustices. Communities need to heal the body of the Earth.

AN This interview will be part of a chapter on the politics of solidarity. How can we advance from local alliances to global solidarity?

PT Today, everything is at the same time local and global, grounded and planetary. So local alliances are always also forms of global solidarity. Spatial politics need to be framed across scales, taking the ground as the Earth, the Earth as a planet, and the planet as our home.

American Indian Center of Chicago, *Land Acknowledgment*

Chicago Architecture Biennial 2019,
curated by Yesomi Umolu, Sepake Angiama, and Paulo Tavares

1   Rafi Segal et al., eds., *A Civilian Occupation: The Politics of Israeli Architecture* (London: Verso, 2003). See also the interview with Eyal Weizman, "Architecture and negative planning in the West Bank," *Cabinet* 9 (Winter 2002/03), accessed November 18, 2022, www.cabinetmagazine.org/issues/9/kastner_najafi_weizman.php.

2   Mário Pedrosa, "Reflexões em torno da nova capital," *Brasil: Arquitetura Contemporânea* 10 (1957), 2–5, quoted in Paulo Tavares, "Brasília: Colonial Capital," *e-flux*, October 2020, accessed November 18, 2022, www.e-flux.com/architecture/the-settler-colonial-present/351834/braslia-colonial-capital.

3   More on this in Paulo Tavares, "Stratoshield," in *Textures of the Anthropocene: Vapor*, eds. Katrin Klingan et al. (Berlin: Haus der Kulturen der Welt, 2015), 61–71.

4   Paulo Tavares, "Forest Alliances in the Amazon," *The Funambulist* 35, *Decolonial Ecologies* (2021), accessed November 18, 2022, thefunambulist.net/magazine/decolonial-ecologies/forest-alliances-in-the-amazon.

5   Fabricio Araújo, "Film Details How Bolsonaro's Policies Stimulate Mining in Yanomami Land," *Instituto Socioambiental*, September 6, 2022, accessed November 18, 2022, www.socioambiental.org/en/socio-environmental-news/film-details-how-bolsonaro%27s-policies-stimulate-mining-in-the-land.

Radical Roots

Oxana Timofeeva in conversation with Alex Nehmer, Milica Topalović, and Nazlı Tümerdem

Chto Delat, *The Tower: A Songspiel*, 2010

Oxana Timofeeva is part of the artist collective Chto Delat, founded in 2003 in St. Petersburg; its members use various media to link political theory, art, and activism. The 30-minute musical movie *The Tower: A Songspiel* hinges on the conflict around the planned Okhta Center in the historical heart of St. Petersburg, in whose 400-meter-high tower the Gazprom head office was to be located. After massive protests, the project was moved to the city limits.

Philosopher Oxana Timofeeva was still in St. Petersburg when she spoke with Alex Nehmer, Milica Topalović, and Nazlı Tümerdem in early July 2022, before she had to leave Russia. What are the possibilities of resistance under totalitarian regimes? Can solidarity be a response to the catastrophic times we live in?

Alex Nehmer Let us start with a diagnosis. In March 2022, you organized the panel *Burning the Archives of the Earth: From Capitalist Extraction to War Destruction* at Haus der Kulturen der Welt in Berlin, which you opened by describing the catastrophic triangle caused by the climate crisis, the COVID-19 pandemic, and war in Ukraine, which we are currently trapped in but from which we can also learn. How do the sides of this triangle relate to each other? And can the concept of repair offer us a way out?

Oxana Timofeeva Imagine you are a vagabond. After walking for a long time, you find a house in the woods. You enter and find a mess; everything is broken and out of place, so you start cleaning and making repairs. Repair is a mode of being. It absorbs you completely; you become a workhorse. Your relationship with the world does not fit into traditional modes of production and destruction. This work of repair can be taken as a metaphor that functions on different levels. This triangle of war, pandemic, and climate crisis is situated at the planetary level of existence, the highest level we can comprehend. But because our imagination is limited, we tend to look at things separately. In our minds, we sever war from the climate crisis and the pandemic from other disasters. But repair as a mode of existence offers a way out in that it works between these broken relations and messy states of affairs. It also works in between the different scales of this triangle, from local to planetary.

We can think, for example, about the work of repair in relation to the cities destroyed by war. I live in St. Petersburg, and every day I see in the news that my army, my country, is bombing another country. More and more images of ruins emerge before my eyes. Ruins in cities, some of which I visited many years ago when they were still blossoming. I have never been to Mariupol, but I saw the image of the theater that was bombed in March 2022 and where many people died in the ruins of the collapsed building. How reconstruction can succeed is still completely unclear. Drawing on the experience of countries like Germany, Serbia, and others, we know that every war has an end. Then the Great Repair will begin, and it will be time for our solidarity, to help them rebuild their cities. But we cannot repair their lives; we cannot resurrect the dead. Such trauma makes the idea of ghosts very real; they are nothing more than the haunting of places and people by the memory of extreme injustice. Any work of repair and recovery must therefore also address the injustice of destruction.

This is the level of war. At all levels, repair comes as a third phase. It is always preceded by production, followed by destruction, which are in a dialectic relation to each other. Something is produced, then destroyed, and then the process of repair comes into play; previous discourses did not consider this third phase. Repair is a new, feminist concept. While it may not sound as impressive as production or creation, it aims to compensate for the negative impacts of destruction.

On the level of the natural world, the speed of destruction is comparable to war but is not as visible. We think we are capable of repairing the natural world. Still, sometimes it feels as if all our efforts to save nature are pointless, at least on the level of our individual lives and everyday ecological awareness. We can do so little compared to the harm a single factory or airplane causes in just one day, and there are millions of factories and tens of thousands of airplanes. The world is going to hell, and we cannot stop it by simply using more eco-friendly soap. In this regard, we can take a lesson from Donna Haraway. We all "live in disturbing times," she writes; "the task is to become capable […] of response." She points out that "staying with the trouble requires learning to be truly present," taking refuge neither in "awful or edenic pasts" nor in "apocalyptic or salvific futures."[1]

To put it simply: We are living in a catastrophic situation. Nothing will ever be perfect. We will not rebuild a new world where everything is pristine and in full bloom, but this does not mean you have to abandon all effort. We can try to fix things, save those who can be saved, and care for those who cannot care for themselves. We can do small things. Returning to the image of the house in the woods: Anyone who has lived in a house in the countryside knows that repair never ends; you are constantly busy with its upkeep. Repair is an inevitable part of a non-urban way of existence.

Milica Topalović It's interesting that you bring up the non-urban ways of existence. Do these compound crises we are talking about also signify a crisis of urbanization and the urban paradigm? Urban also stands for the modern, for the agglomeration of people and structures, driven by the logic of the industrial capitalist economy. Can non-urban existence, the country way of life, be understood as a mode of repair of the urban?

♂ We need to find a synthesis of urban and non-urban life while also considering that our population is growing and we cannot simply go back to the villages. Cities continue to grow, and presently they can only do so under conditions where inequalities dictate the modes and the quality of life. In Russia, this pattern is very clear. The wealthiest people move to countryside estates, whereas poor people who perform industrial and other kinds of labor get squeezed into ghettos at the periphery of big cities. This dynamic is even more striking in China and other places where global production is concentrated.

That leads me to the third side of the triangle, the pandemic. Here, too, there is stark inequality, between those who are comfortable and safe in their private homes and those who live and work in cramped conditions in the cities. Thinking about the pandemic can help us expand the concept of repair by coupling it with another concept: recovery. Comparable to war but on a global level, the pandemic has led to enormous death. But many people experience recovery, leaving the danger and destruction of their body behind. In this context, the collective dimension of recovery and repair becomes clear. You need others to recover, to bring you water and food to care for you. If we think about repair and recovery as a conceptual pair, it follows that repair is collective work.

♂ With "care," you address a concept that this issue of *ARCH+* addresses in a dedicated chapter. In the discussion about your talk "Solidarity on the Planetary Scale" in 2019, you contrasted care and solidarity, indicating that you view the former with some skepticism. You argued that care brings in psychology, an affective and emotional dimension. Solidarity, on the other hand, is a political strategy and alternative to the sentimentality that often masks a condition of profound alienation in our neoliberal world. But there are different perspectives on care, from the point of view of psychology, as well as a feminist ethics of care, or the Marxist understanding of the invisible and exploited labor of care. How does care relate to the concept of repair for you?

♂ If I said that I don't trust the notion of care, I was referring to a moralizing tendency to make it a cheap metaphor for every-

thing good against everything bad. But indeed, the concept is crucial. Understood fundamentally, it goes against the grain of the individualist idea that every being is autonomous and self-reliant. An obvious example is if we have a plant in our apartment. If we stop watering it, the plant dies. Or we think of ourselves as responsible and caring because we cannot only take care of ourselves but also those who cannot take care of themselves, whom we therefore see as being weaker than ourselves, like older family members, children, pets, etc. In this patriarchal reading of care, those who take care of others also hold power. But in reality, nobody is autonomous; we cannot take care of ourselves alone. Despite what we may think, we are

In his 1993 study *War and Architecture*, dedicated to the citizens of Sarajevo, Lebbeus Woods explores possibilities for repairing war-torn buildings. In his utopian proposals, the US architect advocates a reconstruction that starts from the ruins, acknowledging loss and vulnerability. Gaps and the wounds of war become scars, aiming to allow the urban community to heal through the built environment.

like plants that need watering—we are just not honest enough to admit it. We should embrace this feminist interpretation of care as a principle that can teach us the impossibility of autonomy and separate existence—also of humankind. Even as we think we must save nature, we would also never survive without nature's care. Plants care for us, but they do so without claiming mastery over humans. And these great repairers need our support because they are endangered and dying from human-made damage: global warming and pollution of the air, water, and soil. Solidarity toward us is already present—we need to return it toward all other beings.

♂ Throughout your work, you describe solidarity with nonhuman beings not just as an add-on—to be undertaken once solidarity among humans has been achieved—but as a prerequisite for the latter. How do you see the relationship between the two?

♂ Nature is full of living organisms doing the work of recovery. Mushrooms are exemplary in this regard. As Anna Tsing describes it, mushrooms emerge in places of destruction. On soils devastated by industrialization or even after nuclear catastrophes, they are often the first new life. After the apocalypse, "at the end of the world," mushrooms will do their work of starting new life.[2] However, I would say our most reliable comrades in the process of collective planetary repair and recovery are, ultimately, the plants. Contrary to humans, plants cannot leave a site of destruction. Instead, they just stay, grow, clean the air, and cool it down. Even in the harshest urban environment, plants are constantly doing the work of repair. They are natural repairers and have much more powerful capacities to repair the planet than we do.

In my book *Solar Politics*,[3] I also give the example of the wombats, who sheltered mice, lizards, and other small animals in their enormous burrows during the bushfires in Australia. Natural scientists immediately rushed in with explanations of the worst Darwinian sort. In line with a view of animals as primitive egoistic individuals struggling for survival, they explained that the wombats' behavior was not a result of kindness but a biological survival mechanism, and that to understand it as altruism would just be an anthropomorphization of the wombats. But I see the wombats as an avant-garde, much ahead of contemporary biological science, which is trapped in capitalist ideologies of individualism and the struggle for survival. What if altruism and solidarity are forms of behavior that we cheaply label as instinctual? Animals do not need rules or an ethics for what they do; they do not ask if their actions are good or bad. They simply do the work of solidarity, starting at the organic level. What if they do so because their relationship with their territories differs from humans' obsession with private property? As the Russian anarchist Piotr Kropotkin demonstrated in his book *Mutual Aid: A Factor of Evolution* from 1902, the struggle for survival is not the only driving force of the development of life on Earth; many species survive because they cooperate, communicate, and help each other.[4] Today Timothy Morton calls for solidarity with "nonhuman people," arguing that solidarity is not specifically human but "the default affective environment of the top layers of the Earth's crust."[5] We should be thankful for the work other beings do, and we can learn from them. Our solidarity is different because we are conscious of it. But we can take nonhuman behavior as a model and elevate it into a self-conscious human strategy. For instance, the war gives us a chance to be generous: We should be more like a wombat and share our home with those who don't have one anymore.

♂ Another chapter in our issue centers on the politics of "sufficiency." Much of the ecological discourse in architecture and other

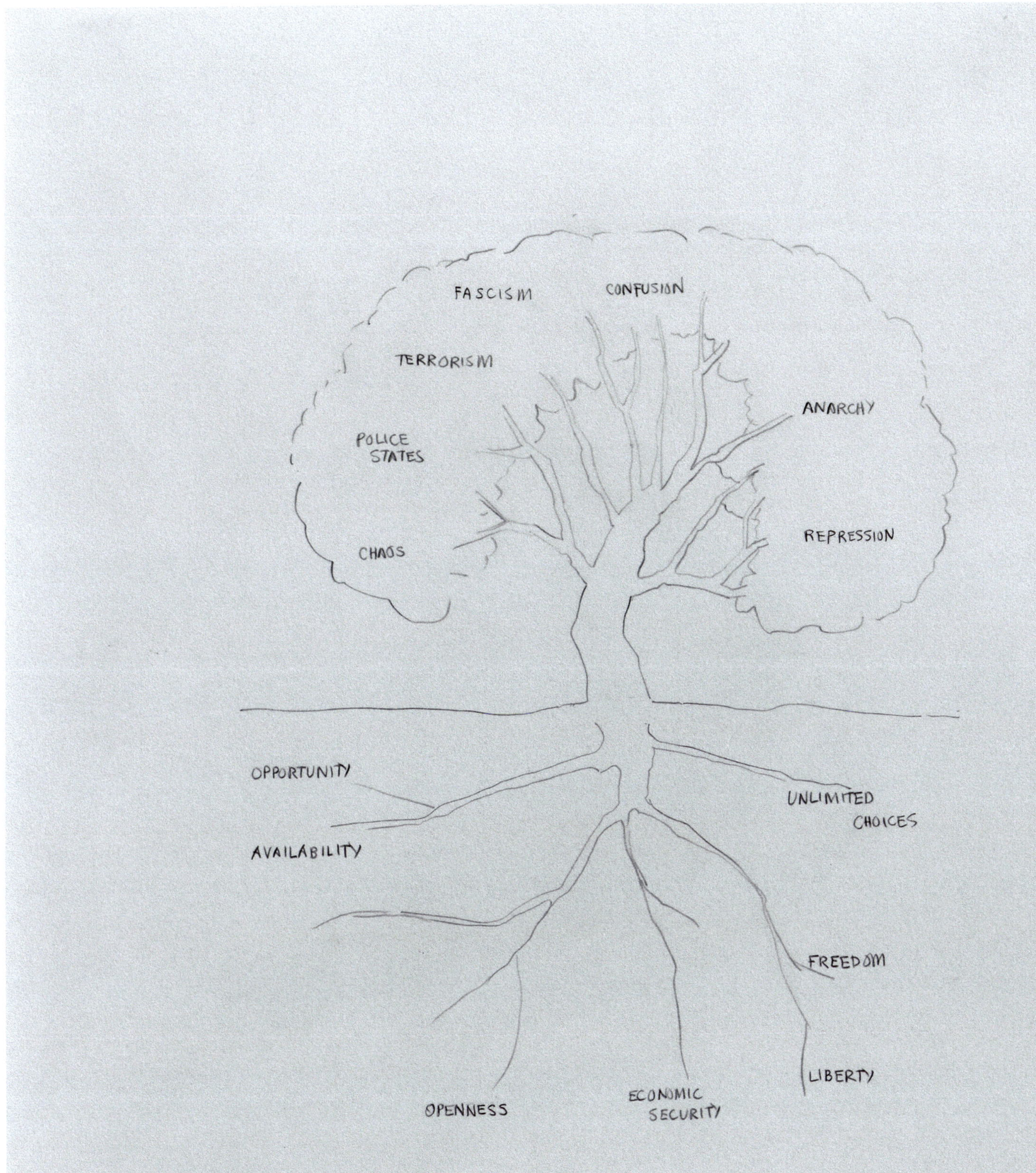

David Byrne, *Social Transformation*, 2002

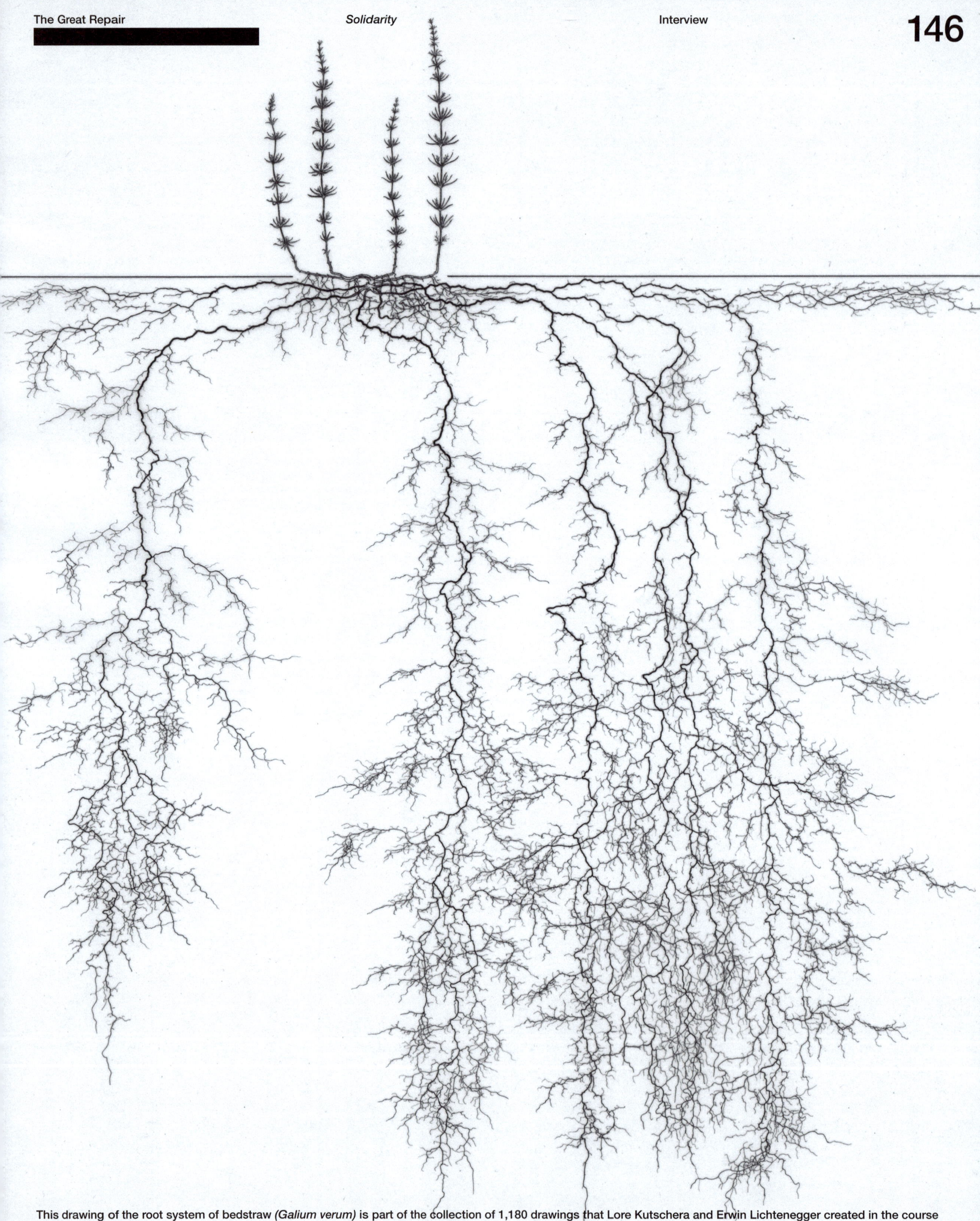

This drawing of the root system of bedstraw *(Galium verum)* is part of the collection of 1,180 drawings that Lore Kutschera and Erwin Lichtenegger created in the course of decades of research at the Pflanzensoziologisches Institut in Klagenfurt, Austria.

fields is based on concepts of scarcity and limits, striving to curb resource consumption and emissions. Your ecological thinking is partly inspired by the philosopher Georges Bataille, who explored the logics of abundance, exuberance, and generosity. When we think of the Great Repair, what role can these values play?

MT In other words, repair calls for counter-narratives to the paradigm of limitless growth and imagined progress that has characterized the history of modernity in architecture. So, is the alternative deindustrialization and demodernization, or can we reimagine progress in other ways?

OT That is such a difficult question. Of course, transformation should not be a step back to preindustrial times. That would just start the same cycle with the same methods of producing energy and supplies. Bataille suggests a more fundamental paradigm shift that I think can be helpful. Put very simply, there is a logic of greed that stands behind the capitalist economy, and there is a logic of generosity that Bataille ascribes to nature. This generosity is not necessarily good; it can also be destructive. But, in general, the logic of greed has led us to financial capitalism and the extractive industrial and post-industrial technologies we have now. They can only treat nature as a resource, which will always end in destruction. Wars are also the direct result of this extractivist and imperialist logic of constant appropriation and accumulation of goods, territory, and resources. Imperialist states are trapped within this logic. Instead, we could take the generosity of nature as a starting point for human societies, learn from it, and devise intentional ways of translating this principle into our actions. A reversal of ethics alone is not enough; we must translate it into a politics of generosity. On this basis, we could develop gift economies as opposed to economies of exchange—these are already anticipated in the concept of sharing and common use. Based on this, we can think about how to build cities that include nonhuman citizens, cities where worms and insects can thrive, and where pigeons will feel comfortable and welcome. We can think about how to build a city not only of solidarity but of justice for all, human and nonhuman, who have not been taken into account so far.

Nazlı Tümerdem In your book *How to Love a Homeland*, you use the image of "resisting like a plant."[6] What do you mean by this? Can this mode of resistance help us in contexts of authoritarian politics, technological control, and militarization, as we are currently experiencing in Russia and Turkey?

OT I wrote that book in 2019, before the war and before the pandemic. In the book, I asked how you can love your homeland under totalitarian regimes without falling into the trap of nationalism and fascism. This was a reference to Bertolt Brecht, especially his essay "Writing the Truth: Five Difficulties," in which he addresses German comrades who didn't immigrate but stayed in fascist Germany and worked in the underground resistance.[7] How do you do antifascist work when there is Gestapo all around? You need to write between the lines and struggle for truth. In that kind of context, the concept of truth takes on new meaning.

While writing the book, I didn't know that this would become my reality in just two years. That I would wake up and struggle to decide whether I should stay or go. Russian intellectuals are now having these discussions. At least half of them have left, and the other half have stayed. Those who remain learn to write between the lines, to evade censorship through code. If you emigrate, you will often have a more comfortable life and a new job; you are generally safe. You can also be more honest and openly state that you are against the war. But in Russia, you cannot do that without risking arrest. Those who have left sometimes accuse those who stay of collaboration, saying that if you remain, you are upholding the rules of this society. I am in between. I am here and there, always traveling. I'm a nomad; I can either leave or stay.

Before the war, I experienced my city, St. Petersburg, as a colorful place. But when the war began, the city somehow lost its color. It became gray, like the corridors of the KGB. I have a particular fascination for the city. The city is a complex symbiotic structure, and there is an ongoing struggle among its various signs. Pedestrians, for instance, can consciously transform themselves into a sign. If you wear an outfit with something like "No War" written on it, you know it's dangerous and that you can be arrested. But it represents an act of re-signifying, a small battle in the struggle for the city, to return color to it. These acts range from subtle gestures and indirect actions to bigger gestures and direct actions by the partisan movement in the city. This work remains when your city is already ruined—not bombed but ruined existentially. As in the example of the house in the woods, you repair these existential ruins little by little, so you can still inhabit the place.

And in doing so, you become like a plant. The state might say: "There will be only strawberries here." You are not a strawberry, you are just a weed, and you grow, nevertheless, through the strawberries. They always cut you down, but you grow back. This is a plant skill; plants literally take root underground. We should reclaim the metaphor of roots from the conservatives because it is revolutionary. You grow where they cannot find you. They may cut down what's on the surface and throw you in jail, but more will rise up from the same root. That is the work of the underground; it is a special kind of architecture.

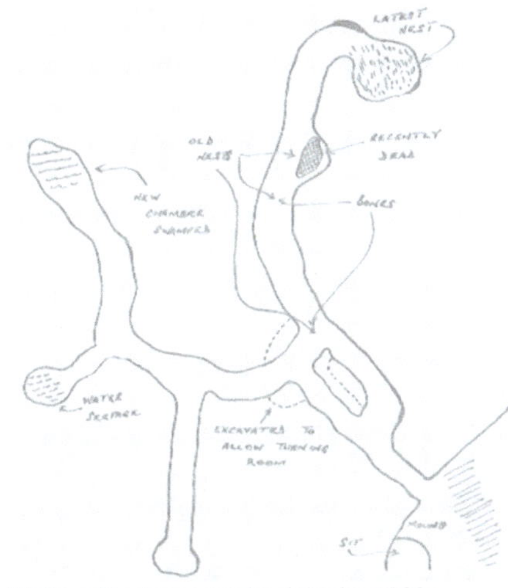

While still a teenager, back in the 1960s Australian Peter Nicholson started crawling on his knees to investigate wombat burrows and mapped the tunnel systems he found underground. In 2004, he launched the Wombat Foundation dedicated to the protection of the northern hairy-nosed wombat, which is threatened with extinction due to expanding cattle farming.

1   Donna J. Haraway, *Staying with the Trouble: Making Kin in the Chthulucene* (Durham: Duke University Press, 2016), 1.
2   Anna Lowenhaupt Tsing, *The Mushroom at the End of the World: On the Possibility of Life in Capitalist Ruins* (Princeton: Princeton University Press, 2015).
3   Oxana Timofeeva, *Solar Politics* (Cambridge: Polity Press, 2022).
4   Piotr Kropotkin, *Mutual Aid: A Factor of Evolution* (New York: McClure Phillips & Co., 1902).
5   Timothy Morton, *Humankind: Solidarity with Nonhuman People* (London: Verso, 2017), 14.
6   Oxana Timofeeva, *How to Love a Homeland* (Kayfa ta, 2020).
7   Bertolt Brecht, "Writing the Truth: Five Difficulties," in *Galileo*, ed. Eric Bentley, trans. Richard Winston (New York: Grove Press, 1966), 133–50.

plurality

Text: Santiago del Hierro

For a long time, the Western mainstream saw government control and privatization as the only two ways of managing common-pool natural resources. Elinor Ostrom, however, was able to prove in 1990 that many communities worldwide relied on institutions other than the state or the market to govern the commons.[1] Ostrom arrived at this conclusion only after several years of empirical research across the world, by taking the slow path of understanding how "others" tackled the problem of the commons. This case for theoretical and empirical plurality is merely one example of how the more we open up and think outside of the hegemonic box, the more we will find multiple approaches to commonly faced issues in different parts of the world.

Yet many of us are still (often unconsciously) trapped within the "one-world world" logic, which is dominated by Western capitalist modernity and negates other ways of seeing the world.[2] From the "one-world" perspective, plurality can be seen as

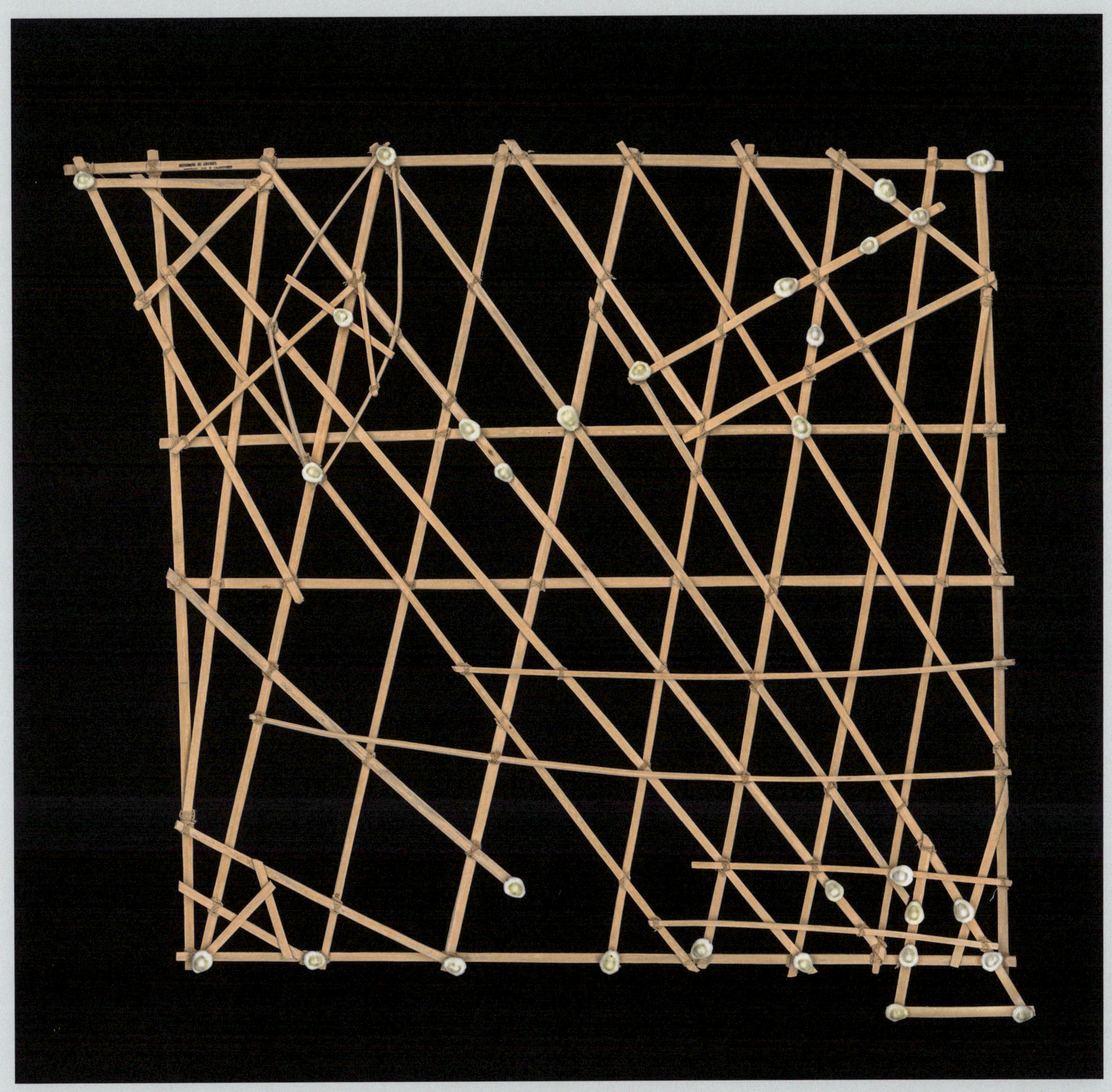

Rebbelib are navigational charts that were used by the Indigenous inhabitants of the Marshall Islands when moving through the island atolls by canoe. The straight sticks represent currents, while the cowries identify the locations of the atolls and islands. The Marshall Islands are located in the Pacific Ocean between Papua New Guinea and Hawaii and today are among the parts of the world most under threat by climate change.

The film *La Montaña* documents how a delegation of Zapatistas sailed from Mexico to Europe—in the opposite direction to the route of the Spanish conquistadors—to mark the 500th anniversary of Spanish colonization. The press photo was taken in 2019 before their departure on Isla Mujeres curin Mexico.

a sociopolitical challenge to a stable society.[3] Decolonial theorists, however, mainly from the Global South, argue that a move towards a decolonial form of plurality, better described as "pluriversality," is crucial for leaving behind Western universalism that subsumes all other forms of knowledge production.

Pluriversality draws inspiration from the Zapatista axiom of a "world where many worlds fit."[4] It highlights the multiplicity of possible worlds or ways of knowing, acting, and being while emphasizing the importance of thinking beyond human plurality. The environmental crisis calls for new ways of relating to our natural context. In many Indigenous cosmologies, the nature-culture continuum (instead of a dichotomy) has been self-evident for millennia.[5] Countries like Ecuador and Bolivia have already begun to include the rights of nature, independent of human interests, within their legal systems, coinciding with a rise in political power for Indigenous groups.[6] The thought of a pluriversal future that thrives in difference raises hope. There are other ways. There are many ways.

1   Elinor Ostrom, *Governing the Commons: The Evolution of Institutions for Collective Action* (Cambridge: Cambridge University Press, 1990).
2   Aníbal Quijano, "Coloniality and Modernity/Rationality," *Cultural Studies* 21, nos. 2–3 (2007): 168–78; Israel Holas Allimant and Eugenia Demuro, "Reading the World Anew: Zapatista Stories, the Denial of Singularity, and the Creation of a Plural World," *Journal of Postcolonial Writing* 56, no. 6 (2020): 830–44. Édouard Glissant, "For Opacity," in *Poetics of Relation*, trans. Betsy Wing (Ann Arbor: University of Michigan Press, 1997).
3   Andrea Blair Vasconcelos and Fran Martin, *Plurality, Plurilogicality, and Pluriversality: A Literature Review* (Exeter: Creativity and Emergent Educational-futures Network (CEEN), Graduate School of Education, University of Exeter, 2019).
4   Walter D. Mignolo, foreword to *Constructing the Pluriverse: The Geopolitics of Knowledge*, ed. Bernd Reiter (Durham: Duke University Press, 2018). Arturo Escobar, *Designs for the Pluriverse: Radical Interdependence, Autonomy, and the Making of Worlds* (Durham: Duke University Press, 2018).
5   James Clifford, *Returns: Becoming Indigenous in the Twenty-First Century* (Cambridge: Harvard University Press, 2013).
6   Gwendolyn Gordon, "Environmental Personhood," *SSRN Electronic Journal*, March 7, 2017, 6.

A World

Text: Iván Darío Vargas Roncancio

Uaira Uaua / Benjamín Jacanamijoy Tisoy, *En un lugar de las hojas del árbol de viento* (detail), 2018   Acrylic on canvas, 120 × 150 cm

where Many worlds Fit

Radiating the serene joy of decades of experience and struggle, an Indigenous elder from a local community in Bajo Putumayo in the Colombian Amazon was seated on an old-looking stool. He held something that looked like a piece of cord. "Pedro passed away," he said, and then went silent. As I introduced myself and paid my respects, I recognized that the cord in his hand was in fact the skin of a plant. At that moment, I realized that he was not talking about a person, but the plant, *yoco*.[1]

Paullinia yoco is a tropical climbing vine that grows up to 15 meters long. Usually it is harvested in the wild and sometimes cultivated in *chagras*—an Amazonian slash-and-burn cultivation system. Often referred to as the forest's sap, yoco is important to the diet and rituals of communities across the Amazonian regions of Peru, Ecuador, and Colombia to this day. Conventionally used as a breakfast infusion, yoco allays hunger and stimulates the muscles.[2] To prepare yoco as a beverage, one carefully rasps the phloem layer of the plant with a knife and dissolves the resulting particles in cold water. Besides its tonic properties, yoco is an antipyretic for treating malaria fever and a remedy for treating bilious disease, which is common in the Putumayo region.[3] Yoco has emetic, psychoactive, contraceptive, and even abortive properties, and people in Amazonia maintain that it provides advice to those who ingest it. More than a plant, however, yoco is a person. And more than a person, it is a mode of relation, of learning, and co-participating in forest life.

An encounter

The bitter and earthy taste of the yoco infusion sparked an instant sensation of warmth in my limbs and head, before igniting a mild *chuma* (dizziness) as my body quivered in slow motion. The chuma grew stronger, and my stomach turned in on itself, expelling both the bile and the plant with the urgency of powerful relief. Bewildered and grateful, I imagined the vibrant presence of gentle song sprouting from the surrounding trees …

The concept of plants as teachers is a well-established trope in Amazonian ethnology.[4] In Luis Elvira Belaunde's and Juan Alvaro Echeverri's ethnological study, the Indigenous Airo-pai (Secoya) know the cuacuiyó bird as the *ëjaë* or owner of the plant. The cuacuiyó feed their offspring by swallowing the yoco's fruit, or *guayo*, and then spitting out the seeds to retain the pulp for their chicks. In this way, the birds distribute the seeds in the forest. Much like the cuacuiyó using the yoco to raise and nurture their chicks, the Secoya people employ this plant to educate their human children about how to live in the forest.[5]

"Yoco is like morning coffee for us, because you drink it fresh and cold very early in the morning before you go to work, and it'll give you *fuerza* (strength)," a Cofán Indigenous elder once told me. To be sure, given the concentration of caffeine and theobromine,[6] a single cup of the infusion is an effective stimulant to endure long hours working in the forest. More crucially, however, yoco teaches an ethics of living well by cultivating a fresh mind (*mente despejada*): The tonic and purgative properties of the plant train the human "to get rid of laziness (to work and think) and to purge the anger"[7] in their dealings with others—human and not. This form of education conceptualizes learning as purging to remove what inhibits the expression of a fresh mind to think, say, act, and live well with the forest.

However, contrary to Western notions of spiritual purification, which are human-centered, this is a multispecies perspective. The former aim to cleanse the body by removing all that is nonhuman in order to approach a state of purity that will help achieve clarity of mind. By this notion, detachment from the world leads to the attainment of an ideal of human self-awareness and self-realization. But for the Secoya, a clear mind is attained not through separation but through human connection with other species—engagement with the nonhuman.

Call of the cuacuiyó bird

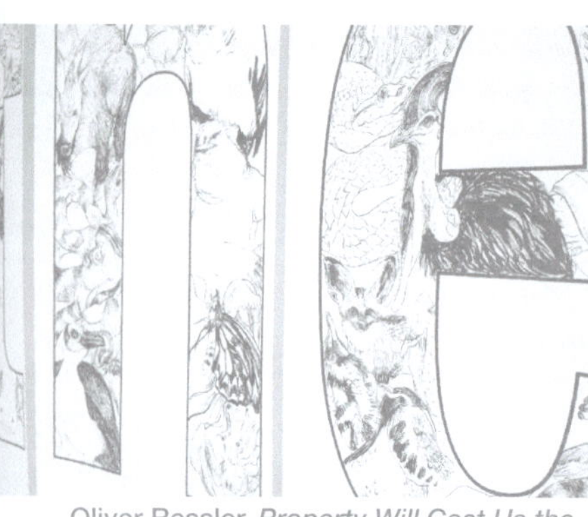

Oliver Ressler, *Property Will Cost Us the Earth* (Detail), 2021
With his ink-drawn words *Property Will Cost Us the Earth*, artist Oliver Ressler quotes human ecologist Andreas Malm, who views the logics of property and capital as the cause for wide-scale species extinction. Within the contours of the individual letters, hundreds of animal species acutely threatened with extinction force their way into the foreground.

Like the cuacuiyó bird feeding her chicks, the plant feeds us through the embodied experience of acquiring a fresh mind by ingesting a vegetal body. Learning with yoco, however, exceeds liberal deference toward a vegetal "other." It is about learning how to engage with the yoco's perspective and being able to see the world from this vantage point. More than the representation of an external reality, this learning process requires the ingestion of the plant as a some*body* rather than a some*thing*. *Chuma*, the feeling of dizziness, is both physically cleansing and a learning technique to listen to the forest. It brings about a distinct form of attunement to and unity with forest life. It is an interspecies form of communication through the material engagements of mixing bodies, a form of co-participation in the larger mind of the forest. Learning with yoco is quite explicitly a form of ethical training to become better partners for our wounded and flourishing Earth.[8] Through incessant acts of embodied engagement with the nonhuman, this multispecies cleanse teaches us an ethics of coexistence, co-responsibility, and care for the nonhuman within and outside ourselves.[9]

This is urgent at the present time because, to paraphrase the sociologist Boaventura de Sousa Santos, we are facing modern problems for which there are not (only) modern solutions.[10] In the forest fires that ravaged the Brazilian Amazon in 2019, the destructive consequences of modernity came to a catastrophic climax: biodiversity loss, illegal grabbing of Indigenous lands, and racialized violence against local populations. To break out of this vicious loop, we can learn from Indigenous and vegetal territorial logics of care. I firmly believe that other-than-human knowledge practices and lifeways should be at the forefront of contemporary debates around socio-ecological challenges and transitions worldwide. Our vegetal friends in particular can teach us new pathways to "mutually enhancing relationships" between humans and Earth,[11] towards a new epoch of repair, care, and co-responsibility where all beings are regarded as social agents and members of the community of life. These new relationships require new conceptual tools. The notion of the "pluriverse"[12] is a worldmaking alternative to the present "modernist ontology of universalism"[13] and may offer guidance as we reimagine learning and teaching for our catastrophic times.

Contesting universalism

The "modernist ontology of universalism"[14] is based upon a dualist principle that separates human and nonhuman beings, body and mind, bio and geo, the living and the non-living. This "ontology of separation"[15] determines how people produce knowledge, how they act, experience the world, relate to one another, and organize collectively. For example, the discipline of physics presupposes the separation between an objective universe and the subjective experience and cultural beliefs of an independent human observer; similarly, the discipline of economics separates markets from the socio-ecosystems where they are actually embedded,[16] and the same is true for almost all descriptive and normative disciplines of the modern learning/teaching apparatus. In this regard, anthropologist Eduardo Viveiros de Castro suggests that in the modern scientific paradigm, one knows something when one is able to see it from the outside, that is, when the world is de-subjectivized and no intentions are attributed to the object of study (e.g., plants, animals, complex tropical ecologies). In contrast, for traditional medicine people (*sabedores*) in the so-called Americas, to know something well is to be able to attribute intentionality to this object of study, namely when this object is rendered a subject.[17]

The modern ontology of universalism, then, is about creating "One World"[18] based on two core ideas: first, the notion of a single world made up of discrete and separable entities rather than interdependencies, and second, the notion that this world can be revealed only by science at the expense of other knowledge systems, or by relegating them to the status of cultural beliefs and/or myths of non-modern peoples.[19] The idea of the One World thus suggests the primacy of one local experience (the "West") and system of knowledge ("Science") as the only veritable source of knowledge of an external world as observed by a particular kind of human: the Western Man. The modernist ontology of universalism is at the root of the ongoing colonization and destruction of ecological and cultural systems throughout the world, among other reasons, because it turns life itself into an object of knowledge and a resource of economic value. This ontology of universalism shapes everything from worldviews to socioeconomic, political, and legal systems by which peoples organize their lives and their relationships with their territories.

But alternatives to this paradigm proliferate everywhere. The pluriversal alternative, for example, challenges this modernist orientation in favor of a multiplicity of possible worlds or ways of knowing, doing, and being.[20] Following the Zapatista dictum, the pluriverse can be best described as "a world where many worlds fit" (*un mundo donde quepan muchos mundos*),[21] namely a world where many ways of being, doing, and knowing are rendered possible and are put at the service of repairing or, better yet, "healing the web of life."[22]

Searching for answers to the ongoing global crisis of climate and justice, the pluriversal alternative contests universalism without falling into cultural relativism. Cultural relativism arose as a counter-project to Western universalism and attributes to all cultures their own ways of thinking and value systems. But it still presupposes the existence of an external and thus universal reality, shared across different cultural groups. This theory allows these different cultural groups to have different views of reality—but assumes that there is only one reality.[23] Seen from the perspective of cultural relativism, culture thus remains separated from this external nature; nature is perceived as the passive backdrop of human action and the human as the only cognitive and meaning-making self in the cosmos.[24]

Conversely, the pluriverse presupposes a relational view of life. It acknowledges that nonhuman beings, such as animals, plants, rivers, mountains, and forests, are sentient and cognitive,[25] and that the human is part of the web of life and, therefore, only one subject in the community of life.[26] The pluriverse seeks to bring forth different "ways of worlding,"[27] namely a meshwork of practices, ways of producing knowledge, doing things, and contributing to a regenerative web of life. In that sense, the pluriverse has more to do with learning to create worlds beyond the human[28]—or beyond the culture/nature divide—than with creating knowledge about a world outside of us.

Amerindian cosmologies exemplify this way of worlding in the pluriverse. For example, in Amazonia, animals, plants, mountains, and rivers, among other beings, are endowed with a form of interiority or "a soul (*wakan*) similar to that of humans. This constitutes a faculty that classifies them as 'persons' (*aents*) in that it provides them with a reflexive awareness and intentionality that enable them to experience emotions and exchange messages with their peers and members of other species, including humans."[29] In this region, the world is not intrinsically organized through the stable categories of nature and culture since all beings (human and not) share a common interiority concealed beneath the mask of their own bodies. The pluriversal project thus suggests that individual humans as such *do not exist*, that is, the individual is a modern fiction based on the premise of separation

Paullinia yoco

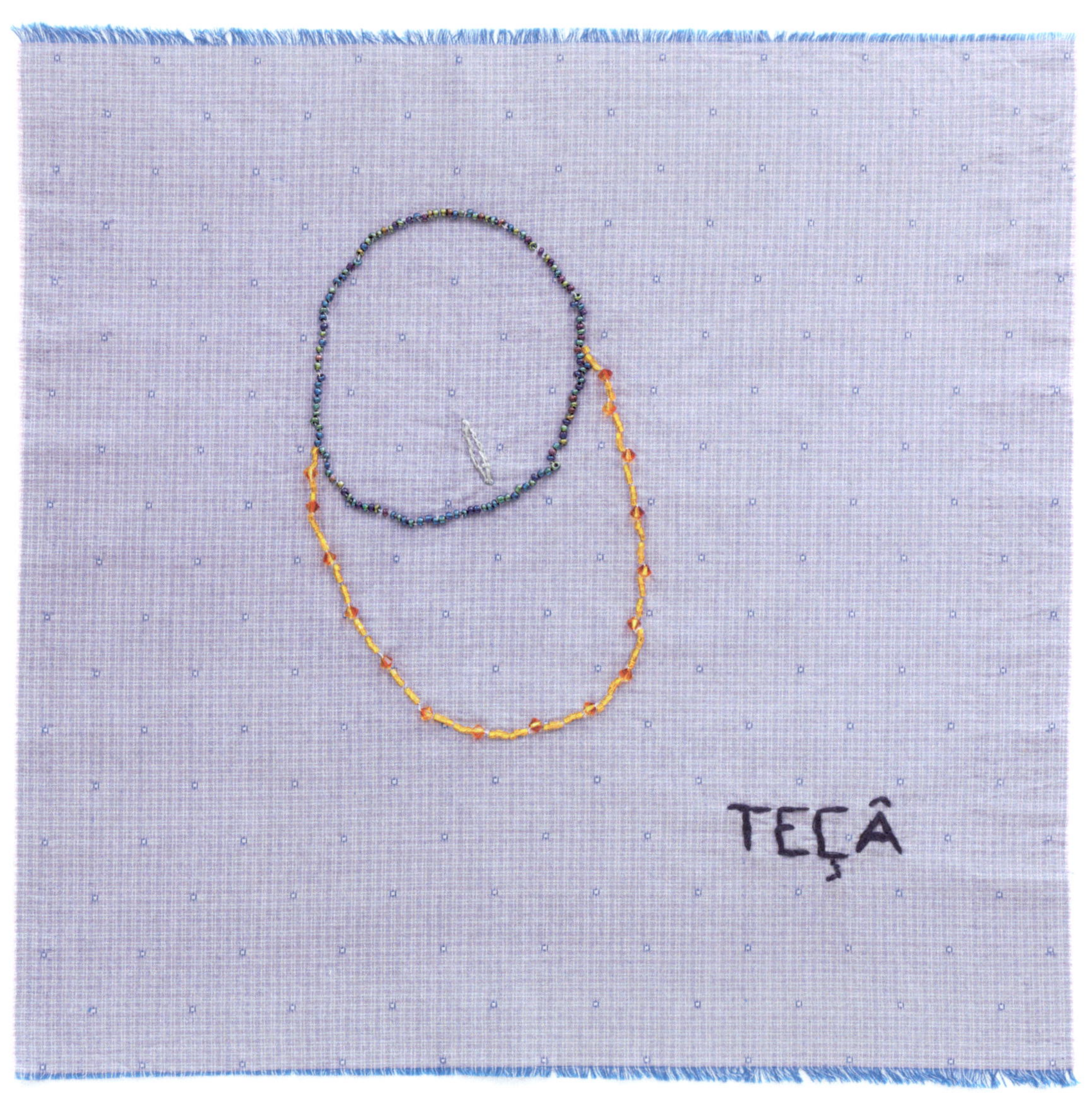

Maria Thereza Alves, *Invisible Shadows: Teçâ* (Eye), *Apigçâ* (Ear), *Jurû* (Mouth), 2015
Fabric, thread, glass beads, each 37 × 37 cm

With the almost complete eradication of the Tupinambá, an Indigenous people originally at home in the Brazilian Atlantic rainforest, by the European colonizers, their language, Tupi, likewise disappeared, as did knowledge of the natural region and all its species. The bead embroideries by Maria Thereza Alves recreate seed pods that the artist found during her visit to the city of Ubatuba from where parts of her Tupinambá family originate.

JURÛ

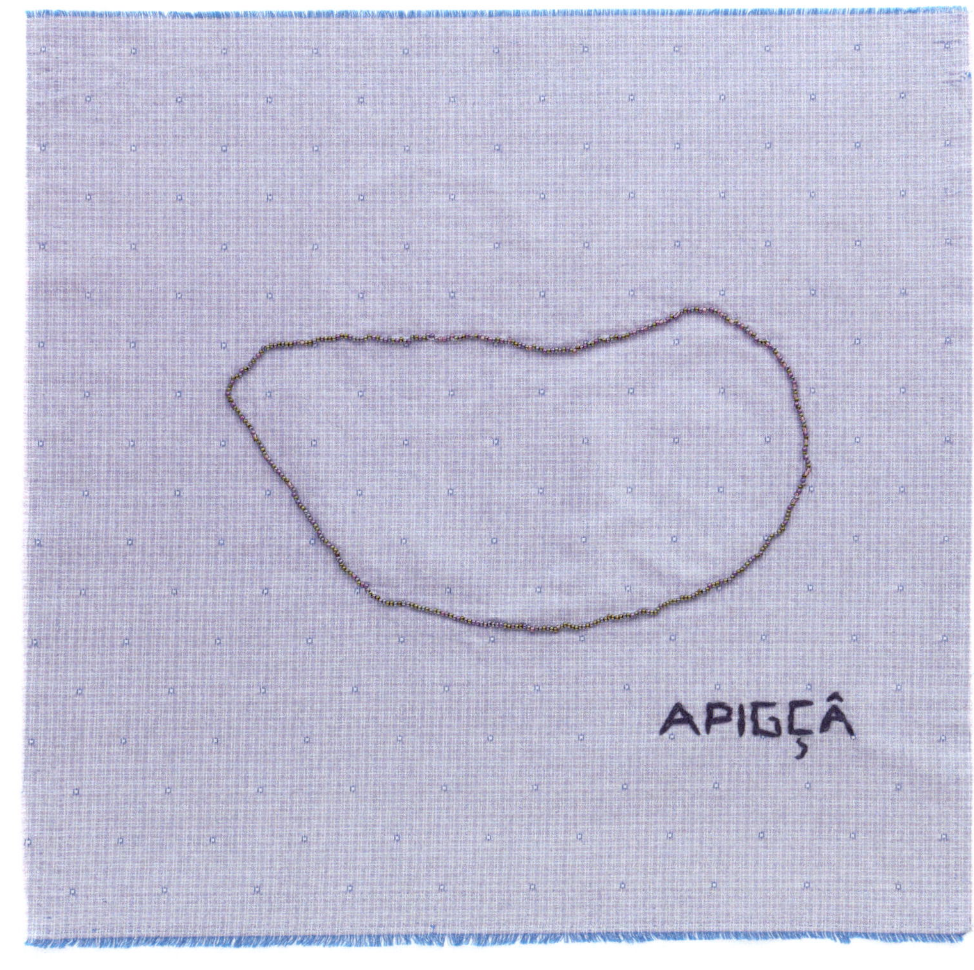
APIGÇÂ

The Kamukuwaká cave is a sacred site of the Wauja people in Brazil. The Indigenous community used carved cave drawings to pass down its history and culture. In 2018, these drawings were destroyed by unknown persons. The background to the act may have been conflicts between the Indigenous communities and the incursion of the agro-industry. In 2020, the Factum Foundation used high-res 3D imaging techniques and the knowledge of the Wauja and Kuikuro community to create a true-to-scale reconstruction of the cave.

1   This text is a revised and expanded version of Iván Darío Vargas Roncancio, "The Pluriverse and the Ecozoic: a Convergence of Agendas? Towards a Pluriversal Learning," *L4E Ecological Law Blog*, accessed November 7, 2022, www.l4ecozoic.org/post/the-pluriverse-and-the-ecozoic-a-convergence-of-agendas-towards-a-pluriversal-learning-by-iv%C3%A1n-v.

2   Luisa Elvira Belaunde and Juan Alvaro Echeverri, "El yoco del cielo es cultivado: perspectivas sobre Paullinia yoco en el chamanismo airo-pai (secoya-tucano occidental)," *Anthropologica* 26, no. 26 (2008): 87–111.

3   See Ken Fern, *Tropical Plants Database*, accessed November 7, 2022, tropical.theferns.info/viewtropical.php?id=Paullinia+yoco; William T. Vickers and Timothy Plowman, "Useful Plants of the Siona and Secoya Indians of Eastern Ecuador," *Fieldiana: Botany New Series* 15 (1984): 1–63; Richard E. Schultes, "Plantae Colombianae IV. Una planta estimulante del Putumayo," *Revista de la Facultad Nacional de Agronomia* (1943): 59–79; Richard E. Schultes, "Recognition of Variability in Wild Plants by Indians of the Northwest Amazon: An Enigma," *Journal of Ethnobiology* 6, no. 2 (1986): 229–38; Richard E. Schultes, "Plantae Colombianae II. Yoco: A Stimulant of Southern Colombia," *Botanical Museum Leaflets* 10, no. 10 (1942): 301–24; Luke M. Weiss and James K. Kearns, "Caffeine and Theobromine Analysis of *Paullinia yoco*, a Vine Harvested by Indigenous Peoples of the Upper Amazon," *Tropical Resources* 34 (2015): 6–15.

4   Luis Eduardo Luna, "The Concept of Plants as Teachers among Four Mestizo Shamans of Iquitos, Northeastern Peru," *Journal of Ethnopharmacology* 11, no. 2 (1984): 135–56.

5   Belaunde and Echeverri, "El yoco" (see note 2), 87.

6   See William F. Coleman, "Chocolate: Theobromine and Caffeine," *Journal of Chemical Education* 81, no. 8 (2004): 1232. Yoco intake seems to be decreasing in this region. Factors involve the accelerated deforestation of Amazonian forests for cattle, monoculture, and other forms of extraction.

7   Translation by the author from the Spanish expression "para [botar] la pereza y [purgar] la rabia" in Belaunde and Echeverri, "El yoco" (see note 2), 107.

8   Eduardo Kohn, *How Forests Think* (Berkeley: University of California Press, 2013).

9   A longer version of the discussion about yoco can be found in Iván Darío Vargas Roncancio, "Yoco *(Paullinia yoco)*," in *The Mind of Plants*, eds. John C. Ryan et al. (Santa Fe: Synergetic Press, 2021).

10   Boaventura de Sousa Santos, *Epistemologies of the South: Justice against Epistemicide* (Boulder: Paradigm Publishers, 2014).

11   Thomas Berry, *The Great Work: Our Way into the Future* (New York: Bell Tower, 1999), 61.

12   Zapatistas, "Cuarta Declaración de la Selva Lacandona," January 1, 1996, accessed November 7, 2022, enlacezapatista.ezln.org.mx/1996/01/01/cuarta-declaracion-de-la-selva-lacandona Zapatistas; Arturo Escobar, *Designs for the Pluriverse: Radical Interdependence, Autonomy, and the Making of Worlds* (Durham: Duke University Press, 2018).

13   Ashish Kothari et al., eds., *Pluriverse: A Post-Development Dictionary* (New Delhi: Tulika Books, 2019), xviii. Broadly speaking, we define ontology as a set of claims about what the world is, as well as a set of practices through which the world comes into being for a people that is part of it. Epistemology here stands for how people represent the world, for example, through language and/or images.

rather than the premise of radical interdependence of all that exists. This theory of the self—as multiple natures or bodies sharing a common interiority or culture across different kinds of beings—affords a quite different understanding of experience and knowledge as something beyond cultural or human meaning only.[30]

While the pluriversal alternative offers a multiplicity of ways of knowing, it is not only about knowledge creation. It is also about learning how to create new worlds and possibilities, namely different ways of feeling, being, and doing. Today, Indigenous peoples resist the modernist ontology of separation described above when they mobilize on behalf of mountains, rivers, spirits, and forests, arguing that these are sentient beings rather than cultural beliefs, objects, or resources to be exploited for capitalist expansion.[31] From the central ethical claim of the pluriversal project—that human and other-than-human beings constitute a community of subjects endowed with cognitive abilities, affective life, and rights—a movement has emerged that fights for the recognition of nature as a legal subject.[32]

But the project of a pluriverse as an ethical and political alternative can also encompass a set of other, quite different practices, knowledge systems, and ways of being, all informed by the principle of "radical interdependence of everything that exists."[33] Examples of these are Indigenous ancestral and innovative practices with the land and food production; post-development economies such as degrowth and *Buen Vivir*; care work; healing practices beyond allopathic medicine based on the regeneration of local ecosystems; commons and communing. Several scientific practices also share a belief in a plurality of realities, following from a commitment to mind–world monism (rather than dualism), such as the notion of the "embodied mind" in the work of Francisco Varela, Evan Thompson, and Eleanor Rosch.[34] In a wider sense, the endosymbiotic theory of biologist Lynn Margulis can also be counted among them, which proposes a view of evolution as based on cooperation and symbiosis rather than competition.[35] Many of these practices "echo the autopoietic dynamics and creativity of the Earth," as the Columbian anthropologist Arturo Escobar writes, "and the indubitable fact that no living being exists independently of the Earth."[36]

Thinking-feeling

How, then, might new, pluriversal forms of learning and teaching be designed to contribute to an ethic of care for today's times? In a footnote to "Thinking-Feeling with the Earth: Territorial Struggles and the Ontological Dimension of the Epistemologies of the South," Escobar describes the noun *sentipensamiento* or thinking-feeling— first reported by Colombian sociologist Orlando Fals Borda[37]—as "the

living principle of the riverine and swamp communities of Colombia's Caribbean coast." *Sentipensar*, the verb, implies "the art of living based on thinking with both heart and mind. *Sentipensamiento* was later popularized by the Uruguayan writer Eduardo Galeano as the ability found among popular classes to act without separating mind and body, reason and emotion."[38]

The Mexican community of Santa María Natívitas was devastated by an earthquake in 2017. The idea was to rebuild it using traditional knowledge and techniques. Feminist practice Comunal: Taller de Arquitectura from Mexico City supported the community in assessing traditional architecture's ability to withstand earthquakes and improve it. On the basis of jointly conducted mappings of the territory, a production strategy was devised to produce the 100,000 clay bricks needed to rebuild the houses.

The aspirational ethics of this form of learning is based on a crucial ontological assumption: The One World of colonialism, modernity, and development is only one among many worlding possibilities. *Sentipensar*, as Fals Borda learned with the riverine communities of Northern Colombia, is a methodological principle for what he called a *ciencia propia* (our own science) as a response to intellectual colonialism and cognitive injustice in the relationship between the Global South and the Global North.[39]

Planetary crises such as the climate catastrophe and biocultural loss are not only insistent and painful reminders that the One World feeds off of the destruction of other worlds. Yet, this One World, paraphrasing the Zapatista adage, is already a "world of many worlds, a world where many worlds can (and should) fit" across deeply disturbed socio-ecologies. These times of acute "interrelated crisis of energy, climate, food, justice and meaning"[40] call for old and new forms of *sentipensar*—for a new science of relationships and plurality that reckons with the sentience and cognitive affordances of other members of the "community of subjects" that include plants like the yoco. To do this, we must decenter established systems of human-centered perception, meaning, and identity, and instead co-create the world with plants and other beings. We need to create a vision of the future that seriously and skillfully weaves together the strands of self-critical Western science, Indigenous cosmologies, and other-than-human modes of presence and action. How can we translate this vision into new forms of inquiry and action for the pluriverse? Perhaps plants and trees can give us some guidance.

14   Ibid.
15   Iván Darío Vargas Roncancio et al., "From the Anthropocene to Mutual Thriving: An Agenda for Higher Education in the Ecozoic," *Sustainability* 11, no. 12 (2019): 3312.
16   Peter G. Brown and Peter Timmerman, *Ecological Economics for the Anthropocene* (New York: Columbia University Press, 2015).
17   Eduardo Viveiros de Castro, *La mirada del jaguar: Introducción al perspectivismo amerindio* (Buenos Aires: Tinta Limon, 2013).
18   John Law, "What's Wrong with a One-World World?," *Distinktion: Journal of Social Theory* 16, no. 1 (2015): 126–39; see also Escobar, *Designs for the Pluriverse* (see note 12).
19   Marisol de la Cadena, *Earth Beings: Ecologies of Practice* (Durham: Duke University Press, 2015).
20   Kothari et al., *Pluriverse* (see note 13).
21   Zapatistas, "Cuarta Declaración" (see note 12).
22   Arturo Escobar, "Healing the Web of Life: On the Meaning of Environmental and Health Equity," *International Journal of Public Health* 64 (2019): 3–4.
23   Tim Ingold, *Being Alive: Essays on Movement, Knowledge and Description* (Abingdon: Routledge, 2011).
24   Kohn, *Forests* (see note 8).
25   Monica Gagliano, *Thus Spoke the Plant: A Remarkable Journey of Groundbreaking Scientific Discoveries and Personal Encounters with Plants* (Berkeley: North Atlantic Books, 2018).
26   Berry, *Great Work* (see note 11).
27   Kothari et al., *Pluriverse* (see note 13).

28   Kohn, *Forests* (see note 8).
29   Philippe Descola, *Beyond Nature and Culture*, trans. Janet Lloyd (Chicago: University of Chicago Press, 2013), 5.
30   Kohn, *Forests* (see note 8).
31   Kothari et al., *Pluriverse* (see note 13).
32   Anthony Zelle et al., eds., *Earth Law. Emerging Ecocentric Law: A Practitioner's Guide* (New York: Wolters Kluwer, 2021).
33   Escobar, *Designs for the Pluriverse* (see note 12).
34   Francisco J. Varela et al., *The Embodied Mind: Cognitive Science and Human Experience* (Cambridge: MIT Press, 1999).
35   Lynn Sagan (Margulis), "On the Origin of Mitosing Cells," *Journal of Theoretical Biology* 14, no. 3 (1967): 225–74.
36   Arturo Escobar, "Transiciones: A Space for Research and Design for Transitions to the Pluriverse," *Design Philosophy Papers* 13, no. 1 (2015): 14.
37   Orlando Fals Borda, *Resistencia en el San Jorge* (Bogotá: Carlos Valencia Editores, 1984).
38   Arturo Escobar, "Thinking-Feeling with the Earth: Territorial Struggles and the Ontological Dimension of the Epistemologies of the South," *Revista de Antropología Iberoamericana* 11, no. 1 (2016): 14.
39   In education today, there are many practices of worldmaking that oppose the regime of the One World. See for example the network PeDAGoG (Post-Development Academic-Activist Global Group), accessed November 7, 2022, globaltapestryofalternatives.org/pedagog.
40   Escobar, "Thinking-Feeling" (see note 38).

Repairing the

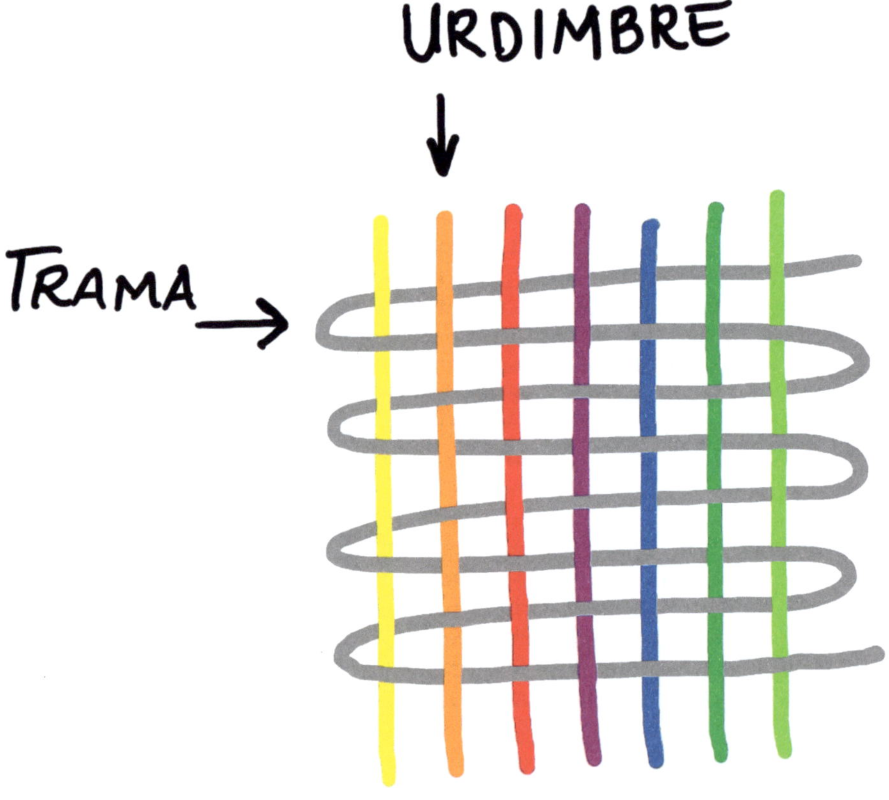

This is a text composed of nine threads from a conversation we had with five women and two men belonging to the Inga people of Colombia. The focus is on the multiple meanings that repair has in Inga thought and tradition. We, Santiago and Álvaro, met with Agripina, Antonia, Liliana, Mariela, Yeni, Pablo, and Pedro in several sessions. They shared with us their thoughts about the present, their concerns about the future, and their view of what needs to be fixed and what repair means to them.

The word "text" comes from the Latin *textum*, which means fabric. Creating a text with nine voices means interweaving different perspectives into the fabric of a single discussion that follows a continuous narrative. Considering the importance of verbal communication for the Inga people, we faced the challenge of finding a way to transmit the strength of the spoken word through the written word. We have called this a "pluritext" to highlight the plurality of thoughts and the method of collective coproduction.

The Inga people of Colombia are widely recognized for the richness of their material culture, expressed primarily in their textiles. The fabrics they wear daily are at the same time woven artworks, expressing their way of thinking and seeing the world. In some way, Inga fabrics are a representation system, a living script that helps them to understand the world and express life in its multiple dimensions.

There are two main components of any fabric: the weft *(trama)* and the warp *(urdimbre)*. The weft intertwines the warp and gives it consistency, but it is the warp that creates the original shapes. In this exercise, our seven Inga companions will be the warp, the heart of thought and expression, while we, Santiago and Álvaro, will be the weft of the text, looking for common forms within the multiplicity.

Text: Antonia Agreda, Liliana Armero, Pablo Cuchalá, Santiago del Hierro, Agripina Garreta, Álvaro Hernández Bello, Yeni Yolanda Jacanamijoy, Pedro Jajoy, Mariela Pujimuy   Transcription support: Lizeth Córdoba

Fabric of Life

WHAT SHOULD BE REPAIRED?

Repairing is an act, a process, an event that is critical and proactive at the same time. Repair requires the courage to change and care, and the will to not cause new harm. The first step, the first thread necessary for repair, however, is to develop an awareness of the damage itself. This first section is just that: a call to consciousness from the point of view of a group of people who live in a corner of the world where one thinks and feels about the world in a very particular way.

A disharmonized territory

The Andean Amazon, a territory with great biological diversity, lives in a delicate balance. But due to internal and external causes, this territory is in disharmony. In light of this situation, the Inga are convinced that repair and reparation must begin locally, in their home, in their territory. They view with concern

> "the disharmony that exists within the territory. [Thus] one of our tasks has been to begin by repairing all our internal relations with the spiritual guidance of our elders through the sacred plant of yagé."

Ancestral wisdom guides the Inga people through the yagé or ayahuasca ceremony, a ritual to repair spirit and thought.

> "We first have to repair our way of life before we can repair what is around us."
> *Yeni Yolanda Jacanamijoy*

Some are concerned that corrections might happen in a way

> "that could further damage the territory or cause Inga culture to be forgotten. We have to transform past problems into opportunities." *Mama Antonia Agreda*

Many of the external threats to the territory share the same logic, reducing the value of life to a price and setting profit as the primary purpose of all human activity.

> "The state is only usufructuary of our Mother Earth (we call her Alpa Mama): She does not belong to it, but it makes a profit from her. This has greatly harmed our Alpa Mama."
> *Mama Agripina Garreta*

The logic of usufruct has a lot to do with the logic of colonization, which was and still is felt in the territory today.

> "When we talk about repairing our Mother Earth, our Alpa Mama, I think of colonization. Since the arrival of what we call *iurakuna*, white people, tremendous upheavals have taken place that have led to the worse. From the perspective of the Inga, our Alpa Mama used to be a healthy territory, and now it's not."
> *Yeni Yolanda Jacanamijoy*

Broken relationships

To repair is to reweave, to intertwine again. Fundamentally, it consists of restoring a relationship—the relationship with animals, plants, rivers, other humans, and all other living beings with whom we share our common home. In Colombia, armed conflict has been the main factor of disharmony within communities and territories.

> "We know the strengths of our community and the wealth of our territory. We are therefore convinced that we Inga people can help repair the social fabric destroyed by the armed conflict. If we recognize our wealth, we can all mutually support each other, build coexistence, and enable participation so we can develop together as one."
> *Mama Agripina Garreta*

A disjointed society loses its values, traditions, and ways of life that otherwise ensure harmony in the territory.

> "A rewoven society is a sum of connections that extend over time: we

must continue accompanying the life process of our children, even our grandchildren! It is up to us to claim that ancestral connection, especially because our future generations have the right to know about their cultural origin."
Mariela Pujimuy

An ancient culture

Harmony in the territory arises from the harmony between beings and their ways of life. A central principle in the worldview of the Inga people is *suma kausay* (good living or well-being), an ancient philosophy shared with many other native peoples throughout the continent. It teaches ways to relate harmoniously with all beings. Thought is inseparable from language; it is the backbone of Inga culture. Consequently, revitalizing the Inga language is crucial:

> "A fundamental element we have to repair and rectify at this time is our language. Its recovery is urgent because all our knowledge is transmitted through our language. Losing language means losing knowledge. With language, we classify, recognize, express, and share all of the elements of our thought." *Mama Antonia Agreda*

REPAIRING MEANS…
valuing our knowledge

How can we value what we do not know? Knowledge, spirituality, and medicine share the same space in the worldview of various peoples of the Andean Amazon. Recently, the Inga people have revived their spirituality.

> "For a while, we had forgotten the knowledge and wisdom of our traditional doctors, our *curacas*, our *sinchi iachas*, who many years ago were our guides." *Yeni Yolanda Jacanamijoy*

Like many other Indigenous communities, the Inga people have struggled to preserve their knowledge and culture through oral tradition. Education from the West, mainly through religious missions, has been one of the main challenges in conserving the ancient cultures. Currently underway is a revaluation of Indigenous thought, which the Colombian sociologist Orlando Fals Borda tried to capture with the term *sentipensamiento* or *sentipensar* (thinking-feeling). It is a thinking that does not separate but connects spirit and body, mind and emotion. In this context, audiovisual media have a special value for recording Indigenous knowledge. There is hope that new generations will have renewed access to their ancestral worldviews.

> "Our elders show us the way through what they call seeds of life and pass them on to our children. Through oral tradition, they have left us many experiences, lessons, and advice. Although I live far from my territory, I am fortunate as I have been dedicated to saving those experiences and those memories through technological means."
> *Mariela Pujimuy*

protecting our territory

Legally recognized Indigenous territories occupy 30 percent of the Amazon basin. Together with the protected natural areas, they conserve approximately half of the tropical rainforest. Their contribution to mitigating climate change is immense. Yet Indigenous communities remain the most disadvantaged segment of the population, with even their basic needs often not met. Frequently, the international support that reaches their territory comes with conditions that do not align with their worldviews.

> "How do we make visible that Indigenous peoples are the guardians, the caretakers of Mother Earth? Through our actions, our spirituality, our traditional medicine, and our self-governance systems, we have managed to maintain the natural resources of our territories. That was already acknowledged at the UN Climate Conference in 2015. Indigenous peoples are known for conserving their territories. Where Indigenous communities live, the forest is better preserved." *Pablo Cuchala*

listening to different voices

To repair also requires valuing the individual as well as the multiple, the unity of nature and its diversity, the community of cultures amid its heterogeneity:

> "In Colombia, there are more than 104 Indigenous ethnic groups that maintain their customs and traditions. We each have our languages and clothing that make us different and unique. But we all share a common thought that unites us as a community."
> *Liliana Armero*

Despite all the damage European colonization has caused since its beginning five centuries ago, the Inga people continue their journey with optimism and respect for the plurality of cultures with whom they share the territory. They are aware of the importance of strengthening their identity and defending the forest, while at the same time listening to others in order to find ways together to achieve harmony for the Alpa Mama, peace between humans and nonhuman beings.

> "For Indigenous peoples, the forest is not an infinite resource that can be fully exploited. It is an integral space because there are spirits, medicine, food; there is everything! In contrast, what many non-Indigenous peoples see in the forest is a piece of land where trees must be cut down and replaced with pastures and cows. Despite these different ways of looking at the same space, we must come together and listen to each other." *Pablo Cuchala*

The social movements of the 20th century were critical in advancing the state's recognition of the rights of Indigenous peoples. After many years of struggle, Colombia's pluriculturalism has finally been officially recognized.

> "The 1991 Constitution recognizes Colombia as multiethnic and multicultural. But only recently has the state begun to develop a political vision with processes of representation and sharing of power to truly embrace multiculturalism and think of it broadly." *Pedro Jajoy*

Sharing our way of life

Western academia has not always been ethical in working with Indigenous communities. Cognitive injustice is very present in the minds of several Inga leaders, who consider that ancestral knowledge can be shared with the outside as long as it respects their collective intellectual property. Today, more than ever, it is important for the entire planet to learn about the way of life of the Amazonian peoples and their complex relationship with the forest.

"We are seeing that the consequences of global warming affect not only the West. They are also affecting our Indigenous territories. Those of us who still have the possibility of conserving nature also have the task of sharing our experiences and ways of life with others, so they will also begin to change their way of life. As Inga people, we are rightfully suspicious that sharing knowledge could lead to our natural wealth being stolen. But we must share our experiences so that other cultures also begin to recognize the connection they have with our Mother Earth." *Yeni Yolanda Jacanamijoy*

Several members of the Inga people are leaders in national and international spaces. As descendants of the Incas, they consider themselves "travelers" who have been in contact with other Indigenous and mestizo cultures in the region for several centuries.

"For many Indigenous peoples, participating in globalization is a survival strategy. The Inga people have been contributing and can continue to contribute to the world as long as they are aware of their strength as a community." *Liliana Armero*

Forgiving

The armed conflict of recent decades has left a great wound in Colombia society. For many Indigenous peoples, it has meant forced displacement and loss of their ancestral territories. In 2016, a slow reparation process began with the signing of the peace agreement between the state and the Revolutionary Armed Forces of Colombia (FARC). The region is now relatively safer, but this is a fragile peace that must be protected on a daily basis.

"In Colombia, the desire to vindicate life has grown in recent years. To repair is to reweave, to tie together what has been broken, to reshape it, give it new roots and structure, to help what was once shattered, burned, or destroyed to flourish again." *Pedro Jajoy*

Indigenous peoples of Latin America have repeatedly demonstrated their resilience and ability to move forward in the face of adversity. In many ways, Colombia has taught the world that positive change is possible. The majority's will is to advance toward sustainable peace in harmony with nature.

"To move forward, the first step is to look back and forgive. In Colombia, armed violence and internal war have taught many territories to repair themselves. In the face of all this, Colombia is an example of life, healing, and the possibility of forgiving." *Pedro Jajoy*

Once the fabric is finished, it is time to use it, put it on, show it off, and wear it like a suit that gives us character and identity. The polyphony that we have tried to translate in this text is meant to be an example of how to perceive, value, protect, and enjoy the great plurality that exists on the planet. The way people in the Andean Amazon respond to the challenges of our time is worth knowing and sharing. We are convinced that dialogues like these will help us weave and reweave our relationships—our culture—in order to develop a different, healing relationship with our territories.

Re
an
gue

Self-RePair

Text: Marija Marić

While the contemporary problems of architecture as a profession have been in the making for a long time, architects have historically dedicated little attention to the inner crises of their discipline. Thus its alliances with the extractive practices of construction industries and real estate markets, as well as the labor, gender, social, racial, and other internal inequalities, have long remained unchallenged. The last decade, however, saw a growing body of research and practical work addressing the toxicity of architectural practice and training.

To name just some, the project *Spatial Agency* (2011) represents one "early" example of a systematization of possibilities of practicing architecture beyond the design of a singular object and instead as a political activity.[1] Similarly, the 2015 exhibition *The Other Architect* framed historical examples of architectural initiatives critically tackling different social, political, and environmental issues since the 1960s.[2] More recently, publications like *Architects after Architecture: Alternative Pathways for Practice* (2020),[3] or ongoing projects such as *Architecture after Architecture: Spatial Practice in the Face of the Climate Emergency*,[4] have built on these traditions, rethinking more particularly the role of architects within the challenges of the climate crisis.

A number of authors and initiatives have built on existing intersectional feminist debates to highlight different toxic traits in architectural education—from exploitation in architectural schools to gender imbalance and power hierarchies as reflected in design studio pedagogies, to the overlooked role of women and other marginalized people in architectural histories.[5] Other authors tackle labor exploitation in architecture and construction industries. Notably, books like *The Architect as Worker: Immaterial Labor, the Creative Class, and the Politics of Design* (2015)[6] and *Asymmetric Labors: The Economy of Architecture in Theory and Practice* (2016)[7] have not only opened up a crucial debate about these issues but have also set the foundation for different initiatives, such as The Architecture Lobby. This international organization of architectural workers is one of the first nodes in an emerging network of architectural worker unions. They successfully bridge the gap between debates on the principles of more just architectural design and urban planning with the liberation of architectural work itself.

1   Published as a book and an online database, accessed November 2, 2022, www.spatialagency.net; Nishat Awan et al., eds., *Spatial Agency: Other Ways of Doing Architecture* (London: Routledge, 2011).
2   Curated by Giovanna Borasi at the Canadian Centre for Architecture, accompanied by a book of the same name: Giovanna Borasi, ed., *The Other Architect* (Leipzig, Montreal: Spector Books, Canadian Centre for Architecture, 2015).
3   Harriet Harriss et al., eds., *Architecture after Architecture: Alternative Pathways for Practice* (London: Routledge, 2020).
4   Research Project at the Technical University of Braunschweig, Institut für Geschichte und Theorie der Architektur und Stadt, *Architecture after Architecture: Spatial Practice in the Face of the Climate Emergency*, accessed November 2, 2022, www.gtas-braunschweig.de/researching/detail/spatial-practice-in-the-face-of-the-climate.
5   ARCH+, *Contemporary Feminist Spatial Practices* (Spring 2023); Jay Cephas et al., eds., *JAE* 76, no. 2, *Pedagogies for a Broken World* (2022).
6   Peggy Deamer, ed., *The Architect as Worker: Immaterial Labor, the Creative Class, and the Politics of Design* (London: Bloomsbury Academic, 2015).
7   Aaron Cayer et al., eds., *Asymmetric Labors: The Economy of Architecture in Theory and Practice* (New York: The Architecture Lobby, 2016).

From Architectural Work of Repair

Text: Marija Marić

to the Repair of Architectural Work

Architecture, its workers, students, institutions, and resources, are burned out. Recognized by the World Health Organization as an "occupational phenomenon," burnout can be considered not only a physical or mental condition but also a historical condition, a point of culmination in which bodies refuse to cater to the exploitative logic of capitalist production.[1] Characterized by a general sense of exhaustion, fatigue, detachment, and, consequently, limited productivity, burnout has been recognized as a set of symptoms that goes beyond the scale of the human body. Instead, it exists as a social condition, shared across different sites and environments of labor exploitation, including the discipline of architecture. Infamous for its toxic work culture involving simultaneous overwork, underpayment, and a general "disciplinary fatigue,"[2] architecture as a discipline has already proven an illustrative case for a better understanding of systemic exhaustion, and vice versa—its broken work and educational practices have already been effectively framed in terms of the burnout symptoms.[3]

Still, burnout, as a genuine product of the dysfunctional work environments of the global capitalist economy, could serve as more than a metaphor for the brokenness of the labor of architecture or a wake-up call to organize architectural workers against the conditions of their oppression. Being a syndrome and not a disease, burnout is a condition without a singular cause and cure. Operating between the individual body and its social context, burnout could provide architecture with a lens to better understand what the rehabilitation of the discipline could look like. It reminds us that we should think of repair beyond returning to a previous or "normal" state. And without a one-size-fits-all cure, those affected by burnout have no other option than to act as the main protagonists in overcoming the symptoms—and causes—of their condition. Similarly, recovering from architectural burnout would imply the return of both responsibility and power to architectural researchers and professionals in redefining the conditions of their work and their role in society.

Architecture: a brief history of stress management

In line with burnout as a condition "resulting from chronic workplace stress that has not been successfully managed," we can contextualize the current state of crisis in architecture in the history of its previous disciplinary responses to various political, economic, cultural, and environmental crises.[4]

Architects already began to partake in acts of capitalist exploitation and dispossession during the Industrial Revolution. That period, as Alicia Carrió noted, was characterized by a new division of labor and a mechanization of skills previously held by workers and artisans that laid the groundwork for the emergence of modern professions. Architects too, by "investigating, fragmenting and decoding this knowledge, made it their own."[5] If the late-18th century provided the foundations for the birth of experts and institutions for the (re-) production of this naturalized knowledge, the ensuing decades were marked by the struggle of the newly emerged professionals in constructing their social relevance. In her essay "Can Architects Be Socially Responsible?" the architectural historian Margaret Crawford discusses the professionalization of architects in the United States during the 19th century. She shows how, in this period, the educated middle class worked on establishing a "monopoly of competence," claiming their particular set of skills that would differentiate them from other professions in order to secure their social status and economic benefits.[6] For architects, this process was not easy. The unclear scope and definition of architecture-specific knowledge, stuck between the claim of scientific and technical expertise on the one hand and artistic creativity on the other—an inner friction particularly difficult to maintain in that period of intensive knowledge specialization—placed architecture under immense stress. As Crawford further points out, the profession responded to this crisis by "invoking superior aesthetics rather than superior building," leaving "architecture, a luxury rather than an indispensable service within a premodern model of elite patronage," and its services dependent on and shaped by economic forces.[7]

Poster of the National Association of Local Government Workers / National Union of Public Employees, Great Britain 1982

Following a period of architecture's close entanglements with state power during the 20th century, political detachment and disinterest again came to characterize the development of the discipline. The 1970s saw a turn from industrial, Fordist forms of labor and production to post-industrial, post-Fordist forms of labor and production. As the architectural theorist Tahl Kaminer has observed, this marked a turn "in which 'the cultural' came to dominate the society, highlighting everything that is in the territory of 'the Ideal' [...] at the expense of realist-materialist concerns," at the same time putting additional pressure on architecture to cater to the growing middle class and segmented consumer markets that now demanded (commodity) difference and authenticity.[8] Architecture responded to this crisis by shifting its attention from "the Real" to "the Ideal," detaching from broader social and political issues of its time—a withdrawal best depicted in the discipline's renewed interest in historical styles, "paper architecture," and the search for "architectural autonomy."[9] This, as Kaminer further points out, "aided the restoration of the self-confidence and credibility of the discipline and propelled it to a popular status, positioning architecture at the fore of culture," at the same time keeping it protected from reality.[10]

During the 1990s, architecture confronted "the Real" again. But the new, disinterested architecture of the Real, with Rem Koolhaas at the vanguard, now exhibited a new kind of "distance from social issues and its autonomy from the city."[11] It accepted the reality of cities as developed and determined by real estate developers and property markets, and elevated "the absence of moralizing, of imbuing modernist art and architecture with overbearing social and political responsibilities" to become a maxim of architectural practice.[12] This disciplinary cycle, as Kaminer effectively describes, started with a crisis, evolved through withdrawal, and ended with acceptance of the new social and economic landscape as unchangeable and given, keeping architecture isolated from social issues. Not only did this contribute to the loss of its design and planning authority and control over the production of the built environment, it also made the discipline and its workers more vulnerable to external financial pressures.[13] Throughout this process, architecture as a discipline successfully internalized the exploitative logic of capitalist production, both in terms of its objects of work (buildings, cities, landscapes, territories) as well as its working subjects—architects and urban planners.

These and other disciplinary responses, coupled with a lack of collective reflection about the external pressures and internal relationships and value system, ultimately made architects particularly susceptible to self-exploitation. The neoliberal economization of architecture brought about a new level of competitiveness and commodification of architectural knowledge and labor. Hiding behind the paradigm of the "entrepreneurial self"—a position in which all aspects of subjectivity, both professional and personal ones, are seen as a form of "human capital"—it successfully managed to undermine the importance of professional support systems that could protect architectural workers from precarity.[14] In failing "to conceptualize our work as work," and instead, continuously obliterating the material aspects of architectural labor by describing it as "a calling," as the architectural theorist Peggy Deamer notes, architects have actively participated (and continue to do so) in the systemic depoliticization of their own profession, thus allowing and normalizing exploitative practices both within and outside architecture as a discipline.[15]

From repair to care

This raises the question: Where do we start repairing architectural work? How do we move from repairing broken objects toward repairing broken professional subjectivities, social relationships, and infrastructures of class alliances? It seems that the first step in this process must involve a rethinking of repair, abandoning its sometimes universalizing character while reimagining it as a messy process without fixed notions of beginning or end, of the broken and the repaired. Repair must cut across different temporalities in a nonlinear manner, not moving towards the future only, but also reaching back to the past while rectifying the causes of the broken present. We must find an understanding of repair whose goal is not the restoration of normality and the totalizing authority of the repairman, but instead seek answers within the community of care. In this process, we must learn to abandon the prescriptive, sometimes violent, technocratic solutionism that has for so long shaped the politics of architecture—its practice, discourse, hierarchies, and role in society—and instead embrace a more nuanced and emancipatory *politics of cure*, as put forth by the writer and activist Eli Clare. Instead of managing and controlling bodies, whether they are individual, collective, human, or non-human, we must acknowledge the multiple possibilities of what healing might mean. We must think of repair as a way of working with existing memory, trauma, and scars of brokenness, and in doing so, as Clare points out, "encouraging and reshaping (ecological) interdependencies" that link these bodies.[16]

Writing on the history of nostalgia, the cultural theorist Svetlana Boym observed how nostalgia, as a social syndrome of longing for a different rhythm of time, emerged as a refusal to adapt to the pace of progress, growth, and acceleration brought about by modern capitalism. As Boym shows, nostalgia came from medicine, not poetry or politics, and was first described in 1668 in a medical dissertation by the Swiss medical student Johannes Hofer. During the 17th century, nostalgia was considered a curable disease, with "opium, leeches, and a journey to the Swiss Alps," commonly prescribed by Swiss doctors to treat its symptoms.[17] But, as Boym further shows, it was the radical act of bodily refusal to cater to the dominant ideologies of production and the fast pace of time, combined with its often prospective and not only retrospective character, that could give nostalgia its political agency: "Nostalgic time is that time-out-of-time for daydreaming and longing that jeopardizes one's timetables and work ethics."[18] Learning from Boym's reading of nostalgia, we might start thinking of burnout as an initial act of refusal and the starting point for what recovery perhaps needs the most: *taking time* (back).

If we see burnout as a refusal of the individual body to work under the premises of collective exploitation, in overcoming it the collective body must refuse the exploitative nature of work that led to this condition in the first place. Looking beyond immediate symptoms to instead find common ground, a shared struggle of all architects as workers, means not falling for the myth of the "creative" but unpaid, "flexible" but constant work. It means understanding that "there is no 'architectural' struggle, but there is a labor struggle, to which we all belong."[19] Moving on from hcrc, as United Voices of the World – Section of Architectural Workers (UVW-SAW) suggests in its call for collective action of architects as workers—it is not the street nor the parliament but the workplace that should become the starting point for the launch of this struggle.[20]

Burnout thus reminds us that, in resisting the exploitative practices characteristic of our contemporary modes of production and in refusing the conditions of our oppression, we need to act within networks of solidarity, consciously building alliances with those with whom we share politics. Here, Jodi Dean's unpacking of the notion of *comradeship* might prove helpful. Describing comrades as "more than survivors" and instead as "those on the same side of a struggle for an emancipated egalitarian world," Dean underlines the distinction between comradeship and friendship: "Comradeship has nothing to do with the person or personality in its specificity; it's generic. […] Comradeship isn't personal. It's political."[21] In overcoming burnout, we need both friends and comrades, as well as new words and discourses to describe and build other conditions of shared political agency.

1   World Health Organization, "Burn-Out an 'Occupational Phenomenon': International Classification of Diseases," May 28, 2019, accessed September 26, 2022, www.who.int/news/item/28-05-2019-burn-out-an-occupational-phenomenon-international-classification-of-diseases.
2   The Editorial Board of *Ardeth*, "Burn-out after Burn-out," *Ardeth* 8 (2021): 6, accessed September 26, 2022, journals.openedition.org/ardeth/2099.
3   See the project *Burn-Out: Exhaustion on a Planetary Scale* (2019–20) by Het Nieuwe Instituut in Rotterdam and issue no. 8 of the journal *Ardeth*, titled *Burn-out: On Planetary Exhaustion and Alternative Public Infrastructures*, published in 2021 (see note 2).
4   World Health Organization, "Burn-Out" (see note 1).
5   Alicia Carrió, "The Hunger Games: Architects in Danger," in *The Architect as Worker: Immaterial Labor, the Creative Class, and the Politics of Design*, ed. Peggy Deamer (London: Bloomsbury, 2015), 172.
6   Margaret Crawford, "Can Architects Be Socially Responsible?," in *Out of Site: A Social Criticism of Architecture*, ed. Diane Ghirardo (Seattle: Bay Press, 1991), 28.
7   Ibid., 29 and 31.
8   Tahl Kaminer, *Architecture, Crisis and Resuscitation: The Reproduction of Post-Fordism in Late-Twentieth-Century Architecture* (Abingdon: Routledge, 2011), 85.
9   Ibid., 87.
10   Ibid., 5.
11   Ibid., 113.
12   Ibid.
13   The division of labor and architects' loss of professional authority, especially since the second half of the 20th century, allowed for the rise of professions such as real estate developers and media strategists to the forefront of architectural and urban design. On the professionalization of real estate developers, see Sara Stevens, *Developing Expertise: Architecture and Real Estate in Metropolitan America* (New Haven: Yale University Press, 2016). On the emergence of specialized real estate media experts since the neoliberal turn in the 1970s, see Marija Marić, "Real Estate Fiction: Branding Industries and the Construction of Global Urban Imaginaries," PhD diss., ETH Zürich, 2020.
14   For discussions on "neoliberal economization" and the rise of the "entrepreneurial self," see Andreas Rumpfhuber, "The Architect as Entrepreneurial Self: Hans Hollein's TV Performance 'Mobile Office' (1969)," and Manuel Shvartzberg Carrió, "Foucault's 'Environmental' Power: Architecture and Neoliberal Subjectivization," both in Deamer, ed., *The Architect as Worker* (see note 5).
15   Peggy Deamer, "Work," in Deamer, ed., *The Architect as Worker* (see note 5), 61.
16   See Eli Clare's essay in this issue, and Eli Clare, *Brilliant Imperfection: Grappling with Cure* (Durham: Duke University Press, 2017).
17   Svetlana Boym, "Nostalgia and Its Discontents," *The Hedgehog Review* 9, no. 2 (2007): 7.
18   Svetlana Boym, *The Future of Nostalgia* (New York: Basic Books, 2001), 16.
19   Marisa Cortright, *"Can This Be? Surely This Cannot Be?" Architectural Workers Organizing in Europe* (Prague: VI PER Gallery, 2021), 91.
20   See the statement by United Voices of the World – Section of Architectural Workers (UVW-SAW) in this issue.
21   Jodi Dean, "Four Theses on the Comrade," *e-flux Journal*, no. 86 (November 2017), accessed September 26, 2022, www.e-flux.com/journal/86/160585/four-theses-on-the-comrade/.

Negotiating worldly Relationships

or Unionizing for the planet

Text: United Voices of the World—
Section of Architectural Workers (UVW-SAW)

"We are tired" was one of the first protest slogans devised by the architectural workers who have joined forces in the union United Voices of the World.

UVW-SAW opposes the precarious working conditions in the architecture sector. Together, its members fight against the exploitation of human labor and of natural resources in the construction industry.

The first year of our organization is coming to an end. Over the last 18 months we have joined picket lines, self-trained in employment law, formulated press releases denouncing the fraud and abuse in our workplaces, stood up to the employers who were taking advantage of us, and organized support networks with our colleagues and peers. One of our posters shown here, a graphic of a weary eye, a clock in lieu of the iris, serves as a reminder of where the project began.

Of all the possible things architectural workers wanted to change about their jobs, overwork seemed as good a place to start as any. "WE ARE TIRED" was among the first slogans we stuck onto placards to promote the cultural shift we wanted for our industry, calling out a burnout culture, its pervasiveness and glorification. Our friends in the Marx reading group kept noticing descriptions of Victorian factories that sounded strangely like contemporary architectural offices. "No 9-to-5 mentality. The working day contains the full 24 hours, with the deduction of the few hours of rest without which labor-power is absolutely incapable of renewing its services." The game of guessing which was which (*Dezeen* Jobs or *Das Kapital*?) did not distract us from the realization that workers today are still living out the logic of the maximum extraction of labor power. "It is self-evident that the worker is nothing other than labor-power for the duration of their whole life, and that therefore all their disposable time is by nature and by right labor-time, to be devoted to the ~~self-valorization of capital~~ *architecture*."

Never far from the exploitation of the worker lurks the exploitation of nature—another resource equally subjected to the extractive rationale of capital. Every practitioner, school, and professional institute today flaunts their awareness of architecture's capacity for environmental destruction: from the production, transportation, and construction of material elements, to energy consumption throughout a building's lifetime. Over the last few years, in the UK alone architectural workers like many others have joined the protest movements demanding immediate climate action. Petitions and declarations have abounded, and every firm expressed its "commitment to addressing the climate and biodiversity emergency." Yet despite all the pledges, it seems that the initial impetus is running out of steam. Major design practices are already reframing their individual responsibility to the environment to suit their commercial ambitions, greenwashing their way back into business-as-usual. And it is in no way surprising. After all, the discourse on the necessary transformation in the face of environmental collapse still conceives of *architects* as the agents of change, when in fact architects cannot so easily grant themselves the autonomy from capital they require to have a meaningful effect on the climate emergency.

Meanwhile, the fundamental link between natural and worker exploitation remains untapped. Once we realize that architecture's social and ecological damage is only made possible by our labor as workers, that planetary exhaustion is indeed fed by worker exhaustion, then radical possibilities emerge. Just imagine if all of those who marched for the climate and expressed support of a Swedish pupil going on school strike also refused to work on projects that opposed their beliefs and ethics: prisons, airports, high-end housing, unsafe construction sites … "WE ARE TIRED—ON STRIKE FOR SOCIAL & CLIMATE JUSTICE!" The site of the struggle against ecological breakdown is not the parliament nor the street, but the workplace; and agents of change are therefore not the architects but the architectural workers, a term inclusive of all those necessary for the production of architecture: the receptionists, the draftspeople, the assistants, the office cleaners, administrative staff, clerks of works, security guards, technicians, the construction workers, the BIM managers, document controllers, bid coordinators, architects… the list goes on. The distinction is subtle but profound, as it shifts our attention towards a plural understanding of agency, where power relies not on individual deeds but on collective responses to collective issues. This holds the possibility of a radical restructuring of power relationships, in the workplace and in the worlds produced in these workplaces.

To build such collective political agency among workers necessitates a particular kind of infrastructure, one we might call a worker-led union. We have been coming together as the Section of Architectural Workers (SAW) for the last 18 months and call upon all workers to join. SAW does not exist independently of us, its members, and therefore cannot act on our behalf: It is merely the vehicle of our empowerment as architectural workers, a space to autonomously organize and negotiate our professional and worldly relationships—in the workplace, across society, and indeed at a planetary scale. Through our union we upskill each other and develop the resources necessary to organize collectively, in order to effect the changes we want to our working conditions, the city, and the environment. In concrete terms, we train and support each other through workplace disputes and legal battles against our employers; we organize ourselves to obtain better terms of employment; we develop our connections to other organizations and campaigns, to support them, and find common ground; we map the world of work and develop the appropriate language and tools to navigate existing power structures; very importantly, we broadcast our voices to inspire other workers to take action for themselves and in solidarity with others.

For this is the project: to transform the landscape of architectural labor, with ramifications beyond the boundaries of our industry. It is about ending the endemic exhaustion of human and Earth resources, the reproduction of overwork, precarity, and discrimination, and rebuilding the balance of power from the bottom up, in order to produce, at last, the responsible architecture of which we are capable.

The text was written in December 2020 for the Annual General Meeting of the Section of Architectural Workers of the UK trade union United Voices of the World. It first appeared in Ardeth 8 (2021).

Land as Key

Artist Simone Leigh in front of her evolving artwork *Brick House* (2019) from her *Anatomy of Architecture* series. The bronze sculpture, which was produced in the Stratton Sculpture Studio in Philadelphia, is at once body and house and (as so often in Leigh's work) refuses the return of the gaze.

Text: Hollyamber Kennedy

to Repair and Reparations

In an interview in 2018, Achille Mbembe was asked for his response to the removal of the Cecil John Rhodes statue at the University of Cape Town (UCT). The disassembling had occurred three years earlier in response to the parallel actions of the Rhodes Must Fall (RMF) and Fees Must Fall movements, which sought a decolonization of education and the public sphere.[1] "I interpret the toppling of his statue," Mbembe stated, "as a small, symbolic victory, in the long and protracted struggle for universal justice."[2] Rhodes, a British mining magnate who amassed a fortune from the acquisition and extraction of mineral wealth from the South African, Zimbabwean, and Zambian earth, served as Prime Minister of the Cape Colony from 1890 to 1896. During his tenure, he worked to expropriate African land entitlements, establishing a legal precedent for the structural brutality and racialized violence that later defined South Africa's apartheid regime.[3]

The 900-kilogram, 2-meter-high bronze sculpture of Rhodes was designed by the British artist and engraver Marion Walgate. It was presented to the University in 1933 by the Rhodes Memorial Committee. Lifted by crane from its pedestal on April 9, 2015, it is now entombed in a storage unit at UCT. The sculpture depicted a seated Rhodes, his gaze, like a survey, coldly mapping and administering the landscape. Let us call his a calculative and not a contemplative eye, drawn from and attesting to a set of practices that helped shape the epistemological traditions of the West and that also form the foundation of the planning disciplines. Practices in which territory supersedes place, turning a space of habitation into an annexed unit that could be mapped, calculated, projected, and managed.[4] Cast out over the Cape Flats, his expression is resonant of the knowledge protocols that structured the violent forms of globalism created by European empires and capitalism.[5] It marked and memorialized the historical introduction of a gendered and racialized administrative analytic rooted in colonial political economy and military governance.

Walgate's rendering was accurate in this regard, for Rhodes was nothing if not a covetous aggregator of territory: The region of the Rhodesias, present day Zimbabwe and Zambia, carried his name after having been appropriated through treaties, concessions, and bloodshed by his syndicate, the British South Africa Company, in 1889. One year earlier, he and his partner, Charles D. Rudd, formed the diamond company De Beers Consolidated Mines—today, the corporation pursues a planetary-scale project of extraction with operational mines in over 30 countries, working divergent terrains: coastal, open-pit, alluvial. Its scale of territorial intervention recalls (and exceeds) other enterprises devised by Rhodes, such as the Cape to Cairo railway line, a failed campaign that would have spanned the African continent from south to north, a seamless passage for the transfer of raw materials, the mineral wealth of empire. The plan was later revived, after 1927, by the German architect Herman Sörgel in his fever dreams of Atlantropa, which envisioned lowering the water level in the Mediterranean Sea with gigantic dams to merge Europe and Africa into a new supercontinent. It was a world project reminiscent of the developmentalist and infrastructural turn of empire, coauthored by figures such as Rhodes, that prevailed after the colonial interventions of the 1890s.[6] The physical and often violent acquisition of territory and its on-the-ground administration had become increasingly central to imperial systems at this time. The heightened role that infrastructure played as an imperial-governmental technology, one shaped by architects, planners, and civil engineering specialists in colonial contexts across the globe, underscores the urgent need to decolonize planning disciplines today, steeped as they have been in the spatial histories of the theft and regrafting of place.

Rhodes was "a ruthless actor in the mercantile expansionism that characterized 19th century settler colonialism in the southern part of Africa," as Mbembe describes him,[7] and an embodiment of the kind of resource imperialism that extended alongside these developments—denoting a legacy of practice that, too, is indivisible from imperial and colonial structures, from their architectures of settlement and their brutal displacements. When asked about the lineage that descends from Rhodes to the neoliberal order of capital that we see today, Mbembe responded: "There is an explicit kinship between plantation slavery, colonial predation, and contemporary forms of resource extraction and appropriation. In each of these instances, there is a constitutive denial of the fact that we, the humans, coevolve with the biosphere, depend on it, are defined with and through it and owe each other a debt of responsibility and care."[8]

The grammar of colonization which flowed through the actions of Rhodes has shaped today's economics of extraction. Its damages and depredations have brought us to the cusp of a planetary climate emergency, while its deterritorializations and reterritorializations have captured and mined laboring bodies, as Kathryn Yusoff showed us in *A Billion Black Anthropocenes or None*.[9] These grammars of

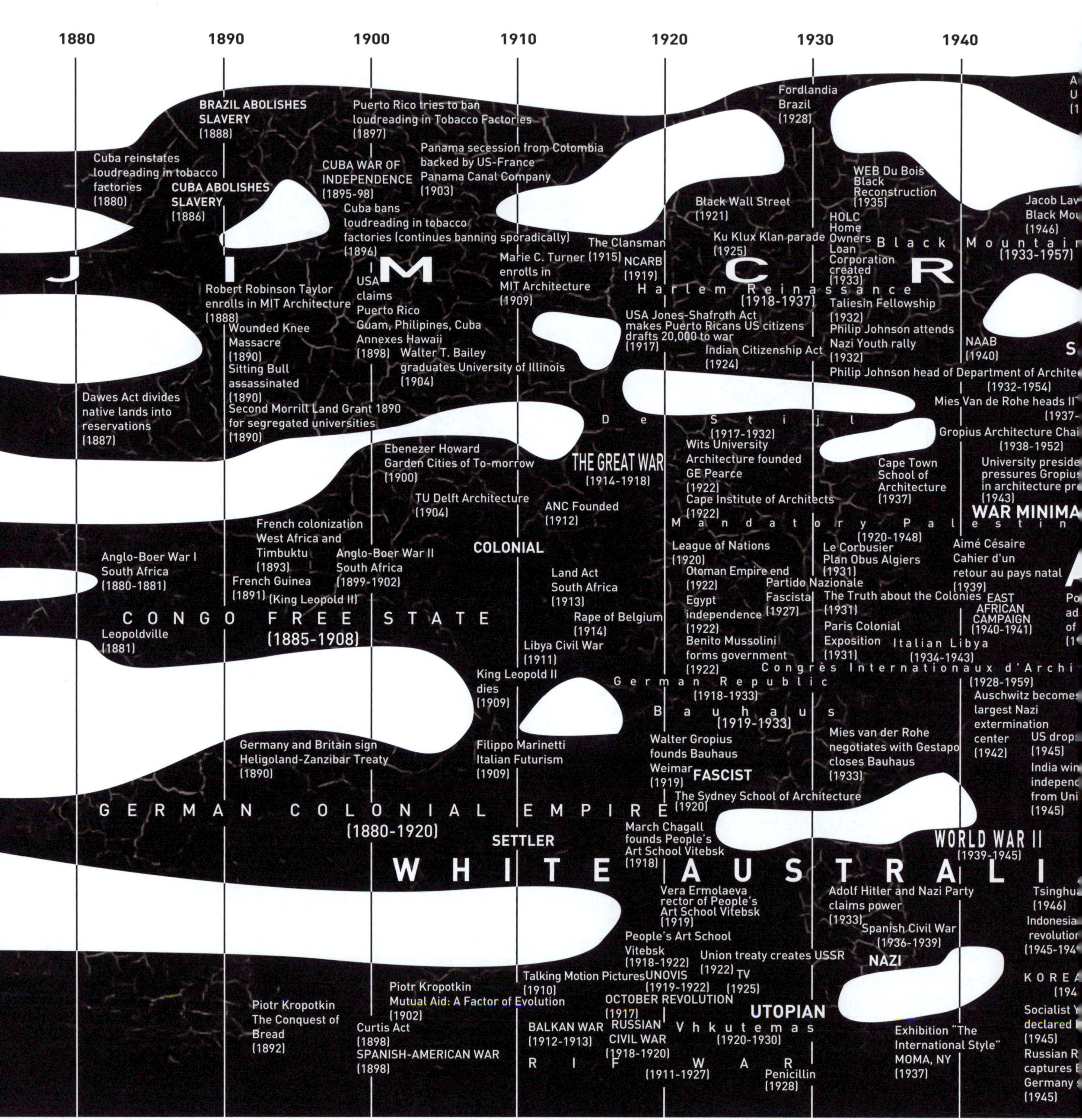

For the work *A Manual of Anti-Racist Architecture Education* WAI Think Tank revised Charles Jencks's *Evolutionary Tree to the Year 2000*. In it, they expose racist relations as the underlying condition for certain canonized architectures and reveal how perpetuating the same discourses serves to consolidate and maintain power.

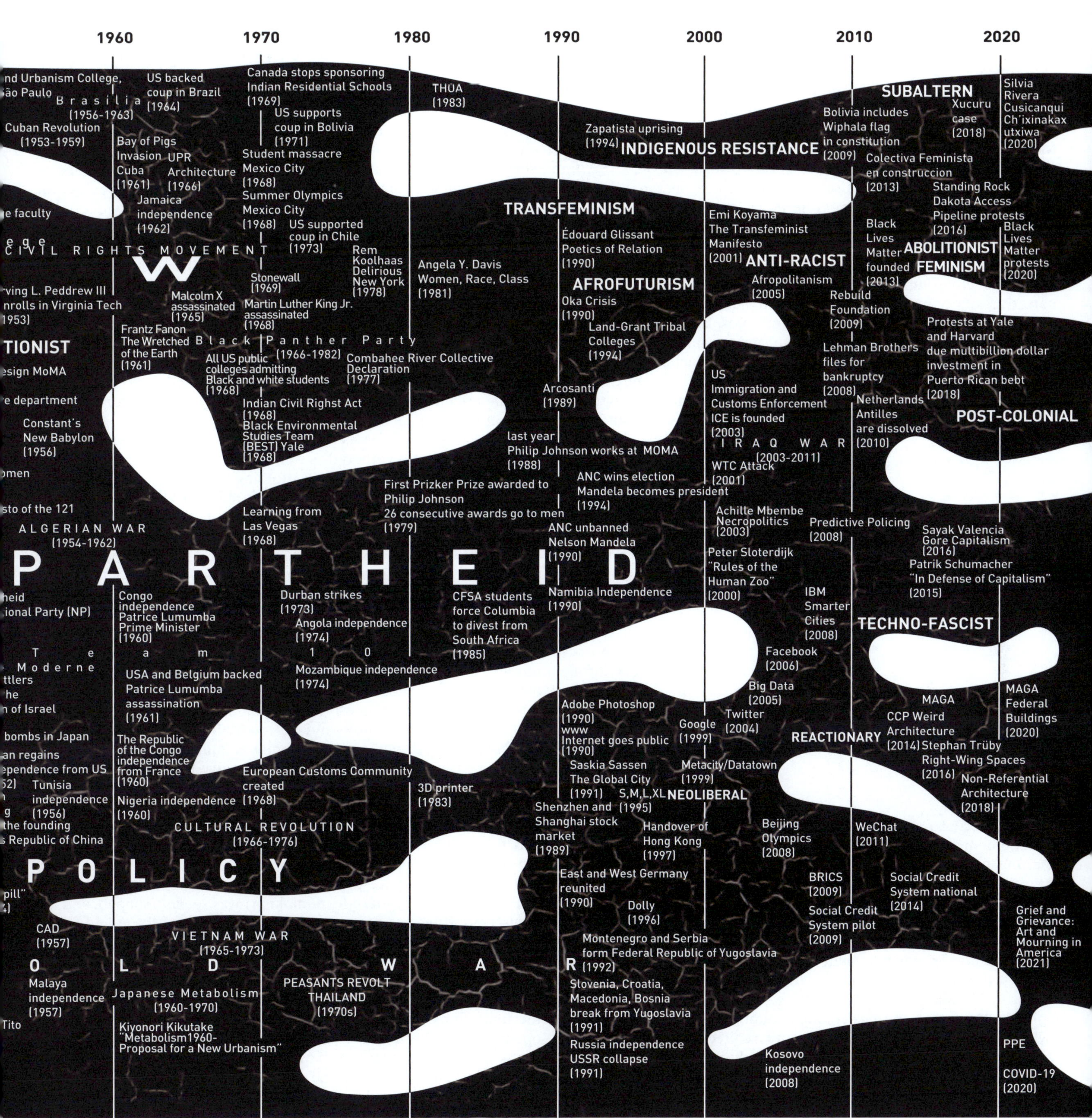
1960
1970
1980
1990
2000
2010
2020

nd Urbanism College, São Paulo
Brasilia (1956-1963)
Cuban Revolution (1953-1959)
US backed coup in Brazil (1964)
Canada stops sponsoring Indian Residential Schools (1969)
THUA (1983)
SUBALTERN
Bolivia includes Wiphala flag in constitution (2009)
Xucuru case (2018)
Silvia Rivera Cusicanqui Ch'ixinakax utxiwa (2020)
Bay of Pigs Invasion Cuba (1961)
UPR Architecture (1966)
US supports coup in Bolivia (1971)
Student massacre Mexico City (1968)
Zapatista uprising (1994)
INDIGENOUS RESISTANCE
Colectiva Feminista en construccion (2013)
Standing Rock Dakota Access Pipeline protests (2016)
e faculty
Jamaica independence (1962)
Summer Olympics Mexico City (1968)
TRANSFEMINISM
Emi Koyama The Transfeminist Manifesto (2001)
Black Lives Matter founded (2013)
Black Lives Matter protests (2020)
ege CIVIL RIGHTS MOVEMENT
W
US supported coup in Chile (1973)
Rem Koolhaas Delirious New York (1978)
Angela Y. Davis Women, Race, Class (1981)
Édouard Glissant Poetics of Relation (1990)
ANTI-RACIST
Afropolitanism (2005)
ABOLITIONIST FEMINISM
ving L. Peddrew III nrolls in Virginia Tech 1953
Malcolm X assassinated (1965)
Stonewall (1969)
AFROFUTURISM
Oka Crisis (1990)
Rebuild Foundation (2009)
Protests at Yale and Harvard due multibillion dollar investment in Puerto Rican bebt (2018)
TIONIST
Frantz Fanon The Wretched of the Earth (1961)
Martin Luther King Jr. assassinated (1968)
Black Panther Party (1966-1982)
Combahee River Collective Declaration (1977)
Land-Grant Tribal Colleges (1994)
Lehman Brothers files for bankruptcy (2008)
esign MoMA
All US public colleges admitting Black and white students (1968)
US Immigration and Customs Enforcement ICE is founded (2003)
Netherlands Antilles are dissolved (2010)
POST-COLONIAL
re department
Indian Civil Righst Act (1968)
Arcosanti (1989)
Constant's New Babylon (1956)
Black Environmental Studies Team (BEST) Yale (1968)
last year Philip Johnson works at MOMA (1988)
IRAQ WAR (2003-2011)
WTC Attack (2001)
omen
ANC wins election Mandela becomes president (1994)
sto of the 121
First Prizker Prize awarded to Philip Johnson 26 consecutive awards go to men (1979)
Achille Mbembe Necropolitics (2003)
Predictive Policing (2008)
Sayak Valencia Gore Capitalism (2016)
ALGERIAN WAR (1954-1962)
Learning from Las Vegas (1968)
ANC unbanned Nelson Mandela (1990)
Peter Sloterdijk "Rules of the Human Zoo" (2000)
Patrik Schumacher "In Defense of Capitalism" (2015)
PARTHEID
heid ional Party (NP)
Congo independence Patrice Lumumba Prime Minister (1960)
Durban strikes (1973)
CFSA students force Columbia to divest from South Africa (1985)
Namibia Independence (1990)
IBM Smarter Cities (2008)
TECHNO-FASCIST
Team Moderne
ttlers he n of Israel
Angola independence (1974)
1 0
Mozambique independence (1974)
Facebook (2006)
MAGA
CCP Weird Architecture (2014) Stephan Trüby
MAGA Federal Buildings (2020)
bombs in Japan
USA and Belgium backed Patrice Lumumba assassination (1961)
Big Data (2005)
an regains ependence from US
The Republic of the Congo independence from France (1960)
Adobe Photoshop (1990) www Internet goes public (1990)
Google (1999)
Twitter (2004)
REACTIONARY
Right-Wing Spaces (2016)
52) Tunisia independence (1956)
European Customs Community created
3D printer (1983)
Saskia Sassen The Global City (1991)
Metacity/Datatown (1999)
S,M,L,XL (1995)
NEOLIBERAL
Non-Referential Architecture (2018)
Nigeria independence (1960)
g the founding s Republic of China
Shenzhen and Shanghai stock market (1989)
Handover of Hong Kong (1997)
Beijing Olympics (2008)
WeChat (2011)
CULTURAL REVOLUTION (1966-1976)
POLICY
East and West Germany reunited (1990)
BRICS (2009)
Social Credit System national (2014)
pill" 4)
Dolly (1996)
Social Credit System pilot (2009)
Grief and Grievance: Art and Mourning in America (2021)
CAD (1957)
VIETNAM WAR (1965-1973)
Montenegro and Serbia form Federal Republic of Yugoslavia (1992)
O L D W A R
Malaya independence (1957)
Japanese Metabolism (1960-1970)
PEASANTS REVOLT THAILAND (1970s)
Slovenia, Croatia, Macedonia, Bosnia break from Yugoslavia (1991)
Tito
Kiyonori Kikutake "Metabolism1960-Proposal for a New Urbanism"
Russia independence USSR collapse (1991)
Kosovo independence (2008)
PPE
COVID-19 (2020)

colonization to this day remain deeply inscribed in the disciplines of architecture and planning.

However, the planetary, ecological repercussions of these damaging grammars have already begun to pierce architectural discourse and education. In a decolonial turn, built upon critical movements within architectural historiography that have been slowly coalescing in recent decades, architecture's geography of thought has started to shift radically. This, I would suggest, can be read as a sign of an unfolding recognition of the debt of care described by Mbembe, and the politics of repair, responsibility, and reckoning that enfold it.[10] Within studies of the built and landscaped environment increased scrutiny is being placed on the common heritage that territorial formations such as the plantation, the colony, and their planetary afterlives share, informed by the same recurring themes that define the Anthropocene. Those themes include entrenched forms of racialized violence, land alienation, environmental degradation, and large-scale species loss—narratives of occupation that have etched themselves into the land and the landscape, and more broadly into our biosphere.

Yet, developing a new, expansive, and reparative grammar with which to write, to teach, to research, and to learn inclusively about the histories of the built and imagined environment remains an open and urgent project. Understanding architecture's interdependence with and embeddedness in histories of land, terrain, and territory, allows us to challenge the constraints—as descending from colonial practices and imperial conditions—that have disciplined our thinking on the subject. Drawing on the vital framework of *unlearning* that Ariella Aïsha Azoulay and Swati Chattopadhyay have done so much to advance, I would propose that we might also think through *unsettlement*—of existing orders of knowledge, but especially of territorial orders—in equally transformative ways. To seek a way of reading the built environment that is grounded in the centrality of land as a key site of repair and reparations.[11]

Rural Studio was founded in 1993 by Samuel Mockbee und D. K. Ruth at Auburn University in Alabama. It offers a form of architecture training in which students are supported from the first design through to realization of their project. Primarily it is homes for people in need that are built, utilizing recycled or donated materials.

Unsettling territory

My recent research on the history of rural land reclamations,[12] resettlement, and internal colonization leads me to ask: How can we see and center the terrains, scales of experience, and agencies that have been obscured by territorial processes and by the knowledge protocols that structure how we understand them?[13] In recent years as an instructor at the Institute for the History and Theory of Architecture at the ETH Zürich, my students and I have sought other ways of knowing and observing the built environment. We engaged with Indigenous spatial ontologies, following for example Leanne Betasamosake Simpson's reading of the Nishnabeeg practice of land as pedagogy, and Black feminist and postcolonial counter-mapping.[14] We followed Sylvia Wynter and Saidiya Hartman's redirection of subterranean forms of resistance forged in slavery and subjugation.[15] Through them, we have traced the ways in which those territorial orders, such as the one administered by Rhodes, have been disrupted, unsettled, and reimagined, highlighting the core need for methodologies and practices rooted in intersectional approaches that privilege marginalized voices, situated experiences, and Southern geographies. Guided by such insight, the spatialities of territory take on other resonances—spaces, in the words of Walter D. Mignolo, of "interconnected dispersal in which decolonial futures are being played out."[16]

Yet as a paradigm shift, the vital task of unlearning imperialism and centering what for too long have remained peripheral subjects has been embraced unevenly. In the place from which I write, in central Europe, long-standing curriculum and disciplinary debates continue to be waged over the value and place of the traditional Eurocentric canon of architectural history, and, in certain corners, ignored altogether. Here, we must continue to scrutinize still-entrenched beliefs about the origins of architectural modernity, the global contexts in which it emerged, and the kinds of labor that gave it form. My own work in this regard has been enriched and deepened by an ongoing collaboration with the architectural historian Anooradha Iyer Siddiqi. Over the course of the last decade spent in conversation with one another, we have sought to make visible the link between migration and colonial modernities.[17] The movement or transfer of individuals and populations, both free and forced, is indivisible from colonial and imperial structures and their land practices, and has been central to the development of modern architecture, yet continues to remain isolated as a subject within the architectural humanities. In the context of the present climate crisis and extended forms of environmental racism, the need to better understand the historical entanglements between modern architecture and mass migration in formerly colonized places and the attendant production of increasingly precarious forms of settlement takes on a heightened significance.

But around processes of dispossession and displacement, insurgencies have always gathered as well, which as wellsprings of anticolonial thought could become the scaffolding for new architectural pedagogies. We must question the historiographical traditions that inform architectural studies, which continue to sideline such marginalized histories. Even in the midst of architecture's decolonial pivot, a body of critical scholarship in postcolonial architectural history, largely forged in the work of non-Euro-American immigrant women scholars in US institutions beginning in the 1980s, continues to be overlooked, as Itohan Osayimwese calls attention to in an important new essay.[18] We therefore urgently need to "disentangle architectural historical traditions from colonial practices," as my collaborator Siddiqi argues. This requires a critical and unsentimental understanding of their entanglement, of how architectural historical traditions draw on and rearticulate colonial epistemologies.[19] Samia Henni, thinking alongside Aníbal Quijano, Walter D. Mignolo, and Nelson Maldonado-Torres, has made a similar point, in her essay "Colonial Ramifications," interrogating the extent to which the colonial past, as a lived coloniality, is still inscribed in architecture's prevailing historical, linguistic, ethno-cultural, and geographical self-understanding.[20]

For a true decolonial shift, we must move even deeper, and subvert the cultural techniques at the very core of our disciplines which are the same through which the Earth's landscape under colonialism and slavery (as a space of dispossession, extraction, negotiation and resistance, and of modern form making) was seeded, shaped, and administered. If we are to be committed to anticolonial thought in our history writing, in our story telling, and in our teaching, then our starting point, as Katherine McKittrick has argued, must be one of disobedient relationality that ruthlessly questions the conditioning inscribed in analytical reasoning, and to creatively move beyond, or contravene, the limitations and recursivities of its conventions. The possibilities opened up by Black studies and insurgent thought, she notes, are rigorous and at the same time full of wonder. "This is a way of living," she writes, "and an analytical frame, that is curious and sustained by wonder (the desire to know). This is a method that demands openness and is unsatisfied with questions that result in descriptive-data-induced answers."[21] We must unsettle the grounds of analytical reason in order to read in more reparative ways.

The urgency of this radical reframing is growing daily. It grows alongside intensifying global inequalities, rapidly escalating climate breakdown, continued land enclosures, unprecedented mass migrations, ecological collapse, and species extinction—systemically interconnected and recursive patterns of depletion and dispossession. These developments raise the stakes of research focused on the long histories of colonialism and the enduring legacies of colonization, on the traces of the latter's land practices and its architectures of settlement and resource mobilization, on the ways it has shaped the modern world through violent geographical transformations and the transvaluation of Indigenous places, as well as the knowledge protocols and systems of value that prevailed in conjunction with such disruptions. Thus, more than ever we need decolonial reframings and reparative reimaginings, a transformational shift in practice and in thought.

1   Torbjørn Tumyr Nilsen and Sindre Bangstad, "Thoughts on the Planetary: An Interview with Achille Mbembe," *New Frame*, September 5, 2019, accessed July 15, 2022, www.newframe.com/thoughts-on-the-planetary-an-interview-with-achille-mbembe/. For a more detailed discussion of the protest, see Anooradha Iyer Siddiqi, "The University and The Camp," *Ardeth* 6 (2020): 137–51. On the parallel RMF movement in Oxford, England, see Akwugo Emejulu, "Another University is Possible," Verso blog, January 12, 2017, accessed November 4, 2022, www.versobooks.com/blogs/3044-another-university-is-possible. I would like to thank the architectural researcher and designer Khensani de Klerk for her powerful and nuanced presentation on the actions that unfolded at the UCT around the Fees Must Fall movement and for introducing our class to the practice and concept of the imbizo.
2   Nilsen and Bangstad, "Thoughts on the Planetary" (see note 1).
3   Among the hallmarks of Rhodes's disenfranchisement efforts are the Glen Grey Act of 1894 and the notorious Natives Land Act of 1913, which placed severe restrictions on the areas where Black Africans were permitted to settle.
4   Stuart Elden, *The Birth of Territory* (Chicago: The University of Chicago Press, 2013); Stuart Elden, "Land, Terrain, Territory," *Progress in Human Geography* 34, no. 6 (2010): 799–817; Stuart Elden, *Terror and Territory: The Spatial Extent of Sovereignty* (Minneapolis: University of Minnesota Press, 2009). For alternative readings of territory and terrain within the field of critical geography, see Sam Alvorsen, "Decolonising Territory: Dialogues with Latin American Knowledge and Grassroots Strategies," *Progress in Human Geography* 43, no. 5 (2018): 1–25; and Sam Halvorsen, "Cartographies of Epistemic Appropriation: Critical Reflections on Learning from the South," *Geoforum* 95 (2018): 11–20.
5   For more on this notion of the global as rendered by empire and capitalism, see Dipesh Chakrabarty, *The Climate of History in a Planetary Age* (Chicago: University of Chicago Press, 2021).
6   For more on this turn, see Dirk Van Laak, *Imperiale Infrastruktur: Deutsche Planungen für eine Erschließung Afrikas, 1880 bis 1960* (Paderborn: Ferdinand Schöningh, 2004). On the legacy of Rhodes in Herman Sörgel's Atlantropa project, see Peter Christensen, "Dam Nation: Imaging and Imagining the 'Middle East' in Herman Sörgel's Atlantropa," *International Journal of Islamic Architecture* 1, no. 2 (2012): 325–46; Hollyamber Kennedy, "Modernism's Politics of Land and the 'Cult of the Colossal'," paper presented at Society of Architectural Historians, 71st International Meeting, Saint Paul, Minnesota, April 18–22, 2018; Hollyamber Kennedy, "Binding Power Lines: Notes on Herman Sörgel's World Project," paper presented at European Architectural History Network, Thematic Conference *Tools of the Architect*, Rotterdam/Delft, November 22–25, 2017; Hollyamber Kennedy, "A Secure Interior: The Ecological Imaginary of Herman Sörgel's Atlantropa Project," paper presented at European Society for Environmental History, International Meeting, Versailles, June 30–July 3, 2015. See also *ARCH+ 239, Europa: Infrastrukturen der Externalisierung* (July 2020), particularly the chapter "Erschließung," 160–97.
7   Nilsen and Bangstad, "Thoughts on the Planetary" (see note 1).
8   Ibid.
9   Kathryn Yusoff, *A Billion Black Anthropocenes or None* (Minneapolis: University of Minnesota Press, 2019).
10   See the *Caregiving as Method* series organized by Anooradha Iyer Siddiqi on the digital forum SAH Connects, September 2021, accessed September 13, 2022, www.sah.org/conferences-and-programs/sah-connects/2021/caregiving-as-method.
11   Ariella Aïsha Azoulay, *Potential History: Unlearning Imperialism* (London: Verso, 2019); Swati Chattopadhyay, *Unlearning the City: Infrastructure in a New Optical Field* (Minneapolis: University of Minnesota, 2012).
12   Reclamation acquires a dual meaning here, both signaling the technical process of "reclaiming" arable and "productive" land through, for example, the draining of submerged wetlands, and, simultaneously, describing state claims asserted over historically contested lands through such "civilizing" reclamation projects.
13   See for example *The Ecological Turn in Architecture*, Annual Research Day in the Department of Architecture, ETH Zürich, May 12, 2022.
14   Leanne Betasamosake Simpson, "Land as Pedagogy: Nishnabeeg Intelligence and Rebellious Transformation," *Decolonization: Indigeneity, Education & Society* 3, no. 3 (2014): 1–25. I am grateful to Rafico Ruiz for drawing my attention to this important essay. Katherine McKittrick, "Plantation Futures," *Small Axe* (November 2013): 1–15.
15   Sylvia Wynter, "Novel and History, Plot and Plantation," *Savacou* 5 (1971): 95–102; Sylvia Wynter, "Unparalleled Catastrophe for Our Species? Or, to Give Humanness a Different Future: Conversations," in Sylvia Wynter, *On Being Human as Praxis*, ed. Katherine McKittrick (Durham: Duke University Press, 2015), 9–89; Saidiya Hartmann, *Scenes of Subjection: Terror, Slavery, and Self-Making in Nineteenth-Century America* (Oxford: Oxford University Press, 1997).
16   Walter D. Mignolo, "Epistemic Disobedience, Independent Thought and Decolonial Freedom," *Theory, Culture & Society* 26, no. 7–8 (2009): 162.
17   See for example Anooradha Iyer Siddiqi and Hollyamber Kennedy, *Migration and Colonial Modernities*, Session convened at College Art Association 2019, Annual Conference, New York, February 13–16, 2019. Collaborators include Samia Henni, Huma Gupta, and Manuel Shvartzberg Carrió.
18   Itohan Osayimwese, "From Postcolonial to Decolonial Architectural History: A Method," *Kritische Berichte* 44 (March 2021): 16–38.
19   Siddiqi, "The University and The Camp" (see note 1).
20   Samia Henni, "Colonial Ramifications," in the History/Theory series, *e-flux Architecture*, October 13, 2018, accessed July 31, 2022, www.e-flux.com/architecture/history-theory/225180/colonial-ramifications/.
21   Katherine McKittrick, *Dear Science and Other Stories* (Durham: Duke University Press, 2021), 5.

Frameworks for

Text: Charlotte Malterre-Barthes, Dubravka Sekulić

Internal call for proposals for a more inclusive curriculum at the Department of Architecture at ETH Zürich, spring 2020

Curriculum Repair

"I have never lived, nor has any of us, in a world in which race did not matter. Such a world, one free of racial hierarchy, is usually imagined or described as dreamscape—Edenesque, utopian, so remote are the possibilities of its achievement. […] How to be both free and situated: how to convert a racist house into a race-specific yet nonracist home."[1] This quote by Toni Morrison is useful to start to think about fixing Architecture and all of its houses. Only if institutions acknowledge that their origin is grounded in racism, classism, and patriarchy, i.e., exclusion, can it be possible to transform institutional design through spatial design. This change has to happen where it matters most for the future: how we teach it. Thus to ensure that the future of architecture will be based on an ethics of equity, we need a curriculum revolution.

To unpack the complexities inherent to these efforts, the work of the Parity Group at the Department of Architecture at ETH Zürich is a telling example and, perhaps too, a cautionary tale. What started as a local rebellion against white male academia quickly turned into articulating a political agenda demanding profound corrections to architecture education, with the ambition of carrying these into the profession and the industry. When the effort began in 2014, the situation was bleak. All-male juries were a sad, recurring banality, and those who complained a marginalized minority. Despite a relatively diversified and gender-balanced student body, diverse faculty was non-existent, with female and BIPOC professors an exception. Blatant sexism and racism, social injustice, classism, and lack of diverse representation were rampant.

These appalling conditions triggered a grassroots movement among teaching assistants, doctoral students, and junior researchers within the Department of Architecture that became the Parity Group. This politicized, fluid, in-house body grew to include staff, students, and a few professors and is intensively active to this day, fully committed to changing the situation to foster parity and diversity in the conservative context of architecture education in Switzerland—by deploying institutional activism. Hundreds of hours of free labor went into the organization work that created a remarkable space for dissent, conflict, accountability, and negotiation, allowing other groups to emerge, inside and outside the institution, challenging hierarchies, teaching methods, and academic content. Grounded within the larger struggle for diversity in architecture, stressing the importance of sharing information and creating tactics and strategies within the institution, the group evolved from demanding gender parity at all events and in the hiring of professors (an unachieved goal) to articulating an intersectional agenda, of which curriculum change is a cornerstone.

While the efforts to reform a fundamentally hostile environment undertaken since 2014 by the Parity Group have been discussed in other instances, its attempts to revise the curriculum is a lesser-known story.[2] This is because it is essentially an unsuccessful one.

In 2019, the in-house call "Towards an Inclusive Architectural Curriculum" was launched by the Parity Group and its official counterpart, the school's Parity and Diversity Commission (PDK), inviting faculty to submit proposals to help improve the school curriculum with the support of a university grant (InnovEDUm). The aim was to "increase the offer of classes located outside of the canon rather than frontally challenging the existing formats and contents."[3] Acknowledging that schools cannot be reformed overnight, the call was carefully crafted to be generous rather than antagonistic. It was based on the semi-independent project *Curriculum Revolution*, which sought "a complete makeover for the architecture school and its curricula toward a fairer future of the discipline,"[4] tailored to the sensitivities of academia.

Curriculum Revolution argued that generations of architecture students have gone through their studies encountering perhaps two or three female architects and even fewer architects from diverse racial and sociopolitical origins as references: "Unaware educators have only served over and over again the same slides, the same icons, and the same architectural references without contextualizing nor questioning the power structures that have heralded some while sidelining others—negating questions of gender, race, and class in their choices."[5] *Curriculum Revolution* thus called for teaching based on inclusive pedagogical strategies and references. It intended to launch an overall assessment of the current state of the curriculum across all architecture schools in Europe—and globally—and offer strategies and tactics for implementing change.[6]

This served as the basis for the ETH call that followed in its steps: "Those who have written the canon suppressed the work and practices of others deemed unworthy because of gender, sexual orientation, geographic origins, ethnicity, social background, etc. But the world is changing, and […] this grant scheme […] offers a framework of support for a new generation of engaged teaching staff to step forward and take a lead […]: From reinventing the studio format, questioning critiques as rigid assessments methods, investigating other forms of teaching […] many formats could find a space in this Inclusive Architectural Curriculum." The proposed new curriculum aimed "to create a parallel 'inclusive' counterpart for each existing credit-given format within the school […], engaging with the issues of gender and diversity within the context of architectural education."[7]

The call was a flop among professors. Recognizing that much of the teaching was delegated to junior faculty, the Parity Group reissued the call a year later, explicitly targeting assistants and students. It invited grassroots initiatives by assistants, doctoral students, and professors from all the department chairs to propose teaching formats to receive additional funding. To entice proposals and offer directions, fictitious and provocative courses were suggested, such as "Colonial Urbanism: The Subaltern and the City (lecture series)," "Alternative Curriculums: Queer Schools of Architecture (personal work)," "Gendered Spaces: The Evolution of Bourgeois Floor Plans in Zurich's Contemporary Housing (seminar week)," "Unable Urban: Zurich for Wheelchairs, Rollators, Strollers (seminar week)," "Contemporary Cultural Constructs: Design Without (studio)," "Architecture of Automation: Cleaning Robots Is Not Done by Robots (seminar)," etc.[8] More than 80 proposals were submitted to this call, demonstrating the vivid interest in changing curricula and the intellectual wealth that resides in the school. Members of the Parity Group then set out to cement the proposals into a grant application in hours of unpaid labor.

Among others, the proposal listed the following changes to impact the teaching of architecture profoundly:
— Make available funds for staff and time needed to revise the basic curriculum spanning the bachelor semesters and required courses to include more diverse protagonists and expand and enrich teaching methods.
— Establish and maintain a discretionary fund to support the diversified curriculum. Chairs could apply for targeted initiatives or pilot projects that would be funded by the chairs themselves in the future.
— Implement at least two to three permanent elective courses on gender and diversity-related topics/methodologies.
— Enable and facilitate, through the support and oversight of the Gender & Diversity officer, specialized units within existing courses to increase the diversity of references and exercises.
— Initiate gender/diversity criteria for all diploma topics.[9]

After being revised, expanded, and amended, the board responsible for allocating the funds necessary to implement these changes rejected the application because it was not evident how it would "contribute to the development of quality education at the school in the long term."[10] The proposal was shelved.

What is striking in this failed attempt is the gap between the pace of progress between discourse and practice. That discourse is advanced in academic institutions is unsurprising, as this is what they mostly traffic in. On the other hand, practical, profound transformation is less tangible, even if many schools have shown progress in hiring diverse candidates. While universities in general, and schools of architecture in particular, are pressured into presenting a facade of progressivism by demands emerging from both within and outside of their institutions, the need to make fundamental changes to their overall approach is not addressed. In keeping with what Olúfẹ́mi O. Táíwò discusses in *Elite Capture*, to respond to the pressing needs of our world, it is not simply optics that need to change.[11] In the case of architectural education, what needs to be revolutionized is also architecture itself. Most of architecture's academic institutions, and even more practices, still end up aligning their understanding of what it means to be an architect with the view established by the economic system. They seem to disregard the warning issued by Robert Goodman in his polemic *After the Planners* that "our economic system has traditionally reduced the architect (the planner as an environmental designer) to the role providing culturally acceptable rationalizations for projects whose form and use have already been determined by real-estate speculation."[12] Acknowledging that the basis of architecture as common knowledge is grounded in white male supremacy means reconsidering all relations anew within and around the profession. What is at stake is unlearning as much as learning and relearning. The curious idea that only a select few should have the prerogative of designing the world to their liking and subjective good taste or its narrow understanding must be put to rest. What is needed is a new spatial social contract centering on racial, social, and environmental justice. This revolution must occur not only at the level of auxiliary courses but across formats, especially within the studio. A true curriculum revolution strives to change power relations in architecture and understands that the education of architects is but one way to foster change.

Moving forward, we propose an incomplete list of frameworks to support processes of curriculum repair as a step toward the revolution, collectively organized changes contextual to the institution in which they are taking place. As bell hooks articulates, "as a radical standpoint, perspective, position, 'the politics of location' necessarily calls those of us who would participate in the formation of counterhegemonic cultural practice to identify the spaces where we begin the process of revision."[13] There is no silver bullet, and what works in one institution does not necessarily work in another. Frameworks are not recipes to be followed to the letter but triggers to inspire action and points of recognition to inspire cross-institutional conversation and collaboration. Frameworks are not organized sequentially or hierarchically. They are what Stefano Harney and Fred Moten call props that enable entering "into some new thinking and into a new set of relations, a new way of being together, thinking together."[14] They should be treated as content for what Ursula K. Le Guin called "a carrier bag"[15] to transform the classroom into a site of emancipated learning. The frameworks follow "the view that reparation is a construction project,"[16] as proposed by Olúfẹ́mi O. Táíwò, and consider spatial education as an ongoing construction site.

Frameworks for Change

Be Situated

The curriculum as situated practice asks where the students in the classroom come from and what kind of practice they want to engage with, what they are prepared to share, and what their specific needs are. Also, how much are the semester fees again?

Prioritize Reuse

Challenge the idea that a good project is something no one has seen before as a form. Prioritize education that looks with fresh eyes at what skills, materials, and structures exist in the local context.

Interrogate Material Flows

It's not just fossil fuels setting the planet on fire. We need to challenge the materials we are force-fed to design with, articulate ways around them, and build without them, with less of them, and with other materials.

Challenge Individual Authorship

Change modalities in which collective and group work by students, and not just students, are recognized and valued. "Writing with" and "togethering"—the feminist frameworks described by Anooradha Iyer Siddiqi for writing architectural history and by Ana Maria Leon for doing things collaboratively—can offer ways to co-think, co-learn, and co-create differently.[17]

Challenge Hierarchies but Accept Responsibilities

As we question educational hierarchies in the classroom, do not dismiss the asymmetries of power we bring in. The quest for the horizontality of learning processes should not lead to a teacher abandoning responsibility for the process or privileging those habituated to speak aloud with ease in front of the group.[18]

Address the Classroom as Physical Space

Be in the present and acknowledge that the material objects and set-ups in and around the places we gather to teach, learn, and study in the classroom, studio, or auditorium, shape how we relate to each other and can reinforce or challenge power asymmetries.

Challenge Project Temporalities

Look beyond the work of an architect as a sole designer to compute the project's maintenance, post-occupancy, and afterlife. As Mierle Laderman Ukeles asked: "After the revolution, who's going to pick up the garbage on Monday morning?"[19]

Understand Education as an Emancipatory Praxis

Become students of bell hooks and Paulo Freire: The education of architects in the future has to become an emancipatory praxis, pursuing a "reflection and action upon the world to transform it."[20] Yet emancipatory for whom? Can an emancipatory spatial education lead to the design of spaces that are genuinely emancipatory for those who use them?

Question "Normality"

Denaturalize the idea of "standards" and make designing for all different bodies routine by centering disability justice.[21]

Challenge Property

Property is (neo)colonialism and (neo)imperialism spelled differently.[22] Question it as the only ordering regime of how we think spatially.

Recognize Labor

Acknowledge that architecture is labor, not a calling.[23] Don't fall for the pseudo-democratic narratives of "participation" that ignore that this, too, is work.[24] Know the bodies that make the architecture.[25] Be frank about the working conditions in academia because "our working conditions are your learning conditions."[26]

Adopt an Anticolonial Way of Seeing

Looping back to Morrison and Franz Fanon, the impossibility of spatial innocence must impregnate our curricula as we embrace an anticolonial way of seeing, which Nicholas Mirzoeff[27] sees as a refusal of the "aesthetics of respect for the established order."[28]

Complicate "Neutrality"

Challenge the outdated understanding of architects as professionals and experts. As Alenka Župančič frames it, "a 'neutral' position is always and necessarily the position of the ruling class: It seems 'neutral' because it has achieved the status of the dominant ideology, which always strikes us as self-evident. The criterion of objectivity in such a case is thus not neutrality, but the capacity of theory to occupy a singular, specific point of view within the situation."[29] And not just theory.

Recognize Life as a Source of Knowledge

Make room in the classroom for students to use their lived experience as a source of knowledge rather than devaluing it in favor of abstract canonized knowledge. The classroom should be a safe space where trust is built and not assumed. Building on lived experiences challenges the overrepresentation of the specific experience as the universal; it insists on multiplicity and rejects competitivity.

Unfreeze History

Activate history as a nonlinear critical tool to understand the present.[30]

Mistrust Technologies

Technology increasingly mediates how we love, live, and die; how we interact with students, clients, and future users. Digital tools completely transformed the processes in architecture classrooms and practice, changing the speed and accelerating the deskilling, skilling, and reskilling cycles. It is, therefore, important to resist the unbridled enthusiasm we are conditioned to have for technological innovation and fixes.[31] And, remember, the archive is technology as well.

Critically Engage with Images

Architects pretend to ignore the immense power residing in images produced to sell and conceal. The curriculum should not only focus on teaching students how to produce stunning images but also address the responsibility they have for the futures they create.

Be Entangled with Other Species

The transformed spatial curriculum must challenge extractive relations enacted between humans and by specific groups of humans on nonhumans, other species with whom we share this planet. To accept that "interdependency is not a contract, nor a moral ideal—it is a *condition*."[32] How can we learn to design for and with that condition? Natasha Myers considers *planthropos*, a human-plant relation,[33] as a society's basic political unit. What kind of teaching and design emerge when the human/non-human relation is understood as the basic spatial unit?

Think Intergenerationally

Decentering adulthood to work with those outside of it. Not only are there 2.2 billion children on Earth, but as Olúfẹ́mi O. Táíwò says, "we should think about our ancestors. But we will win and lose our own ethical battles based on what we do for our descendants. We are defined by what kind of ancestors we choose to be."[34]

Interrogate the Idea of Home/House

"Home is where the hatred is," Gil Scott Heron ominously suggests.[35] House is a site of disciplining.[36] Architecture may have started out as a shelter, but it can also be a trap.[37] As Robyn Maynard and Leanne Betasamosake Simpson tell us, there are "one hundred forms of homespace."[38]

1   Toni Morrison, "Home," in *The House That Race Built: Original Essays by Toni Morrison, Angela Y. Davis, Cornel West, and Others on Black Americans and Politics in America Today*, ed. Wahneema Lubiano (New York: Pantheon Books, 1997), 3–5.
2   Charlotte Malterre-Barthes and Torsten Lange for the Parity Group, "Architects Who Make a Fuss: A Speculative Investigation into the Archive of a Grassroots Initiative for Gender Parity at the Department of Architecture ETH Zürich, 2014–2017," *Site Magazine*, accessed October 10, 2022, www.thesitemagazine.com/read/architectswhomakeafuss.
3   Parity Group and Parity and Diversity Commission, "Towards an Inclusive Architectural Curriculum," call for submissions, 2019.
4   Charlotte Malterre-Barthes and Dubravka Sekulić, "Curriculum Revolution: Bringing Intersectionality to Architecture School," call for ideas, 2019, Future Architecture Platform, accessed October 10, 2022, futurearchitectureplatform.org/projects/765b75fd-0e46-4879-aa8d-28a42ed04102/.
5   Ibid.
6   Ibid.
7   Parity Group and Parity and Diversity Commission, "Inclusive Architectural Curriculum" (see note 3).
8   Ibid.
9   Parity Group, Parity and Diversity Commission, "InnovEDUm Degree Programme Initiative," project description, 2019.
10   ETH Zürich, "Innovedum: Fostering innovative teaching and learning at ETH," accessed December 19, 2022, ethz.ch/en/the-eth-zurich/education/innovedum.html.
11   Olúfẹ́mi O. Táíwò, *Elite Capture* (Chicago: Haymarket Books, 2022).
12   Robert Goodman, *After the Planners* (Harmondsworth: Penguin Books, 1972), 133.
13   bell hooks, "Choosing the Margin as a Space of Radical Opennesss," *Framework: The Journal of Cinema and Media* 36 (1989): 15.
14   Stefano Harney and Fred Moten, *The Undercommons: Fugitive Planning and Black Study* (Wivenhoe: Minor Compositions, 2013), 104.
15   Ursula K. Le Guin, "The Carrier-Bag Theory of Fiction," in *Women of Vision*, ed. Denise Du Pont (New York: St. Martin's Press, 1988), 1–12.
16   See the interview with Olúfẹ́mi O. Táíwò in this issue.
17   Ana María León, "Crowdsourcing Knowledge: Cowriting, Coteaching, and Colearning," *Art Journal Open*, November 20, 2018, accessed October 19, 2022, www.artjournal.collegeart.org/?p=10593.
18   Charlotte Grace, "From Students to Comrades," *Cartha* 1 (2022), accessed October 19, 2022, www.carthamagazine.com/issue/6-1/.
19   Mierle Laderman Ukeles, "Manifesto for Maintenance Art, 1969," in *Maintenance Required*, eds. Nina Horisaki-Christens et al. (New York: Whitney Museum of American Art, 2013), 118.

20   Paulo Freire, *Pedagogy of the Oppressed* (London: Penguin Classics, 2017), 52.
21   Aimi Hamraie, *Building Access: Universal Design and the Politics of Disability* (Minneapolis: University of Minnesota Press, 2017).
22   Brenna Bhandar, *Colonial Lives of Property: Law, Land, and Racial Regimes of Ownership* (Durham: Duke University Press Books, 2018).
23   Peggy Deamer, "Work," in *The Architect as Worker: Immaterial Labor, the Creative Class, and the Politics of Design*, ed. Peggy Deamer (New York: Bloomsbury Academic, 2015), 61–81.
24   Andrew Herscher, "Community and the Disavowed Labor of 'Participation'," *Harvard Design Magazine* 46, No Sweat (2018): 222–25.
25   Kadambari Baxi et al., "Who Builds Your Architecture?: An Advocacy Report," *e-flux Journal*, October 2015, accessed October 10, 2022, www.e-flux.com/journal/66/60751/who-builds-your-architecture-an-advocacy-report/.
26   Slogan used in 2021–22 strikes by the members of the RCAUCU Royal College of Art London branch of the University College Union, the largest organizing body of academic workers in the UK.
27   Nicholas Mirzoeff, "An Anticolonial Way of Seeing," *Interventions: International Journal of Postcolonial Studies* 24, no. 7 (2022): 985.
28   Frantz Fanon, *The Wretched of the Earth*, trans. Richard Philcox, reprint edition (New York: Grove Press, 2005), 8.
29   Alenka Župančič, *What Is Sex?* (Cambridge: MIT Press, 2017), 4.
30   Ariella Aïsha Azoulay, *Potential History: Unlearning Imperialism* (London: Verso, 2019).
31   Adam Greenfield, *Radical Technologies: The Design of Everyday Life* (London: Verso, 2018).
32   María Puig de La Bellacasa on the podcast *Cultures of Energy*, July 5, 2018, accessed October 10, 2022, https://cenhs.libsyn.com/133-maria-puig-de-la-bellacasa.
33   Natasha Myers, "How to Grow Livable Worlds: Ten Not-So-Easy Steps," in *The World to Come: Art in the Age of the Anthropocene*, ed. Kerry Oliver-Smith (Gainesville: Samuel P. Harn Museum of Art, University of Florida, 2018), 55.
34   Olúfẹ́mi O. Táíwò, *Reconsidering Reparations* (Oxford: Oxford University Press, 2022), 206.
35   Listen also to Esther Philips's powerful rendition of the same song, reminding that home is not just gendered, but also a gender-producing place.
36   Andrew Santa Lucia, "Disciplined in the House of Tomorrow," *Mas Context* 33 (2021): 224–37.
37   Adrian Lahoud, "Scale as Problem, Architecture as Trap," *The Avery Review* 15, April 4, 2016, accessed October 19, 2022, averyreview.com/issues/15/architecture-as-trap.
38   Robyn Maynard and Leanne Betasamosake Simpson, *Rehearsals for Living (The Abolitionist Papers)* (Chicago: Haymarket Books, 2022), 149.

The work on curriculum repair is never finished. It flourishes in ongoing reorientation, reorganization, and re-articulation. Thus, we would like to invite readers to add their frameworks at the end of this text. If you want to share your frameworks with us, you can reach us at curriculum.repair@gmail.com.

Framework ___________________________

Framework ___________________________

Framework ___________________________

Framework ___________________________

Framework ___________________________

Framework ___________________________

Framework ___________________________

Framework ___________________________

A Moratorium on New Construction

Book by Charlotte Malterre-Barthes

To build is to destroy. From steel bolts to concrete blocks to wood flooring to polyester insulation panels, every single component of the built environment is the product of extractive processes. Driven by greedy economies—finance, real estate, and the corporate construction industry—the global enterprise of space production is expanding, impacting air, climate, soil, geological features, water resources, fauna, flora, food systems, labor, health, farming activities, and vulnerable local populations, humans and nonhumans everywhere. The industry's actors conceal their role in the ongoing devastation by deploying flaccid "sustainability" campaigns and design gimmicks. In reality, little is done to mitigate the harmful acts of excavating, mining, smelting, manufacturing, transporting, assembling, etc. But as housing is both a human right and the mandate of design disciplines, we stand at the difficult threshold between home provision and depletion: How to navigate the need for housing versus the destructive practice of construction?

To pause new construction, even if momentarily, creates a radical framework to conceive alternatives to the current regime of space production and its suspect growth imperative. Engaging with unsettling questions, *A Moratorium on New Construction* envisions a massive value shift for existing buildings, infrastructure, materials, unbuilt land, earth, and the labor that holds our world together. From housing redistribution to reinviting value generation, from anti-extractive measures to profound structural changes, from curricula reforms to purging the exploitative culture of the office, from respecting soil to embracing repair, reuse, and dismantling—an entire rewiring of design processes and construction lays ahead. The task is immense: It demands an alternative way of making worlds, one that requires a careful inventory of current and vacant stock, the revaluation of care tasks, a global demolition ban, state commitment to public housing, equitable zoning plans, robust rent control, anti-vacancy policies, and ownership reform, but also end-of-life etiquette for materials and maintenance protocols, to be imagined, designed, formulated, planned, and implemented according to context.

Somewhere between a thought experiment and a call for action, *A Moratorium on New Construction* is a leap of faith to envision a less extractive future made of what we have.

Not demolishing, not building new, but building less, building with what exists, inhabiting it differently, and caring for it.

A Moratorium on New Construction is forthcoming with Sternberg Press (fall 2023) in the series *Critical Spatial Practice* edited by Nikolaus Hirsch and Markus Miessen.

Kader Attia
(*1970) is an artist who explores the wide-ranging effects of Western cultural hegemony and colonialism in his work. Central to his inquiry are the concepts of injury and repair, which he uses to connect diverse bodies of knowledge, including architecture, music, psychoanalysis, medical science, traditional healing, and spiritual beliefs. Throughout his multimedia practice, ranging from sculpture to film installation, repair does not mark a return to an intact state, but instead reveals the immaterial scars of psychic injury. This approach is informed by Attia's experience of growing up between Algeria and the banlieues of Paris. Attia was curator of the 2022 Berlin Biennale.

Nitin Bathla
(*1986) is a lecturer and postdoctoral researcher at the Department of Architecture, ETH Zürich, where he coordinates the doctoral program at the Institute of Landscape and Urban Studies. He teaches urban studies and political ecology, with his current research focusing on agrarian questions in the planetary age. In his academic practice, Bathla combines research with artistic practices such as filmmaking and socially engaged art. His film *Not Just Roads* (2020, with Klearjos E. Papanicolaou) has been screened at several film festivals and won the Society of Architectural Historians (SAH) Film Award in 2022.

Anton Brokow-Loga
(*1992) is a political scientist and urbanist. His research and teaching at the Chair of Urban Studies and Social Research at Bauhaus-Universität Weimar focus on degrowth and democratization policies in urban planning. His dissertation addresses translocal climate politics in the context of the climate emergency. Brokow-Loga is part of the I.L.A. collective and has been a member of the Weimar city council since 2019. His writings include the book *Stadtpolitik für alle: Städte zwischen Pandemie und Transformation* (2021, with Frank Eckardt) and *Corona und die Stadt: Beteiligungskultur in der Krise?* (forthcoming, 2023).

Pierre Caye
is a philosopher and, since 2011, director of Centre Jean Pépin at École Normale Supérieure in Villejuif. His research focuses on issues such as the environment and architecture, in particular Vitruvius's *De architectura* and architectural theory in the humanist and classical ages. Caye is a laureate of the Académie française (1996) and the Académie des sciences morales et politiques (2009). He has written numerous books, including *Durer: Éléments pour la transformation du système productif* (2020) and *Critique de la destruction créatrice: Humanisme et production* (2015).

Eli Clare
(*1963) is a writer and social justice educator. He has written two books of essays: the award-winning *Brilliant Imperfection: Grappling with Cure* (2017) and *Exile and Pride: Disability, Queerness, and Liberation* (1999), and a collection of poetry, *The Marrow's Telling: Words in Motion* (2007). He serves on the Community Advisory Board for the Disability Project at the Transgender Law Center in Oakland, California. In 2020 he was a Disability Futures Fellow, funded by the Ford Foundation and the Andrew W. Mellon Foundation.

Charlotte Grace
works on the socio-spatial dimensions of feminist (and) decolonial movements, developing methodologies and solidarity practices that can enable these movements to thrive. She leads Embodied Knowledges and Urban Struggles, the theory component of the City Design master's program at the Royal College of Art in London. She is also completing a PhD on the ongoing revolution in Rojava, Kurdistan, and its commitment to reimagining social and spatial subjectivities.

Katrin Großmann
(*1972) has been Professor of Urban and Spatial Sociology at the University of Applied Sciences Erfurt since 2014. Previously, she was a researcher at the Helmholtz Centre for Environmental Research – UFZ, Department for Urban and Environmental Sociology. Großmann's research deals with issues of sustainable and equitable urban development with a focus on energy and social inequality, neighborhood development, residential segregation, social cohesion, demographic change, and immigration.

Florian Hertweck
(*1975) is an architect and urban researcher. He has been a full professor at the University of Luxembourg since 2016, where he directs the master's program in architecture, and a partner at Studio Hertweck Architecture Urbanism. He co-curated the Luxembourg Pavilion with Andrea Rumpf at the 2018 Venice Architecture Biennale. Hertweck is the author of numerous books and the editor of *Architektur auf gemeinsamem Boden: Positionen und Modelle zur Bodenfrage* (2020). He is a co-curator of *The Great Repair.*

Santiago del Hierro
(*1980) is an architect and researcher. Since 2008, his work has focused on the geopolitics of the Andean Amazon. As a doctoral fellow at ETH Zürich, he is researching the potential connections between intercultural higher education and forest conservation. Santiago holds a master's in architecture from Yale University, which he attended as a Fulbright scholar. Between 2009 and 2010, he was a design researcher at the Jan van Eyck Academie in Maastricht, and between 2011 and 2017, he taught at Pontificia Universidad Católica del Ecuador, where he developed and coordinated the Urban and Territorial Design master's program.

Christian Hiller
(*1975) is a media scholar, curator, and writer. He has contributed to international exhibitions, events, and research projects and has written widely on topics at the intersection of architecture, urbanism, art, and media. Since 2016, he has been an editor at *ARCH+*, where he has led research and exhibition projects, including *projekt bauhaus, An Atlas of Commoning*, and *Cohabitation.* He is a co-curator of *The Great Repair* and of the German Pavilion at the 2023 Venice Architecture Biennale.

Hollyamber Kennedy
is a guest lecturer and senior postdoctoral fellow at the Institute for the History and Theory of Architecture (gta) at ETH Zürich. She holds a PhD in Architectural History and Theory from Columbia University. Her work broadly addresses legal, environmental, and migration histories of land settlement in formerly colonized places. She directs the working group on Architectural and Landscape Histories of Internal Colonization and is a member of the research collective Insurgent Domesticities.

Stefan Krebs
(*1973) is Assistant Professor of Contemporary History at the Luxembourg Centre for Contemporary and Digital History (C²DH). He studied history, political science, and philosophy at RWTH Aachen and Aix-Marseille University. After stints at Eindhoven University of Technology and Maastricht University, he joined C²DH in 2017, where he leads the project *Repairing Technology: Fixing Society?* funded by the Luxembourg National Research Fund (FNR). He is a co-editor of the books *Kulturen des Reparierens: Dinge—Wissen—Praktiken* (2018) and *The Persistence of Technology: Histories of Repair, Reuse and Disposal* (2021).

Markus Krieger
(*1993) is an editor at *ARCH+* and a co-curator of the exhibition and publication project *The Great Repair.* In 2020, he graduated with honors from the Department of Architecture at ETH Zürich.

Silke Langenberg
(*1974) is Professor of Construction Heritage and Preservation with the Institute of Construction History and Preservation and the Institute of Technology in Architecture at the Department of Architecture at ETH Zürich. Langenberg's research and teaching have focused for many years on the topic of repair and reparability in construction. Her book *Reparatur: Anstiftung zum Denken und Machen* was published in 2018, followed by the sequel *Upgrade: Making Things Better* in 2022.

Wilfried Lipp
(*1945) is a heritage conservator and art historian. He was the regional conservator of Upper Austria from 1992 to 2018 and president of ICOMOS Austria from 2002 to 2018. Lipp was an honorary professor at the Institute for Art History and Philosophy at the Catholic Private University (KU) Linz. Since the 1990s, his work has focused on the social relevance of heritage preservation and reassessing traditional cultural heritage values for the present. In 1993, he coined the term "repair society."

Andreas Malm
(*1977) is a senior lecturer at the Institute for Human Ecology at Lund University in Sweden and has been active in the climate justice movement for almost 20 years. In spring 2020, he was a visiting researcher at the Center for Humanities and Social Change at Humboldt University in Berlin. He is a member of the Zetkin Collective, which focuses on analyzing the political ecology of the far-right.

Charlotte Malterre-Barthes
is an architect, urban designer, and Assistant Professor of Architectural and Urban Design at EPFL in Lausanne. She was previously an assistant professor at the Harvard Graduate School of Design. Malterre-Barthes's work focuses on contemporary urbanization, material extraction, climate emergency, and ecological and social justice. In 2020, she started the initiative A Global Moratorium on New Construction. She is a founding member of the Parity Group and the Parity Front, activist networks dedicated to gender equality and diversity in architecture. Malterre-Barthes received a PhD from ETH Zürich with her dissertation on the political economy of commodities in the built environment. During that time, she directed ETH's Master of Advanced Studies in Urban Design program.

Panos Mantziaras
(*1967) is an architect and holds a PhD in planning and urban design. From 2010 to 2015, he was head of the Office for Architecture, Urban and Landscape Research (BRAUP) of the French Ministry of Culture. Since 2015 he has been the director of the Braillard Architecture Foundation in Geneva, where he led prospective consultations for Greater Geneva (2017–19) and Luxembourg (2020–22) in conjunction with The Eco-Century Project®. He currently advises cities and governments on ecological transition.

Elke Marhöfer
(*1967) is an artist working mainly within the medium of film, through which she investigates ecological practices that support human and nonhuman communities. Her work has been presented at festivals and exhibitions such as transmediale, Berlinale, and Berlinische Galerie, Berlin; BFI London Film Festival; International Film Festival Rotterdam; Courtisane Festival, Gent; Images Festival, Toronto; Biennale of Urbanism, Shenzhen; Badischer Kunstverein, Karlsruhe; Kyiv Biennial; Palais de Tokyo and Jeu de Paume, Paris.

Marija Marić
(*1986) is an architect, researcher, and curator. She is also a postdoctoral research associate in the Master in Architecture program at the University of Luxembourg, where she also teaches. In 2020, she obtained her PhD from the Institute for the History and Theory of Architecture (gta), ETH Zürich, with research examining the role of media strategists in the communication, design, and globalization of urban projects. Marić is a co-curator of the Luxembourg Pavilion at the 2023 Venice Architecture Biennale.

Metaxia Markaki
is an architect, urbanist, and educator. She is currently completing her PhD at the Institute of Landscape and Urban Studies (LUS) of ETH Zürich, studying the urbanization of peripheral landscapes in Greece. She has taught research and design at the Herzog & de Meuron Chair at ETH Studio Basel and Harvard GSD, and at the Architecture of Territory Chair of Milica Topalović at ETH Zürich. She is co-author of the book *Achtung: die Landschaft* (2015). In 2019, her team won first prize at Europan 15 with the project *Landscape*

In-Between. In 2022, she co-organized the peer-to-peer writing retreat *Tentacular Writing.* Markaki is part of the collaborative design practice ThatStudio in Athens and Zurich.

Markus Miessen
(*1978) is an architect and professor of Urban Regeneration at the University of Luxembourg. He received his PhD under the supervision of Eyal Weizman at the Centre for Research Architecture at Goldsmiths, University of London. Miessen taught at the AA in London and held professorships at the Städelschule in Frankfurt, the University of Southern California in Los Angeles, and the HDK-Valand Academy of Art and Design in Gothenburg. He was also a Harvard GSD Fellow. He is the author of several publications, including *The Nightmare of Participation* (2010) and *Crossbenching* (2016), both of which have been translated into eight languages. Together with Nikolaus Hirsch, he is co-editor of the *Critical Spatial Practice* book series.

Richard Misrach
(*1949) is a photographer. He is well known for his series *Desert Cantos* (1979–ongoing), which takes a multifaceted approach to studying place and people's complex relationship to it. The chapter *Border Cantos*, produced in collaboration with the experimental composer Guillermo Galindo, explores seldom-seen realities along the border between the United States and Mexico. In the most recent chapters, *Premonitions* and *The Writing on the Wall*, Misrach documents graffiti in desolate areas throughout the American Southwest and southern California, finding an angry and ominous response to the highly charged political climate before and after the US presidential election in 2016.

Jason W. Moore
(*1971) is an environmental historian and historical geographer at Binghamton University, New York, where he is a professor of sociology and leads the World-Ecology Research Collective. His research focuses on capitalism and the environment, with a particular focus on their historical development and their current crisis. He is the author of the books *Capitalism in the Web of Life* (2015) and *A History of the World in Seven Cheap Things* (2017, with Raj Patel).

Alex Nehmer
(*1989) is an editor at *ARCH+*. She studied Cultural Studies at Humboldt University in Berlin and at the Department of Visual Cultures at Goldsmiths, University of London. From 2015 to 2016, she worked for the Haus der Kulturen der Welt in Berlin on the publication series for the exhibition *Wohnungsfrage*, and taught in the Metropolitan Culture program at HafenCity University Hamburg in 2019/20. She co-curated the project *Cohabitation* and is a co-curator of *The Great Repair.*

Anh-Linh Ngo
(*1974) is an architect, writer, and publisher of *ARCH+*. He is a co-curator of *The Great Repair.* He was also co-curator of *projekt bauhaus* (2015–19) and *Cohabitation* (2021–22). From 2010 to 2016, he was a member of the Art Advisory Board at the Institut für Auslandsbeziehungen (ifa), for which he co-curated the touring exhibitions *An Atlas of Commoning* (2018) and *Post-Oil City* (2009). He is currently a member of the board of trustees of the IBA 2027 StadtRegion Stuttgart, the board of trustees of Akademie Schloss Solitude, and the advisory board of the Goethe-Institut. He is a co-curator of the German Pavilion at the 2023 Venice Architecture Biennale.

Sarah Nichols
is Assistant Professor of Architecture at EPFL in Lausanne, where she is also director of the Theory of Environment and Materials in Architecture lab (THEMA). Her scholarly work examines the environmental and political entanglements of construction, particularly through building materials. Her material retrospective *Beton* was shown at the Swiss Architecture Museum in Basel in 2021/22. Nichols is currently working on the book *Opération Béton: Constructing Concrete in Switzerland* based on her dissertation, for which she was awarded the ETH Medal.

Raj Patel
(*1972) is an author, filmmaker, and academic. He is a research professor at the Lyndon B. Johnson School of Public Affairs at the University of Texas, Austin and holds degrees from the University of Oxford, the London School of Economics, and Cornell University. Patel has worked for the World Bank and the WTO, and protested against them around the world. His writings include the books *A History of the World in Seven Cheap Things* (2018, with Jason W. Moore) and *Inflamed: Deep Medicine and The Anatomy of Injustice* (2021, with Rupa Marya).

Pluritext authors
Antonia Agreda is an education officer for the Cities Two area of the Inga People. She lives in Bogotá. **Liliana Armero** is an advisor at Universidad Biocultural Indígena Panamazónica (AWAI) in the Nariño area. She lives in Piamonte, Cauca. **Pablo Cuchalá** is an advisor at AWAI in the Middle and Lower Putumayo area. He lives in Villagarzón, Putumayo. **Agripina Garreta** is an education officer for the Middle and Lower Putumayo area. She lives in Mocoa, Putumayo. **Álvaro Hernández Bello** is a doctoral researcher at the National University of Colombia. He lives in Bogotá. **Yeni Yolanda Jacanamijoy** is an education officer for the Yunguillo and Media Bota Caucana area. She lives in Yunguillo, Putumayo. **Pedro Jajoy** is an advisor at AWAI in the Alto Putumayo area. He lives in Colón, Putumayo. **Mariela Pujimuy** is an education officer for the Nariño area. She lives between Bucaramanga and Aponte.

Bas Princen
(*1975) is an artist and photographer. He was trained as an industrial designer at the Design Academy Eindhoven and later studied architecture at the Berlage Institute in Rotterdam. Since then, his work has focused on urban landscapes in transition, using photography to examine the various forms, outcomes, and perceptions of changing urban spaces.

Andrew L. Russell
(*1975) is dean of the College of Arts and Sciences at SUNY Polytechnic Institute in Utica and Albany, New York. He writes about technology, maintenance, standards, and the history of the internet. His recent work includes two co-authored books, *The Innovation Delusion: How Our Obsession with the New Has Disrupted the Work That Matters Most* (2020, with Lee Vinsel), and *Circuits, Packets, and Protocols: Entrepreneurs and Computer Communications, 1968–1988* (2022, with James L. Pelkey and Loring G. Robbins).

Dubravka Sekulić
is an architect, educator, and author. She is a senior tutor at the Royal College of Art in London after four years as an assistant professor at IZK – Institute for Contemporary Art at Graz Technical University. Her PhD thesis at the Institute for the History and Theory of Architecture (gta) at ETH Zürich focused on the political economy of the non-aligned movement through the lens of the engagement of the Yugoslav construction enterprise Energoprojekt. She is the author of the book *Glotzt Nicht so Romantisch! On Extralegal Space in Belgrade* (2012), and collaborated on the film *Don't Trace, Draw!* (2020) with Ana Hušman. *Curriculum Revolution* was initiated by Charlotte Malterre-Barthes and Dubravka Sekulić in 2019.

Olúfẹ́mi O. Táíwò
is Associate Professor of Philosophy at Georgetown University. He received his PhD in philosophy at the University of California Los Angeles. Táíwò's theoretical work draws from the Black radical tradition, anticolonial thought, and activist thinkers, among others. His public philosophy, including articles exploring intersections of climate justice and colonialism, has been featured in *The New Yorker*, *The Nation*, *Boston Review*, *Dissent*, *The Appeal*, *Slate*, *Al Jazeera*, *The New Republic*, *Aeon*, and *Foreign Policy*. He is the author of *Elite Capture* (2022) and *Reconsidering Reparations* (2022).

Paulo Tavares
(*1980) is an architect, author, and educator. Operating through multiple media, his work opens a collaborative field aimed at environmental justice and counter-hegemony narratives in architecture and visual cultures. His work has been featured in exhibitions and publications worldwide, including *Harvard Design Magazine*, *The Architectural Review*, *Oslo Architecture Triennial*, *Istanbul Design Biennale*, and *São Paulo Art Biennial.* He is the author of several books questioning the colonial legacies of modernity, most recently *Des-Habitat* (2019), *Lucio Costa era Racista?* (2022), and *Derechos No-Humanos* (2022). In 2017, Tavares founded autonoma, a platform for urban research and urban interventions. He was co-curator of the 2019 Chicago Architecture Biennial.

Oxana Timofeeva
is a professor at Stasis Center for Practical Philosophy at the European University at St. Petersburg and is a member of the artist collective Chto Delat. She is author of the books *Solar Politics* (2022), *This is not that* (in Russian, 2022), *How to Love a Homeland* (2020), *History of Animals* (2018), *Introduction to the Erotic Philosophy of Georges Bataille* (in Russian, 2009), and other writings.

Milica Topalović
is Associate Professor of Architecture and Territorial Planning at the Department of Architecture at ETH Zürich. Her work is concerned with territories beyond the city and the transformation processes they are exposed to through the movement of capital, social restructuring, and environmental change. With the Architecture of Territory group, she undertook a range of territorial studies around the world, in remote regions, resource hinterlands, and countrysides, in an effort to decenter and ecologize architects' approaches to the city, the urban, and urbanization. She is a co-curator of *The Great Repair.*

Nazlı Tümerdem
is an architect and researcher. She studied at Istanbul Technical University and Istanbul Bilgi University. In 2018, she defended her PhD, entitled *Istanbul Walkabouts: A Critical Walking Study of Northern Istanbul*, at Istanbul Technical University. During this time, she initiated the independent performance project *Istanbul Walkabouts.* In 2019, she joined the Chair of Architecture and Territorial Planning at ETH Zürich as a postdoctoral researcher and recipient of a Swiss Government Excellence Scholarship.

UVW-SAW
United Voices of the World – Section of Architectural Workers (UVW-SAW) is a grassroots trade union for architectural workers in the UK. SAW collectively takes action and fights against the negative impacts of architectural work on workers, communities, and the environment. Members of SAW organize both in their workplaces and across the sector around overwork, underpay, unstable employment, a toxic workplace, university culture, discrimination, and unethical practice.

Iván Darío Vargas Roncancio
(*1984) is a lawyer and has a PhD in Natural Resource Sciences. He is a postdoctoral fellow (Leadership for the Ecozoic) and Associate Director at the Centre for Indigenous Conservation and Development Alternatives (CICADA) at McGill University in Montreal. He is part of a team of scholars in support of the Universidad Biocultural Indígena Panamazónica led by the Inga people of Colombia. Vargas Roncancio has published on Earth Law and the rights of nature, Indigenous legal traditions and cosmologies in the Amazon, the anthropology of plant-human relations, and critical pedagogies.

Cover image: © Bas Princen
Inside cover flap: Courtesy of the artist and Galleria Continua. Photos: MMK Museum für Moderne Kunst Frankfurt / Axel Schneider

REPAIR AND REPARATION

Interview Jason W. Moore, Raj Patel
pp. 15–18, 21–24: © Bas Princen
p. 19 above: © Ivy Close Images / Alamy Stock Photo
p. 19 below: © Trinity Mirror / Mirrorpix / Alamy Stock Photo

Interview Olúfẹ́mi O. Táíwò
p. 28: © Olúfẹ́mi O. Táíwò
pp. 29–32, 35–38: © Richard Misrach. Courtesy of Fraenkel Gallery, San Francisco
p. 34: © DESIGN EARTH

Interview Wilfried Lipp
p. 46: © Photo: Paulina Kampmann, published in Silke Langenberg, *UPGRADE: Making Things Better* (Berlin: Hatje Cantz, 2022), 269.
p. 49: © Photo: Paulina Kampmann, published in Silke Langenberg, *UPGRADE: Making Things Better*, Berlin: Hatje Cantz, 2022), 367.

POLITICS FOR THE REPAIR SOCIETY

Curriculum: Sufficiency
p. 53: © gta Archiv / ETH Zürich, Hannes Meyer
p. 54: Photo: Lise Gaudaire. Courtesy of Galerie MICA, Saint Grégoire

Essay Florian Hertweck, Markus Miessen
p. 56: © Jumpe Suzuki
p. 58: © ZAS*
p. 60 left: © Peter Liedtke
p. 60 right: Photo: Wien Museum
p. 61: © Jon Broome
p. 62 left: © Peter Kurze
p. 63: © OrganicLea

Interview Anton Brokow-Loga, Katrin Großmann
p. 64: © Evelyn Salt and Material Cultures
p. 65: © Charlotte Malterre-Barthes
p. 66: © Carles Oliver Barceló
p. 68: © baubüro in situ ag. Photo: Martin Zeller
p. 69: "The Doughnut of Social and Planetary Boundaries," in Kate Raworth, *Doughnut Economics: Seven Ways to Think Like a 21st-Century Economist* (London: Random House, 2017). © Kate Raworth and Christian Guthier. CC-BY-SA 4.0

Curriculum: Longevity
p. 71: Courtesy of Artemide

Interview Pierre Caye
p. 74: Photo: Leon Faust. © Countdown 2030
p. 75: Photo: Strata Suomi, CC-BY-SA 2.0
p. 77: Photo: Nils Koenning
p. 78: Photo: Douglas Garcia
p. 79 right: Photo: Adrià Goula

Statement Sarah Nichols
p. 82: © Bas Princen

Interview Andrew L. Russell, Stefan Krebs
p. 86: © Portland Anarchist Road Care
p. 88 above: © Archives New Zealand, Communicate New Zealand Collection, Reference R24809065 AAQT 6539 W3537 142 / B5099
p. 88 below: © Hans Peter Hahn
p. 89: © Johnny Miller
p. 90: © ANSA
p. 92: © Todd McLellan, all rights reserved
p. 93 above: © Platform21
p. 93 below: © MAMA

Curriculum: Care
p. 95: © Mierle Laderman Ukeles. Courtesy of the artist and Ronald Feldman Gallery, New York
p. 96: Photo: Robi Kahn © Mierle Laderman Ukeles. Courtesy of the artist and Ronald Feldman Gallery, New York

Essay Eli Clare
pp. 98, 104: © Elke Marhöfer
p. 102: Courtesy of the Burton Historical Collection, Detroit Public Library
p. 103: Courtesy of Ericson Collection, California State Polytechnic University, Humboldt

Essay Metaxia Markaki
pp. 106, 109 above, 110, 112: © Tokomburu / Piraeus Bank Group Cultural Foundation
p. 108 left: © Sakiya Photo Archive
p. 108 right: © Public Central Historic Library of Koraes Chios, Album: Photographs taken by Philip. P. Argenti (1910–21), p. 117

Curriculum: Reappropriation
p. 115: Photo: Donna Svennevik
p. 116: Photo: Kader Attia. Courtesy of the artist

Interview Kader Attia
p. 118: Courtesy of Kader Attia, Galerie Christian Nagel, Cologne/Berlin, Galerie Krinzinger, Vienna and the Biennale of Sydney. This version of the work was created specifically for the 17th Biennale of Sydney and was made possible through the generous support of the Keir Foundation. Photo: Sebastian Kriete
pp. 120, 122: Courtesy of Kader Attia
p. 123: Courtesy of Kader Attia, Galerie Christian Nagel, Cologne/Berlin
p. 124: Courtesy of Kader Attia. Photo: Tony Hafkenscheid

Statement Andreas Malm
pp. 126, 129: © Tim Wagner

Curriculum: Solidarity
p. 131: © Pamela Singh. Courtesy of sepiaEYE
p. 132: © Raul Walch

Interview Paulo Tavares
p. 134: © WAI Think Tank
pp. 136, 137, 138: © Paulo Tavares
p. 139: © pumfleteers collective / Wolff Architects
p. 141: © Kendall McCaugherty | Hall+Merrick+McCaugherty

Interview Oxana Timofeeva
p. 142: © Chto Delat
p. 144: © Estate of Lebbeus Woods
p. 145: © David Byrne. Courtesy of Pace Gallery. Photo: Doyle Auctioneers & Appraisers
p. 146: © Pflanzensoziologisches Institut
p. 147: © Peter Nicholson, Wombat Foundation

Curriculum: Plurality
p. 149: © Library of Congress, Geography and Map Division
p. 150: Photo: Gladys Serrano © El País

Essay Iván Darío Vargas Roncancio
p. 152: © Uaira Uaua / Benjamín Jacanamijoy Tisoy
p. 154: © Oliver Ressler. Photo: Boris Berc
p. 155: © Field Museum of Natural History
pp. 156–157: © Maria Thereza Alves
p. 158: © Factum Arte
p. 159: © COMUNAL Taller de Arquitectura

Pluritext
p. 160: © Álvaro Hernández Bello

SELF-REPAIR, AN EPILOGUE

Statement UVW-SAW
pp. 173, 174: © UVW-SAW

Essay Hollyamber Kennedy
p. 176: © Timothy Schenck. Courtesy of High Line, New York
pp. 178–179: © WAI Think Tank
p. 180: © AU Rural Studio

Essay Charlotte Malterre-Barthes, Dubravka Sekulić
p. 182: © Charlotte Malterre-Barthes

ARCH+
Journal for Architecture and Urbanism

Publishers
ARCH+ / Spector Books

ARCH+ Publishers
Nikolaus Kuhnert, Anh-Linh Ngo

Advisory Board
Arno Brandlhuber, Beatriz Colomina, Philipp Oswalt, Stephan Trüby, Georg Vrachliotis, Mark Wigley, Karin Wilhelm

Editor-in-Chief
Anh-Linh Ngo*

Managing Director
Arno Löbbecke

Editorial Team
Nora Dünser, Mirko Gatti, Franziska Gödicke*, Christian Hiller*, Felix Hofmann*, Sascha Kellermann, Markus Krieger* (project leader), Victor Lortie*, Melissa Makele, Alex Nehmer* (project leader)

Guest Editors
Florian Hertweck, Milica Topalović

Guest Editorial Team
Santiago del Hierro, Marija Marić (project leader University of Luxembourg), Leo Paulmichl, Nazlı Tümerdem (project leader ETH Zürich)

ETH Zürich D-ARCH
Chair for Architecture and Territorial Planning / Architecture of Territory

University of Luxembourg
Chair for Architecture

Managing Editor
Nora Dünser*

Scholarship
Marlene Huster*, Sarah Knechtel*, Daniel Kuhnert*, Lukas Meyer, Finn Steffens

*Editorial team for this publication, which is based on the German issue ARCH+ 250: *The Great Repair – Politiken der Reparaturgesellschaft. Ein Reader* (December 2022)

Head of Research & Exhibition Projects
Christian Hiller

Head of Events
Sascha Kellermann

Head of Communications & Marketing
Barbara Schindler

Head of Organization
Elke Doppelbauer

Assistant
Friederike Kiko

Ambassadors
Martin Luce, Christine Rüb

Advertising
anzeigen@archplus.net
archplus.net/en/mediakit

ARCH+ Verlag GmbH
Friedrichstraße 23a
10969 Berlin, Germany
Phone: +49 30 340 467 19
verlag@archplus.net
Managing Directors:
Nikolaus Kuhnert, Anh-Linh Ngo

ARCH+ gGmbH (non-profit organization)
ggmbh@archplus.net

Donation Account
GLS Bank
IBAN: DE47 4306 0967 1229 2768 01
BIC: GENODEM1GLS
archplus.net/en/nonprofit

Art Direction
Stan Hema, Berlin

Design
Mattis Bettels, Peer Hempel, André van Rueth, Thomas Spieler

Typesetting
André van Rueth, Daniel Vandré

Project Management Stan Hema
Niki Moreira

Copyediting
Jeremy Gaines (pp. 12–39, 118–25, 172–81)
Alisa Kotmair (pp. 82–93, 106–17, 134–71, 182–92)

Translations
Petra Gaines + Jeremy Gaines (pp. 1–6, 40–81, 94–97, 130–33)

Proofreading
James Copeland

Prepress
max-color, Berlin

Printing
Medialis Offsetdruck GmbH, Berlin

Thanks
We warmly thank Milica Topalović, Professor of Architecture and Territorial Planning at the Department of Architecture at ETH Zürich, with postdoctoral researcher Nazlı Tümerdem and doctoral fellow Santiago del Hierro, as well as Florian Hertweck, Professor of Architecture at the University of Luxembourg, with postdoctoral research associate Marija Marić and student assistant Leo Paulmichl, for working with us to initiate the project *The Great Repair* and for their close and constructive collaboration as guest editors of this issue. We thank Bas Princen for his insightful advice on the visual concept. Special thanks are due to Johannes Odenthal, the former program director at Akademie der Künste in Berlin, and his successor Johanna M. Keller, along with the entire team at Akademie der Künste for their extraordinary support of the project. We would also like to express our sincere gratitude to all our supporters, especially the German Federal Cultural Foundation, and to the authors, interlocutors, and artists who contributed to the issue and the exhibition project.

Direct Orders
of ARCH+ English editions:
archplus.net/en/shop/english-publications

Subscriptions
only German issues: archplus.net/abo

Distribution
Spector Books
Harkortstraße 10
04107 Leipzig
www.spectorbooks.com

Germany, Austria: GVA, Gemeinsame Verlagsauslieferung Göttingen GmbH & Co. KG, www.gva-verlage.de
Switzerland: AVA Verlagsauslieferung AG, www.ava.ch
France, Belgium: Interart Paris, www.interart.fr
UK: Central Books Ltd, www.centralbooks.com
USA, Canada, Central and South America, Africa:

The Great Repair
Akademie der Künste, Berlin
October 14, 2023–January 14, 2024

Artistic Direction:
ARCH+ (Christian Hiller, Markus Krieger, Alex Nehmer, Anh-Linh Ngo) in collaboration with
Florian Hertweck, Department of Geography and Spatial Planning, University of Luxembourg
Milica Topalović, Department of Architecture, ETH Zürich

Curatorial Assistance: Marija Marić (University of Luxembourg), Nazlı Tümerdem (ETH Zürich)
Production Management: Felix Hofmann (ARCH+)
Project Management: Elke Doppelbauer (ARCH+)
Communication: Barbara Schindler (ARCH+)

With the support of the teams of the Chair for Architecture and Territorial Planning / Architecture of Territory, ETH Zürich, and the Chair for Architecture, University of Luxembourg

is a project of

in cooperation with

Funded by the German Federal Cultural Foundation

Funded by the Federal Government Commissioner for Culture and the Media

Die Beauftragte der Bundesregierung für Kultur und Medien

The Great Repair educational program is funded by

bpb: Bundeszentrale für politische Bildung

Additional support from

WÜSTENROT STIFTUNG

Hans Sauer Stiftung

The Experimental Scholarship Program for young architectural researchers is funded by

EXPERIMENTAL

ARTBOOK / D.A.P., www.artbook.com
South Korea: The Book Society, www.thebooksociety.org
Japan: twelvebooks, www.twelve-books.com
Australia, New Zealand: Perimeter Distribution, www.perimeterdistribution.com

Bibliographic information published by the German National Library: The German National Library lists this publication in the Deutsche Nationalbibliografie; detailed bibliographic data is available online at dnb.dnb.de.

Library of Congress Control Number: 2020937306

ISBN 978-3-95905-713-4 (Spector Books)
ISBN 978-3-931435-77-6 (ARCH+)

First edition: 2023
Printed in Germany